W9-BZO-596

NEAFCS

National Extension Association of Family and Consumer Sciences

Living Well

More Than a Cookbook

NEAFCS

National Extension Association of Family and Consumer Sciences

More Than a Cookbook

Published by National Extension Association of
Family and Consumer Sciences
Copyright © 2010 by
National Extension Association of Family and Consumer Sciences
14070 Proton Road
Suite 100LB9
Dallas, Texas 75244
972-233-9107

Photography © by Nancy Schneider, Fort Thomas, Kentucky

This cookbook is a collection of our favorite recipes, which are not
necessarily original recipes.

All rights reserved. No part of this publication may be reproduced in any form
or by any means, electronic or mechanical, including photocopying and recording,
or by any information storage or retrieval system, without prior written permission
from the National Extension Association of Family and Consumer Sciences.
Members of NEAFCS may photocopy recipes for their use.

Library of Congress Control Number: 2009935670
ISBN: 978-0-9841425-0-7

Edited, Designed, and Produced by

Favorite Recipes® Press
an imprint of

RP.INC
A wholly owned subsidiary of Southwestern/Great American, Inc.
P.O. Box 305142
Nashville, Tennessee 37230
1-800-358-0560

Art Director and Book Design: Starletta Polster
Project Editor: Tanis Westbrook

Manufactured in the United States of America
First Printing 2010
25,000 copies

USDA

United States
Department of
Agriculture

Cooperative State
Research,
Education, and
Extension Service

Washington, D.C.
20250-2200

The home economics movement of the early twentieth century had a major role in advancing healthy food and nutrition practices in the United States. A main goal of the movement was to use modern principles of science and efficiency to meet this need. Early pioneers in home economics cooking schools provided instruction in preparing healthful, low-cost meals, and over the years, these cooking schools began to educate the general public in food preparation and safety. It was during this period that some of the first cookbooks—directed at a large popular audience—were published.

From its inception as the National Association of Extension Home Economists, to becoming the leading Extension Family and Consumer Sciences professional organization, the National Extension Association of Family and Consumer Sciences (NEAFCS) has honored the rich tradition of advancing healthy food and nutrition practices begun during the home economics movement.

Today, the critical emphasis on safe, affordable food and a healthy, nutritious diet is evident in every aspect of American life. NEAFCS members have had an extraordinary impact on advancing not only sound nutritional practices, but on sound practices in all aspects of healthful living.

Living Well—More Than a Cookbook, developed by NEAFCS members from across the nation, captures these practices, providing time-tested, healthful recipes and educational information to enhance the quality of life of individuals, families, and communities.

I do hope you enjoy the NEAFCS *Living Well* experience.

Colien Hefferan
Administrator
Cooperative State Research, Education, and Extension Service

Contents

Introduction

The National Extension Association of Family and Consumer Sciences (NEAFCS) educates and recognizes Extension professionals who impact the quality of life for individuals, families, and communities. Over two thousand members strong, NEAFCS is the professional association serving the unique needs of family and consumer science educators working in the Extension system. NEAFCS state affiliates

Serve as a nationwide resource for education, information, networking, and partnerships with communities, families, and individuals

Promote Extension Family and Consumer Sciences and the mission and goals of the Land Grant University Extension System

Build leaders of the future, within the path of Family and Consumer Sciences and related fields of study

Provide innovative development opportunities for professional growth

Develop sustainable human, financial, and technological resources for the delivery of informational programs

Recognize and promote excellence in Extension Family and Consumer Sciences through awards and scholarship

NEAFCS Extension Educators accept the opportunity to empower individuals, families, and communities to meet their needs and goals through the emerging issues of the changing and challenging times. The land grant system established "Extension" through a state college or university as an institution that receives federal support for the delivery of research-based information in agriculture, family and consumer sciences, 4-H youth development, and commercial development. The Cooperative Extension System is the agency within the United States Department of Agriculture that reaches out to present research-based information in a nonformal setting.

Living Well—More Than a Cookbook was developed to provide recipes and research-based information from across our nation, encouraging all to improve their health and well-being by taking advantage of the educational opportunities offered by the local Extension Family and Consumer Sciences professionals through the state and national Cooperative Extension System.

Raising kids, Eating right, Spending smart.

The first four presidents of NEAFCS joined for a picture in 1940 in the yard of the Cedar Point Hotel in Cleveland, Ohio, prior to the National Home Demonstration Agents' Association meeting. Left to right: Anna Searl (Illinois), first president; Nellie Watts (Ohio), second president; Florence Carvin (Missouri), third president; and Clara Brian (Illinois), fourth president.

History

This *Living Well* cookbook is a project of the National Extension Association of Family and Consumer Sciences (NEAFCS), which is celebrating its seventy-fifth anniversary in 2009. NEAFCS has had many names over its seventy-five years of existence, and while the name and methods have changed over the years, the original goal of the association has remained constant: support the efforts of family and consumer science educators and home economists serving families through the federal extension system.

The National Home Demonstration Agents' Association started on June 29, 1933, in Milwaukee, Wisconsin, during the annual meeting of the American Home Economics Association (AHEA). At the last organizational meeting, twenty-one agents discussed the many values of a national association to promote the interest of home demonstration work. The most legitimate reason was planning the pre-convention conference and program in conjunction with the AHEA meeting each year (agents had been attending the conventions but did not have a meeting of their own). Of equal importance was the possibility of giving home demonstration agents a voice in forming policies through a national organization and local affiliates. The constitution was adopted in 1934, and the name of the organization was the Home Demonstration Agents' National Association (HDANA).

In 1958, the National Negro Home Demonstration Agents Association (NNHDAA) was founded. NNHDAA members enriched the home economics movement by providing educational experiences for the family, developing programs and resources, and providing support, leadership, and community development initiatives.

To better reflect the changes in extension on a national basis and put an emphasis on the home economics profession, the name was changed to the National Association of Extension Home Economists (NAEHE) at the annual meeting on November 16, 1964. In November 1965, NNHDAA dissolved and its members joined NAEHE. As a result of the evolution of the profession from Home Economics to Family and Consumer Sciences, the association once again changed its name in 1995 to the National Extension Association of Family and Consumer Science (NEAFCS).

NEAFCS members link research to life experiences by interpreting research and delivering that information to families. Extension Family and Consumer Science Educators help people develop the skills necessary to care for family members, promote individual growth and development, and meet individual and family needs for food, housing, fuel, and other requirements essential to health and safety. Today the association has over three thousand members (2,202 active and 1,055 life).

In October 2002, NEAFCS launched a public service campaign entitled Living Well™ to raise consumer awareness of the valuable educational resources available through Extension Family and Consumer Sciences. The Living Well Web site (http://learningandlivingwell.org) has information by subject matter on successful Extension education programs from around the country.

NEAFCS is pleased to share the best recipes from NEAFCS members through this *Living Well* cookbook.

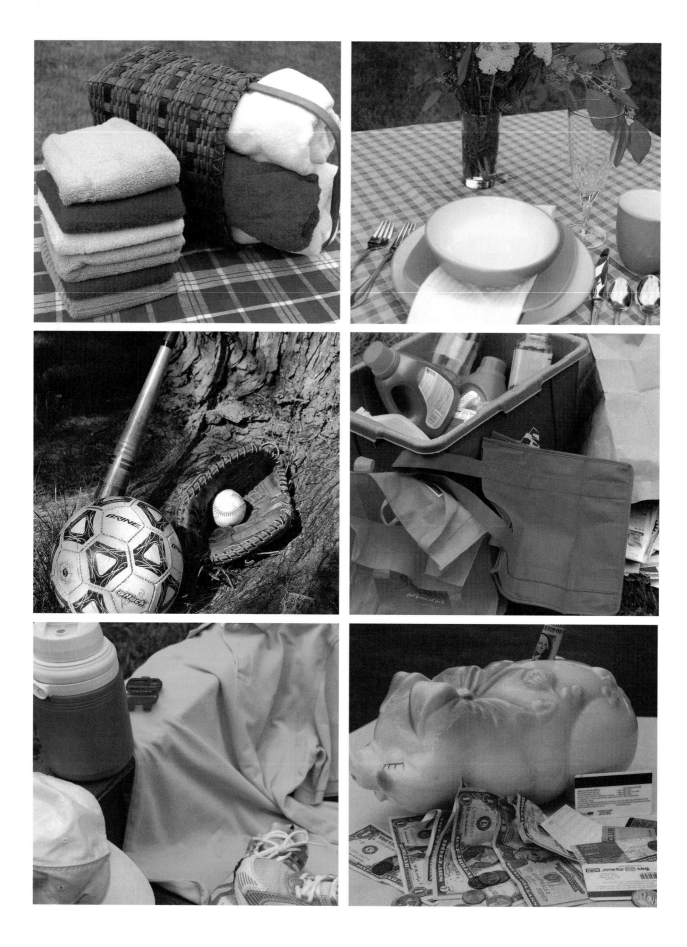

Recipes for Living

Healthy Lifestyles

Many individuals are looking for ways to be healthier and others for ways to manage weight. To lose weight you must maintain a "negative energy balance" by burning off more calories with daily exercise or activities than you consume. Individuals can lose weight and still eat their favorite foods by decreasing their portion sizes. This section will provide you with information on ways to make changes to improve your overall health.

Living Green

Consumers around the world are changing from a resource-consuming lifestyle to a resource-conserving one to help maintain our natural resources and create less waste. This section suggests ways to recycle, reuse, and reduce as we work to lessen our footprints on the environment.

Home Safety

Is your home safe? There are simple steps you can take to protect yourself and your family from household hazards. This section asks questions to help you identify safety issues and potential hazards in each room of your home.

Financial Management

Many individuals are living with less than the recommended three months' emergency fund and little or no money set aside for long-term financial goals. You can take charge of your finances by setting goals and keeping track of where your money goes. The key to your future is in your hands. This section will provide you with tools to help you succeed financially.

Care of Textiles

Manufacturers have responded to consumer demand for textiles with improved and specialized characteristics. Special finishes have been developed to enable natural fibers to compete in care and performance with the rapidly growing number and quality of man-made textiles. Consumers are always faced with the problem of removing stains successfully. This section will provide you with some solutions.

Etiquette

Welcome guests with confidence at a table graced with place settings for any special occasion. Whether you are serving brunch to a few friends or entertaining a crowd, a well-planned table invites your guests to enjoy good food. This section also addresses communication changes for all ages, such as practicing proper manners for public use of cell phones.

For more information, contact your local or state Cooperative Extension Service. Information can also be found on line at eXtension (www.extension.org).

Healthy Lifestyles

Family Mealtime

Mealtimes are so much more than just eating food together—they are about modeling healthy eating, passing along family beliefs, and feeling valued as a person. Families are stretched trying to fit in soccer practice, piano lessons, and other activities, and family time tends to fall to the wayside. Research shows that more positive mealtime experiences can lead to better communication between family members, improved school performance, and better nutrition for children.

Physical Activity Guidelines for Americans

Being physically active is one of the most important steps that Americans of all ages can take to improve their health. The *2008 Physical Activity Guidelines for Americans* provides science-based guidance to help Americans aged six and older improve their health through appropriate physical activity.

Regular physical activity has been shown to reduce the risk of certain chronic diseases, including high blood pressure, stroke, coronary artery disease, type 2 diabetes, colon cancer, and osteoporosis. To reduce the risk of chronic disease, it is recommended that adults engage in at least thirty minutes of moderate-intensity physical activity on most, preferably all, days of the week. You should be able to talk, though not necessarily sing, when exercising at moderate intensity, as your lungs will be demanding more oxygen.

Most health benefits occur with at least 150 minutes a week of moderate-intensity physical activity, such as brisk walking. Both aerobic (endurance) and muscle-strengthening (resistance) physical activity are beneficial. In addition, physical activity appears to promote a sense of well-being and reduce feelings of mild to moderate depression and anxiety. Though benefits occur at 150 minutes, even greater benefits can be obtained with more minutes.

Most adults do not need to see their healthcare provider before starting a moderate-intensity physical activity program. However, men older than forty years and women older than fifty years who plan a vigorous program or who have either chronic disease or risk factors should consult their physician before starting an exercise program. Remember to drink water before, during, and after exercise.

Overcoming Barriers to Physical Activity

Lack of time is often listed as a barrier to physical activity. Setting aside thirty to sixty consecutive minutes each day is one way to obtain physical activity. Another way is to perform short bouts of moderate-intensity physical activity. The accumulated total is what matters. Physical activity can be accumulated through three to six 10-minute bouts over the course of a day. Begin physical activity low and slow. Gradually increase your activity in how often you exercise and how long the activities are done.

Find a buddy with whom to be physically active. It is much easier to keep your activity appointment if someone else is waiting for you. Time also seems to move faster when exercising with a friend.

Physical Activity Guidelines for Adults

For substantial health benefits, adults should complete at least 150 minutes of moderate-intensity, or seventy-five minutes of vigorous-intensity, aerobic activity a week. Aerobic activity should be performed in episodes of at least ten minutes. Adults should also do muscle-strengthening activities that involve all major muscle groups on two or more days a week.

Physical Activity Guidelines for Older Adults

When older adults cannot do 150 minutes of moderate-intensity aerobic activity a week because of chronic conditions, they should be as physically active as their abilities and conditions permit. Older adults should do exercises that maintain or improve balance if they are at risk of falling.

Physical Activity Guidelines for Children and Adolescents

Children and adolescents should do sixty minutes or more of physical activity daily. Most of this time should be either moderate- or vigorous-intensity aerobic physical activity. Muscle-strengthening and bone-strengthening activities should be included on at least three days of the week. One sure way to encourage physical activity is to limit screen time (computer, TV, video games) to two hours or less a day.

Healthy Lifestyles Tip

What you eat—or don't eat—can make a difference in how you feel and your ability to cope with stress. Making sure you get plenty of nourishing food is as important as sleep, relaxation, and exercise to keep a check on your stress level. Be sure to set goals and priorities so that you don't overload yourself. Slow down and catch your breath.

Adding Exercise for Lifelong Health

Medical and fitness authorities emphasize that exercise for health should include three components: cardiovascular fitness or stamina, muscle strength, and flexibility. A good blood and oxygen supply is essential for maintaining good health and healing disease.

Aerobic Exercise or endurance exercise increases stamina and heart rate, which improves heart, lung, and circulatory systems. As a muscle, the heart gets stronger with exercise. A stronger heart also improves circulation and lung function, delivering more oxygen to all parts of the body. This form of exercise can delay diseases associated with aging and diabetes, heart disease, and stroke. Examples of aerobic exercises include swimming, hiking, running, stair climbing, kick boxing, dancing, brisk walking, martial arts, and sports such as volleyball, basketball, and tennis.

Weight-bearing Exercise is an activity practiced on your feet working bones and muscles against gravity. Bone is living tissue that constantly breaks down and reforms. When doing regular weight-bearing exercises, bones adapt to the impact of weight and pull of muscle by building more cells and becoming stronger. This continues to be true as you age. Examples of weight-bearing exercises include brisk walking, jogging, hiking, yard work, team sports such as soccer, baseball, and basketball, dancing, step aerobics, stair climbing, tennis, racquet ball, skiing, skating, karate, and bowling.

Strength Exercise builds muscle and bone, increases metabolism, and can decrease weight and blood sugar. Examples of strength exercises include weight work, martial arts, pilates, cycling, and hiking.

Balance Exercise helps prevent falls, a major cause of broken hips and other injuries that can decrease independence in older adults. Examples of balance exercises include posture exercises like yoga and tai chi; exercise machines that strengthen leg and back muscles; and walking.

Flexibility Exercise keeps the body limber by stretching muscles and tissues that support the structure of the body. Examples of flexibility exercises include tai chi, yoga, pilates, martial arts, calisthenics, and exercises using stretch bands.

Tai Chi is a low-impact exercise program in which individuals work within their personal limits to improve quality of life through movement. The major benefits of a low-impact exercise program include reduced pain and stiffness; better concentration and memory; improved posture, coordination, balance, muscle strength, and stamina; increases in circulation, heart, and lung function; and improved ability to handle stress.

Tai chi looks like a graceful dance in slow motion, but instead is an effective exercise program for the mind and body. The principles include controlled breathing, mental concentration, and fluid movement. Tai chi encompasses many forms and styles. The most common are Yang, Wu, and Chen. The Arthritis Foundation has adopted the Sun style as an effective exercise for people with arthritis. This exercise form was created by Dr. Paul Lam and a team of medical experts. Studies have shown that people with arthritis need regular exercise to improve their muscular strength, flexibility, and fitness. Research of the practice of tai chi has also shown improvement of balance and relaxation. Tai chi forms have been developed for coping with diabetes, osteoporosis, and back pain.

Yoga is a form of exercise that joins mind and body through breathing, meditation, and movement in a series of poses. One of the more popular forms is hatha yoga. This form focuses on improving balance while stretching and strengthening the body. Some of the poses are more physically demanding, as in ashtanga yoga, while raja yoga helps focus the mind. Researchers have found that the regular practice of yoga reduces the incidence of chronic back pain; improves sleep quality and mood; produces a better sense of well-being and quality of life; and improves heart health, rheumatoid arthritis, type 2 diabetes, and overall physical fitness.

For more information, contact your local or state Cooperative Extension Service.

Living Green

Living green. Pursuing sustainability. Embracing environmental responsibility. These phrases have become part of America's social culture, and with each new generation they gain in importance and urgency. In short, we all have a role to play in keeping our homes and our world safe places to live. By addressing topics such as safe and nontoxic cleaning methods, recycling strategies, household chemical safety, and maintaining healthy homes (just to name a few), Extension has kept pace with the need for reliable, nonbiased information that families and communities can use to keep families safe and healthy.

In this section, we provide you with some tried-and-true recipes for alternatives to harsh and toxic commercially produced cleaners. There are also some tips on preventing mold and moisture-related problems, adopting a simpler lifestyle, setting up a recycling center in your home, and decluttering. There are countless ways that we can live a little greener. We can't do it all, but we can certainly take small steps toward improving our environment and protecting our health. See which of these tips might make sense for you and your family!

Easy Nontoxic Cleaning Recipes to Try

When making your own cleaning products, be sure to store mixtures in labeled containers with the recipe attached. Never store cleaners in milk jugs, soda bottles, or food jars that might seem harmless to curious children. Also, never reuse a commercial container; even if you clean them out, residues may mix with your added ingredients, causing harmful gases or other reactions.

Multipurpose Cleaner

1 tablespoon liquid hand-dishwashing soap (or slightly less castile soap)
2 cups water
Several drops of your favorite essential oil (optional, for scent)

Fill a clean squirt bottle with the water, leaving space at the top. Add the soap (a funnel may be helpful). Add the essential oil a few drops at a time—a little goes a long way! Put the nozzle on the spray bottle and very gently and slowly swirl the product to mix. Shaking will cause the product to foam. Try it to see if you are happy with the strength of the scent. This can be used to clean counters, tubs, sinks, baseboards, tile, and more. It is also a great stain treatment for clothing. The same ingredients can even be mixed in larger amounts to wash your car!

Drain Cleaners

When it comes to drains, prevention is best. Purchase metal or plastic screens for drains to prevent hair or food clogs in the pipes. Put fat and grease in a container and throw it away instead of pouring it down the drain. Here are two simple recipes that should help keep your sink draining properly! These recipes should be used as a treatment for slow drains **only**, not for clogged drains.

1 cup baking soda
1 cup salt
1/4 cup cream of tartar

Mix the ingredients in a bowl; then pour 1/4 cup of the mixture into the drain. Follow with 1 cup boiling water. Let it stand before flushing with water from the tap. Store the extra mixture in a covered container. Be sure to label it!

OR

1/2 cup baking soda
1/2 cup white vinegar
1/2 cup boiling water

Mix the ingredients in a bowl. Pour into the drain and let stand for several minutes. Flush with water from the tap. Repeat until the drain clears properly.

If the plumbing continues to drain slowly, there may be a clog in the drain trap. Use a pipe wrench to open the drain at the trap (the U-shaped section of pipe which holds a small amount of water to prevent sewer gas from entering your home). You will then be able to remove any accumulation of hair, grease, food, or debris. To dislodge clogs that are beyond the trap, you may need to borrow, rent, or purchase a plumber's snake to reach it.

Living Green Tip
When replacing appliances, shop for Energy Star rated choices.

Living Green Tip
Carry reusable bags in your automobile for everyday use.

Common nontoxic household products often do an excellent job for everyday cleaning tasks—and they're usually inexpensive! Generally, "basic cleaners" (high pH) like soap, baking soda, or washing soda can be used to clean food stains and general dirt or grime, and "acid cleaners" (low pH) like vinegar, lemon juice, and club soda can be used on water spots, soap scum, and rust.

Baking soda: It neutralizes odors, scrubs soap scum, dissolves dirt, unclogs drains, softens water, and cleans ovens. You can even brush your teeth with it!

Liquid soap: Soap can be used to clean almost anything! There are a few versions from which to choose. Plant-based castile soaps last a long time and work really well. You can also use nontoxic plant-based hand-dishwashing soap. Use unscented versions when making your own cleaning products so that you can add your own essential oils for fragrance, if you choose.

Vinegar or lemon juice: Vinegar is a very mild acid that removes hard water deposits from glassware, grime from windows, rust stains from sinks, and tarnish from brass and copper. It can also be used as a fabric softener. Use white distilled vinegar since apple cider vinegar or other varieties can stain. Lemon juice has mild bleaching properties, so it can be used to whiten or remove stains.

Club soda: Another mild acid, club soda is excellent for cleaning windows, mirrors, or other glass surfaces. Chrome surfaces will shine, too, if you wipe them with club soda on a clean microfiber towel. Club soda is also a great stain remover for clothes or carpets; don't oversaturate the stain or it may spread.

Tips to Keep in Mind When Using Household Cleaning Products

When selecting cleaning products of any type:

- Choose the **least** toxic products for your home.

- Buy only as much as you will use in a reasonable amount of time.

- Store chemicals and cleaning products in locked cabinets out of children's reach (not under the kitchen sink where children can access them easily).

- **Read** the label. It will list the ingredients; give instructions for use, storage, and disposal; and describe hazards associated with use.

- Dispose of toxic products as recommended. Contact your local health department or waste management facility for information about hazardous household waste collection days and disposal options.

Recipes for Disaster

Be sure to read labels when using commercial products (which are reformulated periodically) and use caution preparing mix-at-home cleaning products. No matter how inexpensive a cleaning product might be, the price is too high if an accident occurs due to misuse or improper storage. Think before combining any cleaning product with other household ingredients. Some combinations simply smell bad, but others are dangerous!

Preventing Mold and Moisture

Whether it's from cooking, cleaning, washing hands, spilling, or playing, kitchens are wet! Where there is moisture, there is often mold or mildew.

Here are a few tips to prevent mold growth.

- Keep surfaces clean and dry. Wipe up spills and repair leaks right away.

- When cooking, run a fan that is vented to the outside.

- If you use a humidifier, rinse it with clean water every day and follow the manufacturer's instructions for cleaning it.

If moisture or mold is a problem in any area of your home, it is important to address it immediately because it can spread quickly and may pose serious health risks. It is also crucial to identify the cause of the moisture so that you can correct it to prevent further mold growth.

- When cleaning mold, spores can spread through the air. Wear long sleeves and pants, shoes and socks, gloves, and goggles. Open a window for ventilation.

- Small areas of mold may be cleaned from hard surfaces with a mix of dishwashing soap and water—use a scrub brush, if needed. Rinse the area with clean water before drying it thoroughly with a towel and a fan.

- A mild bleach solution (one cup bleach to ten cups water) will kill the mold on the surface if left on the area for about fifteen minutes. Be sure to dry the area thoroughly.

- A professional should be hired to clean up areas of mold larger than fifteen square feet. Look under "Fire and Water Damage Restoration" in the phone book.

Living Green Tip
Select products based on their durability, ease of repair, and potential for reuse.

Simplifying Your Lifestyle

Living green does not have to be a complicated process. An easy way to become more "green" is to just **simplify**.

Here are some straightforward tips.

- Use natural and/or nontoxic products whenever possible.

- Buy products that have no or minimal packaging.

- Buy products that are made from recycled materials.

- Compost kitchen waste (like coffee grounds, eggshells, orange peels, etc.), grass clippings, and leaves.

- Rent or borrow equipment that you seldom use rather than purchase it.

- Purchase appliances that have the U.S. Environmental Protection Agency's Energy Star and/or WaterSense labels.

- Repair leaky faucets and toilets. Don't let the water run while shaving or brushing your teeth.

- Turn off lights and electronics (TV, radio) when leaving a room. Unplug phone chargers when not in use. Power down or, better yet, turn off computers when they are not being used.

- Install a low-flow showerhead and take five-minute showers.

- Run only full loads in your dishwasher and washing machine (or adjust the water level).

- Use durable, reusable bags in lieu of plastic or paper bags when grocery shopping.

- Carpool, bike, walk, or use public transportation whenever possible. If you must use your vehicle, plan your outing so you are not backtracking or making unnecessary trips.

- Buy locally grown foods and products.

Establishing a Recycling Center in Your Home

A significant part of "green living" includes reducing, reusing, and recycling. If you forgo the purchase or use of any product or service, you'll create the least environmental impact. If you can use a product again and again for its intended purpose, you also help to lessen our impact on the earth. Recycling is a third and important option for lessening impact by reducing the amount of material that must be burned or buried as waste and by reducing the need for natural resources.

Try to participate fully in your community's recycling program. Check with your local solid waste department or go on line to learn where you can recycle batteries, motor oil, computer equipment, sneakers, and eyeglasses.

Set up a recycling center at home. Track the amount of items in your house for about a month to determine what size containers you will need for the items you will be recycling. You can use five or six small plastic trash cans or stackable plastics boxes with lids to create a vertical recycling space.

- Plastic for recycling can be identified by the number in the triangle, usually found on the bottom of the container. Most recyclers accept #1 and #2. Often, because of the plastic formulation used, recyclers will require that the opening of a #2 plastic container be the smallest part of the container—for example, a laundry detergent bottle versus a yogurt cup. Remove tops from the containers to allow the liquid to evaporate, or rinse the container with soapy water to keep from attracting insects and rodents. Follow local directions regarding container cap removal.

- Cardboard comes in many shapes and sizes. Use a pair of heavy-duty scissors to cut tape and score cardboard to flatten. Most centers will not take soiled boxes.

- Glass containers can be recycled whether green, brown, blue, or clear. You can remove the label, but it is not always necessary. Glass containers need to be rinsed out with soapy water.

- Rinse tin cans by hand or clean them in your dishwasher to prevent odors and deter insects before placing them in your home recycling center.

- Almost all community programs will collect aluminum cans because of their traditionally high value in the recycling market. However, you may want to take advantage of the cash value for recycling the cans and/or tabs yourself. The tabs can also be recycled for charitable organizations.

- It's best to reuse clothing by donating no longer needed or outgrown garments to charity, relatives, or friends. Clothing can also be recycled into quilts or other sewing projects.

Living Green Tip
Buy only what you need and avoid accumulating unused products.

Clearing the Clutter

Another excellent way to simplify is to remove clutter. Decluttering and getting organized saves time and reduces allergens. Clutter makes cleaning much more difficult and provides the ideal place for dust and other allergens to accumulate.

Here are a few quick tips for beginning to declutter:

- Designate a time to begin decluttering. If you think it will happen spontaneously, most likely it will not. Do not become defeated if it takes more time than you anticipated.

- Have a place for everything and make sure that everything returns to its place. It is hard to clean counters and spaces of clutter if you do not have places to put everything.

- As you begin to clean and declutter, sort unused items into four piles:

  - Keep
  - Donate
  - Recycle
  - Trash

  If you have not used an item in the past fourteen months, chances are you do not have a need for it and can let go of it.

Once you have your home clutter-free, here are some tips for keeping it clean and healthy.

- Spend a few minutes every day to clean. Cleaning a little every day and putting things away when you are finished with them can go a long way towards maintaining a clean and healthy green home.

- When you leave a room, or leave your car, think about what needs to go with you. Take dishes with you on your way to the kitchen, or shoes with you on your way to the bedroom.

- Adopt the one-in-one-out rule. When you buy something new, think about what you will sell, trash, or give away to make room for the new item.

If you feel you haven't made a dent in getting rid of your clutter, don't get discouraged. On the average, it takes three to six hours per closet or one to one and a half days per room to get organized.

Living Green Tip
Select compact fluorescent lamps (CFL) and bulbs when replacements are needed.

For More Tips on Living in a Healthy Home

Help Yourself to a Healthy Home is a booklet written by Cooperative Extension Service specialists that addresses several home-related environmental health concerns. It is currently available in six languages plus a special edition for Native American audiences. Print a PDF version or order a hard copy on line through the **Healthy Homes Partnership** Web site: **www.healthyhomes partnership.net**. The Healthy Homes Partnership is a HUD/USDA Interagency Partnership.

The **U.S. Environmental Protection Agency (EPA)** is focused on protecting human health and the environment. It has a Green Living section on its Web site (**www.epa.gov**), which covers a variety of topics including green building design, water conservation techniques, and green power.

A nonprofit trade association, **The Soap and Detergent Association** is dedicated to educating the general public on the safety and benefits of cleaning products through research, outreach, and science-based advocacy. Its bimonthly on-line newsletter, *Cleaning Matters*, can be accessed at **www.cleaning101.com**.

Healthy Child Healthy World is a nonprofit organization working to protect children from harmful chemicals. They strive to educate parents, support protective policies, and engage communities to make responsible decisions, simple everyday choices, and well-informed lifestyle improvements to create healthy environments where children and families can flourish. Learn more at **www.healthychild.org**.

*For more information, contact your local or state Cooperative Extension Service and check out the U.S. Department of Energy, **www.energystar.gov**.*

Home Safety

Our homes fulfill many needs. Often the most basic need is for shelter from the elements and intruders. Once we are protected and secure, other needs can be met.

On the following pages, you will find a series of checklists. Use these lists as you go through your home. If there are items you haven't done, place a check next to them and do them as soon as you can.

General Home Safety

- ☐ Emergency numbers and your address are posted by each telephone.
- ☐ Windows open easily from the inside, but have a secure locking system that can prevent someone from entering from the outside.
- ☐ The water heater thermostats are set at 120°F or lower to prevent accidental scalding.
- ☐ Carpeting and rugs are not worn or torn.
- ☐ Small, loose rugs have nonskid backing and are not placed in high-traffic areas of the home.
- ☐ Appliances, lamps, and cords are clean and in good condition.
- ☐ There are no exposed, glaring bulbs in lamps or fixtures.
- ☐ Electrical overload protection is provided by circuit breakers, fuses, or ground fault circuit interrupters (GFCIs). GFCIs prevent electrical shock and are particularly important in areas where water is used, such as kitchens, bathrooms, and outside.
- ☐ Smoke alarms are present in the home and are in working order.
- ☐ Position tables, chairs, shelving, and other furniture so that they cannot be toppled easily.
- ☐ Install screen windows, and make sure they open from the top or have a barricade in front.
- ☐ Provide railings on stairs, porches, decks, and lofts.
- ☐ Equip steps with tread mats or carpet and a handrail that children can reach.
- ☐ Do not store clothing in dry-cleaning bags that are accessible to children.
- ☐ Store all plastic bags, including small bread sacks, out of the reach of children.
- ☐ Do not allow children to use or play with objects that have long cords. This includes pacifiers with strings attached, long telephone cords, old jewelry, necklaces, and long scarves.
- ☐ Tie hanging cords on draperies or blinds up high and out of reach.
- ☐ Install clotheslines out of the reach of children.

Stairs and Hall

- ☐ Steps are in good condition and are free of objects.
- ☐ Steps have nonskid strips. Carpeting on steps is securely fastened and free of fraying or holes.
- ☐ Hallways are equipped with night-lights.
- ☐ Sturdy handrails are on both sides of stairways and are securely fastened.
- ☐ Light switches are located at the top and bottom of stairways and at both ends of long hallways.
- ☐ Inside doors do not swing out over stair steps.
- ☐ It is easy to see the leading edge or nosing of each stair tread while walking down stairs.
- ☐ Stairways and hallways are well lit.
- ☐ Tack down small rugs and runners to prevent slipping.

Bathroom

- ☐ The bathtub or shower has a nonskid mat or strips on the standing area.
- ☐ Bathtub or shower doors are made of safety glass or plastic.
- ☐ The towel bars and the soap dish in the shower stall are durable and firmly installed.
- ☐ A single-lever mixing faucet is used, or faucets are easy to grasp.
- ☐ Bathroom flooring is matte-finished, textured tile, or low-pile commercial carpet.
- ☐ The light switch is near the door.
- ☐ Doors open outward.
- ☐ The bathroom has a ventilation system. Use during and after showers to remove excess moisture and prevent mold and mildew.
- ☐ Perfumes, cosmetics, and other drug products are in high cabinets with safety latches or locks.
- ☐ The outlets are ground fault circuit interrupters (GFCIs) that protect against electric shock.
- ☐ Do not leave children alone in the bathtub.
- ☐ Keep toilet lids closed.

Home Safety Tips
Keep window treatment cords secure and out of the reach of children.

Bedroom

- ☐ A lamp or flashlight is kept within reach of your bed. Check batteries periodically to make sure they are working, and keep a spare package of batteries nearby.
- ☐ A night-light is used to brighten the way to the bathroom at night.
- ☐ Plenty of room is left for you to walk around the bed.
- ☐ You have an adequate-sized nightstand or small table for the telephone, glasses, or other important items.
- ☐ Mesh-sided playpens have holes no larger than ¼ inch.
- ☐ Remove hanging crib toys when infants are able to pull themselves up.
- ☐ Remove the plastic wrap from crib mattresses.
- ☐ Crib mattresses fit tightly with no more than two finger widths in the gap between the mattress and crib frame.

Kitchen

- [ ] Wash hands with warm water, using soap from a pump bottle, and dry hands with disposable towels in all of the following situations: before handling food, immediately after using the restroom, between tasks such as handling raw chicken and making a salad, or any other time necessary to prevent food contamination.
- [ ] Range and sink areas have adequate light levels.
- [ ] Gas range is equipped with pilot lights and an automatic cut-off in the event of flame failure.
- [ ] If you have an exhaust hood for the oven, it has easily removable filters for proper cleaning.
- [ ] When cooking, pan handles are turned away from other burners and the edge of the range.
- [ ] When cooking, do not wear garments with long, loose sleeves.
- [ ] Hot pads and pan holders are kept near the range.
- [ ] If you have a microwave, it is operated only when there is food in it.
- [ ] Small appliances are unplugged when not in use.
- [ ] Knives are kept in a knife rack or drawer.
- [ ] Countertops and work areas are cleared of all unnecessary objects.
- [ ] A sturdy, stable stepladder or step stool is used rather than a chair to reach objects in overhead cabinets.
- [ ] Grease or liquid spills are wiped up at once.
- [ ] Use a refrigerator thermometer—the temperature inside your fridge should stay at or below 40°F.
- [ ] Maintain frozen food in a frozen state. Do not refreeze thawed food items unless they're cooked first.
- [ ] Thaw food products in the refrigerator, under cold running water, in a microwave oven, or as part of the cooking process.
- [ ] Store any leftover foods in containers with tight-fitting lids to avoid contamination.
- [ ] Use tongs or other tools for handling food whenever possible.
- [ ] Never handle food or utensils when you have open sores or cuts on your hands.
- [ ] Do not handle food for your family or friends when you're sick.
- [ ] If you must handle food, use food service gloves to protect you and your family.

Home Safety Tips
There should be enough space to walk through the room leaving clear passageways for traffic.

Child Safety

- ☐ All doors to rooms and closets can be unlocked from both sides.
- ☐ Trash is covered and out of the reach of children.
- ☐ Do not store alcoholic beverages, cleaning supplies, cosmetics, pet supplies, medicines, vitamins, gasoline, paint thinner, fertilizer, weed killer, and other poisons in areas used by children.
- ☐ Store hazardous products in their original containers.
- ☐ Keep purses out of the reach of children.
- ☐ Do not use insect poisons, rat poisons, or weed killers when children are present. Dispose of leftover poisons immediately.
- ☐ Follow directions and caution warnings on drugs, cosmetics, and chemicals.
- ☐ Check to make sure that there is no peeling paint on walls or furniture.
- ☐ Have your home checked for radon—an odorless gas that seeps through the soil into homes. Inexpensive test kits can be purchased at most hardware stores.
- ☐ Check toys and materials to make sure they contain nontoxic, nonpoisonous materials. Look for the "CP" or "AP" seal signifying safe art material for children.
- ☐ Mix prescription drugs with an undesirable substance, such as used coffee grounds or kitty litter, and put them in impermeable, nondescript containers, such as empty cans or sealable bags, and then throw them in the trash. Some community pharmacies have a take-back program that allows the public to bring in unused drugs for proper disposal.
- ☐ Medicines should be stored in a high, locked, or otherwise child-inaccessible space.
- ☐ Cover the sandbox when not in use.
- ☐ Regularly inspect outdoor play equipment for broken, worn, or missing parts. Remove, repair, or replace items immediately.
- ☐ Cover all protruding bolts or screws with plastic safety caps.

Controlling Clutter

- ☐ Spend ten minutes on a quick pick-up around the house.
- ☐ Use a basket and go through the house quickly, picking up and dropping off things where they belong.
- ☐ Things needing to be done should be written on a notepad and shared with whoever will fix the problem.
- ☐ Get the family into the habit of cleaning up as soon as they are finished with something and before another activity is started.
- ☐ Set limits on possessions.
- ☐ Deal with things when they are in your hand, or keep a basket out of sight to hold these items.
- ☐ Magazines can pile up fast. Tear out the articles and recipes you want and donate the rest to a school or recycle them.
- ☐ When a piece of paper comes across your hands, file it, toss it, or deal with it.
- ☐ Put letters in a basket with stamps and envelopes.
- ☐ Before you buy something, ask yourself whether you really need it or if it will just end up as clutter.
- ☐ First eliminate the clutter; then prevent more from coming in.
- ☐ Less clutter means less stuff to clean, clean around, straighten up, reorganize, and worry about.

☐ Simplify your life and be surrounded by only the things you need and love. Removing clutter and maintaining a clutter-free home are major steps to having an organized home and a stress-free life.

Home Exterior and Grounds Maintenance

☐ Steps, paths, and walkways are in good condition.

☐ Doorways, steps, porches, and walkways have good lighting.

☐ Porches, balconies, terraces, window wells, and other heights or depressions are protected by railings, closed with banisters, or are otherwise protected.

☐ Hedges, trees, or shrubs do not hide the view of the street.

☐ Inspect roof for wind, snow, and ice damage from the ground to see that roof shingles are secure, tightly fastened, and in good condition.

☐ Gutters and downspouts are securely anchored to the roof line and house wall and are clean and free of debris such as dirt, leaves, and twigs.

☐ Inspect masonry or brick walls for loose, crumbling mortar joints.

☐ Check weather stripping around windows and doors.

☐ Check to see that insulations are not blocking soffit vents.

☐ Check along the outside and inside of the foundation and along the basement floor for cracks in block and concrete walls and floors for signs of rot/decay, termites, or other damage from wood-destroying pests.

☐ Inspect plastic vapor barrier on dirt floor of crawl space.

☐ Inspect bricks and mortar joints of bricks and lining in the fireplace.

☐ Remove soot and creosote from the chimneys of fireplaces and wood-burning stovepipes and chimneys.

☐ Check outside faucets for leaks.

☐ Inspect electric receptacle outlets and switches to be sure that covers are not cracked or broken.

☐ Clean basement window wells of leaves and other debris to help rain water filter rapidly into the soil, preventing it from backing up and flowing into the basement.

☐ Check vents in the crawl space to make sure that the screen or wire mesh covering is secure and in good repair. Remove insulation and open the vents in early spring.

☐ Gloves should be worn during all gardening activities.

☐ When using garden sprays, always follow the label directions on what to wear to protect yourself.

☐ Mix sprays in an open, well-ventilated area.

☐ Safety goggles should be worn any time you prune, regardless of how simple or involved the job is.

☐ Wear lightweight, light-colored, loose-fitting cotton clothes as well as long-sleeved shirts and pants.

☐ Wear a sunscreen with a minimum SPF 15, protective sunglasses, and a wide-brimmed hat.

☐ Lock storage sheds, barns, and garages.

☐ Check your grill thoroughly for leaks, cracking, or brittleness before using.

☐ Be sure the grill is at least ten feet away from your house, garage, or trees.

☐ Store and use your grill on a large flat surface that cannot burn (e.g., concrete or asphalt).

For more information, contact your local or state Cooperative Extension Service.

Home Safety

Our home should be a place in which we can be safe from accidents and injuries. Home accidents are a major source of injuries and can cause death. Children and older persons are the most susceptible to falls and other injuries in the home. When possessions are regularly cared for and maintained in good working order, they will last longer—saving time and money.

Legal Documents Needed

A variety of legal documents can help us be prepared if we become incapacitated. Some related tools could include a living will, a healthcare surrogate form, and a durable power of attorney. For information relevant in your state, contact your attorney general, your personal attorney, or a regional hospice.

Financial Management

Starting Your Financial Information Binder

A Financial Binder provides a quick reference to your entire financial situation. When complete, your financial notebook will help you manage your personal finances. This information can also help the person who must manage for you in the event that you become temporarily incapacitated or die.

Your Financial Binder should be updated annually as well as whenever a significant change occurs (such as birth, death, marriage, divorce, widowhood, relocation, and purchase or sale of assets). Store a copy of the entire notebook in a fireproof box at home, with a friend, or in a safe-deposit box, and keep the original handy for the ongoing management of your financial affairs.

Guidelines for Starting Your Financial Binder

Your Financial Binder doesn't have to be fancy, but you'll need:

1. A sturdy three-ring binder
2. At least sixteen index dividers
3. Plastic page protectors
4. College-ruled notebook paper

Label the dividers with the titles of your notebook items. Some suggestions are listed below. Add other items as needed.

Suggested Binder Items

List of Goals	Birth Certificates
Budget	Social Security Cards
Paycheck Stubs	Social Security Benefits Statement
Special Expenses	Insurance Policies
Loan Papers	Personal Property Inventory
Credit Report	Rental or Lease Agreements
Net Worth Statement	Personal Directory*
Income Tax Information, Copy of Filings	Professional Directory**
Pension/Retirement Benefits	Immunization Records

* Personal Directory—List each family member and friend who should be notified in the event of a death in your family. Include the executor of your will. Also, include the Social Security and military discharge numbers of immediate family members. These numbers provide a quick reference should you or your representative need to apply for benefits.

**Professional Directory—Together with the Personal Directory, this list would be useful to your representative if you or a family member should die or become incapacitated. Include your employer (and your spouse's employer) and every professional involved in your affairs: physician, dentist, clergy, lawyer, accountant, insurance agent, banker, financial agent, real estate agent, etc.

Organizing Your Records: Where to Store Important Documents

Households should be viewed as miniature businesses. A systematic plan for keeping track of important papers can save hours of anxious searching and can help preserve peace and harmony, as well as make it easier to cope with emergency situations.

Following is a chart of <u>what</u> to store <u>where</u>:

Safe Deposit Box	Fireproof Box or Filing Cabinet at Home	Attorney/ Relative/ Friend
Automobile Titles	Cancelled Checks	Burial Instructions
Birth Certificates	Recent Tax Records	Living Will
Citizenship Papers	Insurance Policies	Power of Attorney
Death Certificates	Living Will	Trust Documents
Education Degrees	Power of Attorney	Will (copy or original)
Marriage Document	Original Will	Copy of Personal and Professional Directories
Legal Documents	Trust Documents	
Property Deeds	Warranties	
Military Documents	Back Tax Records	
Stock/Bond Certificates	Copy of Items in Financial Binder	
Personal Property Inventory		
Mortgage Papers, Title		

Organize your records for safety and accessibility. What's important is that:

- Valuable or hard-to-replace documents are kept in a safe place, such as a safe-deposit box at a bank or a fireproof box at home. A good rule to follow is keep the item at home unless it is a legal document or is difficult to replace or duplicate; then it should be kept in a safe-deposit box or left with your attorney.

- The attorney/friend/relative who would tend to your affairs in the event of your incapacitation or death has easy access to the documents that would be needed.

- When in doubt, **don't** throw it out.

Personal Credit Information

Reviewing your personal credit information periodically is important. One should especially do this before making a large purchase on credit. Telephone numbers for the three major credit reporting agencies are:

Equifax
  1-800-685-1111
Experian
  1-888-397-3742
Trans Union
  1-800-916-8800

Financial Fitness: Exercises to Shape Up Your Spending

How is your financial health? Take charge with an annual financial checkup.

- ■ Do you spend less than you earn?

- ■ Do you spend no more than 15 to 20 percent of your monthly income for credit payments, including car payments, credit cards, and all other debts (excluding mortgage)?

- ■ Do you have an emergency savings fund to cover at least three to six months of your living expenses?

If you answered "yes" to all of the questions above, then your finances should be in great shape! If you answered "no" to any or you are unsure, you may need to complete a few money management exercises to shape up your spending.

Exercise 1: Identify Income

List all sources of income and resources used to pay expenses for one month. Include all household members. List checks separately. *Use **net** income.* Add all income and resources to get your total monthly income.

Family Income

	Source of Income	When Received	Amount Per Pay Period	Amount Per Month
1				
2				
3				
	Total Monthly Family Income $			

Exercise 2: List Debts

Write down each credit account with the monthly payment. Include car payments, credit cards, and all loans except your house. Total the monthly payments and divide that number by your total monthly income.

If the answer is more than 20 percent, it is time to find ways to lower your debt load.

_____ ÷ _____
(Your Monthly Payments)   (Your Total Monthly Income)

= _____
(Your Debt to Income Ratio)

For additional financial management information, contact your local Extension Office.

Exercise 3: Track Expenses

List **fixed expenses**, such as a house payment or rent and car loans or other installment loans, first. Fixed expenses stay the same each month.

Flexible expenses that vary from month to month are harder to estimate. Record how much you spend for one whole month on flexible expenses like food, gas, revolving credit (store or bank credit cards), and utilities.

To track daily expenses, write down every cent you spend every day for one week. It's even better if you track these for a month. This will be an eye-opener!

Fixed Expenses	Date Due	Amount Due
$1/12$ Annual Total of Periodic Expenses*		

Flexible Expenses	Week 1	Week 2	Week 3	Week 4
Back Tax Records				
Gas				
Electricity				
Gasoline				
Personal Care				
Household Supplies				
Other				

Exercise 4: Calculate Periodic Expenses

Complete the Periodic Expense Planner (page 34)

Exercise 5: Compare Income to Expenses

If you are spending less than you earn, you should have money to save for a rainy day and for future goals. Good for you!

If you find you are spending more than you earn, you have two choices: 1) reduce expenses, or 2) increase income.

Total monthly income   _____

                 Minus –

Total monthly living expenses   _____

                 Equals=

Surplus or deficit income   _____

Exercise 6: Compare Expenses to Savings

Financially healthy families have an emergency savings account with enough money to cover at least three months (three to six months preferred) of living expenses. How does your savings account compare?

_____ × 3 = _____
Monthly living expenses   Savings needed for emergency fund

Periodic Expense Planner

Most expenses occur monthly and are easily planned into the monthly budget or spending plan. But expenses which take place periodically may throw off any household budget. By using a periodic expense planner, these periodic expenses such as holidays, birthdays, vacations, car registration/licensing, insurance payments, or income taxes can become more manageable. Take a few minutes to think about your periodic expenses. Write them in the chart below and estimate the amount you will spend on that item, event, or service. Once this is complete, add up all the expenses for the year. Take that number and divide it by 12. This is the amount you can set aside each month. When a periodic expense occurs, you take that amount from this set-aside money. If you find that you have too many periodic payments due at the same time each year, consider negotiating different due dates where possible.

Example

Let's say you had a summer vacation for $1,500, several birthdays totaling $200, and car license tags and insurance payments totaling $700.

Total Annual Expenses = $2,400 ($1,500 + $200 + $700)

$2,400 ÷ 12 months = $200. So each month, this individual or household would place $200 aside to cover the periodic expenses when they occur.

Now it's your turn

January	February	March
April	May	June
July	August	September
October	November	December

Total Annual Expenses ÷ 12 months = Monthly Set-Aside

_____ ÷ 12 months = _____

Smart Goals

Goals are objectives toward which we work and strive. Goals provide a basis for making choices in how money and other resources are used. Spending goals set early in life can serve as a guide to help you spend your money for things that are most important to you. Studies show that those who WRITE goals are more likely to achieve them than those who do not write their goals down. **SMART goals are**

SPECIFIC. Set specific goals that you can clearly name. For example, save enough money to get a new refrigerator. Determine the amount you'll have to pay rather than just saving.

MEASURABLE. Measure goals by the time and money it will take to reach them.

ATTAINABLE. Make sure goals are reasonable and possible. For example, "I know I can save _____ dollars each week to reach my goal in six months."

RELEVANT. Make sure your goals fit your needs.

TIME-RELATED. Set a definite target date.
Write your short-term and long-term saving and spending goals below.

SHORT-TERM GOALS (within six months to one year)

1. By _____ (date) I will have paid off my _____.

2. By _____ (date) I will have saved $ _____ for _____.

3. I will save $ _____ from each paycheck for a total of $ _____

   by _____ (date).

LONG-TERM GOALS (within five years or longer)

1. _____

2. _____

3. _____

Goals are dreams and wishes that could come true.

Specific goals motivate you to balance your spending and saving in order to maximize your happiness from your income.

*If you want to be an effective manager of your life and finances, you need to know **where** you are going, **how** you intend to get there, and **when** you will arrive. Those insights come from your **goals**—your statements of what you want to achieve in life.*

Don't Break the Bank at the Grocery Store

Finding ways to save money is critical for most families. Careful planning and shopping strategies can make a significant impact on the family food budget.

Before Shopping

- Check your pantry to see what ingredients you already have available.

- Plan your meals. Write out recipes and include servings for lunch the following day.

- Consider a couple of meatless days to cut expenses. Dried beans and peas, eggs, and peanut butter are also excellent sources of protein.

- Keep paper and a pen in the kitchen to list items when you are running low. This way you can write down an item right away when you realize it is needed. This will prevent extra trips to the store to pick up those items, and you won't be tempted to buy things that are not needed.

- Make a list. Look at sale ads; if possible look at more than one store's sales.

- Arrange your list by category to make it easier when shopping. If you are familiar with the stores, you can even arrange the list by where items are located in each store.

- Stick to the list. Little items will add up and you will overspend your grocery budget.

- Create a "shopping pool." Agree with family and friends to shop sales for each other.

- Leave your credit cards and checkbooks at home. Bring cash! Cash allows you to spend only the amount you have budgeted for your groceries and helps you ignore impulse buys. If you did not plan for it, do not buy it.

- You have heard this before, but it is so true . . . eat before you go. Don't shop for groceries on an empty stomach!

While Shopping

- Shop for items **BEFORE** you run out of them. If you run out of an item, you'll have to pay whatever the store is charging that week.

- Shop on days when expensive items are on special, or shop at stores that offer frequent shopper programs or double coupon days.

- You may want to tackle the warehouse clubs or superstores when buying in bulk, but buy only what you can use.

- For the best prices on health and beauty products, check the national drugstore chains and superstores.

- Go to the supermarket early in the morning (before 9 a.m.) to have a better chance of getting markdown items. Local stores mark down fresh vegetables and fruits, frozen items, milk, and meats.

- Watch for unadvertised specials, but don't buy just because it's a bargain—make sure you will use it.

- Beware of marketing strategies such as end-of-aisle dump bins, island displays, recipe-related item placement, and middle-shelf items. This is typically where higher priced and impulse products are placed.

- Don't be afraid to try generic or store brands. Most stores will refund your money if you are not satisfied.

- Buy and use in-season vegetables and fruit.

- Always check the expiration date on dairy products. If it is close to the expiration date, ask for a discount.

- Convenience foods are more expensive, as you are trading money for time. Slice, season, mix, and cook it yourself.

- Learn to be a label reader. Ingredients are listed in order by the highest to lowest quantity actually used when making the product. Also, you can get a better idea of what the fat-to-calorie ratio is as well as other valuable nutritional information.

- Watch the scanner. It allows you to stop the checkout process if an item is showing the incorrect price.

After Shopping

- Complete and mail rebates before you forget and lose the potential savings.

- Always return a product that is spoiled.

For more information, contact your local or state Cooperative Extension Service. Information can also be found on line at the eXtension Web site, **www.extension.org**.

Care of Textiles

Textile Fiber Products Identification Act

The Textile Fiber Products Identification Act became effective on March 3, 1960. The purpose of the law is to protect consumers and producers from false advertising and mislabeling of the fiber content of textile fiber products.

This act requires most textile products sold at retail to have labels stating the textile fiber content. To reduce confusion, the law establishes twenty-one generic or family names of textile fibers. For example, polyester is a generic fiber classification. Dacron, Kodel, and Fortrel are all manufacturers' trade names for their polyester fibers.

Each label must give the following information.

1. The generic or family name of the fiber.

2. The name of the manufacturer or a registered identification number or trademark.

3. The percent of each fiber listed in order of its predominance by weight. If a particular fiber is 5 percent or less, it may be designated as "other fiber."

4. The country of origin, if other than the United States.

5. The fiber trade name may be given on the label, if desired. If so, the trade name cannot be used without the generic classification, and the trade name may not be in larger print than the generic.

Rules for Proper Care

The first rule of satisfactory removal of stains is prompt treatment. Spots set by heat or age are almost impossible to remove. Keep in mind the nature of the stain, the fabric, and the process for removing the stain. Follow the instructions and recommendations of the fabric and product manufacturer. Detailed stain removal information and laundry care identification symbol charts are available from local or state Cooperative Extension Services.

Removing Stubborn Stains

Always read the garment's label for care instructions to determine if it is washable or dry-clean only, and follow these general rules.

Apple Cider—Launder with detergent in the hottest water safe for the fabric. To remove old stains, wash with bleach that is safe for the fabric.

Butter, Cooking Oil, Salad Dressing, and Turkey Fat—Light stains can be pretreated with a spray stain remover, liquid laundry detergent, or a detergent booster. Place heavy stains facedown on clean paper towels. Apply cleaning liquid to the back of the stain. Replace towels frequently. Let air dry; rinse. Launder in the hottest water safe for the fabric. Before drying, inspect and repeat the treatment and washing if the stain remains.

Candle Wax—Harden with ice, and then remove surface wax with a dull knife. Place the wax stain between clean paper towels and press with a warm iron. Replace paper towels frequently to absorb more wax and to prevent transferring the stain. Place stain facedown on clean paper towels. Sponge remaining stain with a prewash stain remover; blot with paper towels. Let dry, and then launder. Note: If any color remains, relaunder with bleach that is safe for the fabric.

Chocolate and Hot Chocolate—Treat the stain with a prewash spray or pretreat with a product containing enzymes. Launder. If the stain remains, relaunder with bleach that is safe for the fabric.

Coffee or Tea—Flush the stain immediately with cold water if possible; or soak for thirty minutes in cold water, and then apply prewash spray. Rub the stain with detergent and launder with bleach that is safe for the fabric.

Cranberries—Launder in the hottest water safe for the fabric. Removing old stains may require washing with bleach safe for the fabric.

Personal Clothing Tip
Give your clothing and shoes time to rest between wearing. Launder or dry-clean clothing and household linens only when soiled. Cleaning when unnecessary shortens the life and appearance of the item.

Cream, Egg, or Cheese Sauces—Fresh stains should be soaked and agitated in cold water before washing. If the stain is dried or old, scrape or brush off any crusted matter and soak the stain in cold water up to several hours using a detergent or an enzyme presoak. Launder in warm (not hot) water. If the stain remains, soak an additional thirty minutes and rewash.

Gravy—Treat the stain with a prewash spray or pretreat with a product containing enzymes. Launder. If the stain remains, relaunder with bleach that is safe for the fabric.

Lipstick—Place the stain facedown on paper towels. Sponge the area with a dry-cleaning solvent or use a prewash soil and stain remover. Replace towels frequently; rinse. Rub light-duty liquid detergent into the stain until the outline is removed; launder. Repeat treatment if needed using an all-fabric bleach, which is less damaging to colors and fabric. Use liquid chlorine bleach for tough stains, if fabrics are colorfast.

Pine Resin—Scrape off as much as possible. Sponge the stain with cleaning fluid or pretreatment stain remover; let air dry. Rub with detergent paste and launder as usual. If stains persist, apply a few drops of household ammonia; air dry. Launder using liquid laundry detergent and all-fabric bleach. Use liquid chlorine bleach for tough stains, if fabrics are colorfast.

Smoke or Soot—Shake off excess soot outdoors. Launder in washing machine using heavy-duty detergent or liquid as recommended by the manufacturer and 1/2 cup of all-fabric bleach. Use the water setting appropriate for the fabric; air dry. Inspect for smoke odor. Repeat as necessary. Three or four washes may be needed for cottons and cotton blends.

Wine—Soak the stain in cold water. Pretreat with prewash stain remover, liquid laundry detergent, or a paste of powdered detergent and water. Launder in the hottest water safe for fabric, using bleach safe for that fabric.

Towel Tip

Kitchen towels and dishcloths should be washed often on the hot cycle of your washing machine. Sponges can be washed in the dishwasher.

How to Clean Vintage Linens

Most vintage linens will have some degree of fabric wear, staining, or discoloration. Machine laundering techniques are much too harsh for these linens. The fabrics are simply too fragile, and you could cause further damage. Some may be spot cleaned, but most will require thorough hand washing to remove stains and yellowing.

Examine the item carefully for structural damage. Spot test all cleaning recipes in an inconspicuous spot. While these cleaning methods should be safe for most vintage linens, spot testing will allow you to be sure that the fabric and threads are colorfast.

For normal cleaning, hand wash your vintage table linens with a gentle soap or detergent and rinse thoroughly. Gently ball them into your hands, allowing the water to run through your fingers. Slowly close and open your hands a few times to remove some of the water. Lay the linen flat on a thick clean towel and gently roll up the towel with the linen inside to remove even more of the moisture. Lay flat to dry.

Try lemon juice and sunlight for a natural stain removal solution on your vintage linens. Fill a large pot with water and cut several lemons into slices. Bring your lemon water to a boil and then remove it from the heat. Gently add your linens and press into the water with a wooden spoon. Allow them to soak overnight. Rinse well and wash with mild soap. Lay flat on a towel on the grass in the sun to dry.

For stain removal, add 2 cups of white vinegar and 1/4 cup of salt to a sink of cool water and mix well. Add the fabrics, allowing them to soak with only gentle stirrings for several hours. You may add a couple teaspoons of lemon juice for stain removal and fragrance.

Oxygen bleach products, such as OxiClean powder, work to remove or reduce stains and discoloration. The powder must be activated with very hot water. Then add cold water until the temperature is warm to cool. Add the linens and soak for several hours or overnight. Occasionally, you may gently stir the fabrics around in the solution; but remember to handle with care and definitely do not wring the fabric.

A mixture of peroxide bleach, such as Biz, and a chlorine-free stain remover, such as OxiClean, may work to clean and whiten linens. Combine equal amounts of the two products, two tablespoons of each per one gallon of hot water. Allow the water to cool. Soak the linens for up to two days; rinse. Hand wash with gentle detergent as usual. Sunlight may help with final whitening and stain removal.

Do not use starch before storing linens. Starch could cause discoloration over a period of time. You may make a spray bottle of rose water and lightly mist the linen for a nice fragrance that shouldn't harm the fabric. Allow the linen to dry fully before storing.

To store, wrap or roll your linen in acid-free paper. If the item is small enough, you may roll it into the paper and store it inside a paper towel roll or an empty roll from wrapping paper. The key is to make sure the fabric is fully dry; do not make any hard creases.

For more information, contact your local or state Cooperative Extension Service.

Etiquette Tip
Even in today's electronic environment, a timely handwritten thank-you note is proper and appreciated for both social and business occasions.

Proper Table Etiquette

Practicing good table manners at home will help family members feel more at ease whether dining at a friend's house or in a fine restaurant.

Rules of Table Etiquette

1. Sit correctly at the table; use good posture, keep your hands in your lap or on the table, and keep elbows off the table while eating.

2. Pass food in a counterclockwise movement around the table. Use "please" and "thank you" as you ask the person nearest to an item to pass it to you.

3. Cut meat one piece at a time, and then eat it before cutting another. Take small bites of food and eat quietly and slowly. Do not try to talk while you are still chewing.

4. If you want a second helping in your own home, ask for it. However, if you are a guest in someone else's home, don't ask. If there is more, it will be offered to you.

5. If you are a guest in someone's home, follow your host's lead. Don't eat or drink anything before grace has been said or the hostess is seated and starts to eat.

6. As soon as you sit down at the table, spread your napkin across your lap. If you must leave the table during the meal, place your napkin on the seat of your chair, not on the table. When the meal is finished and everyone is leaving, fold your napkin and leave it on the table.

7. Excuse yourself for all biological functions, including a coughing spell or the need to blow your nose.

8. It is very poor manners to use a toothpick at the table.

9. Lift food to your mouth when you eat.

10. Eat all of the food taken on a fork or spoon at one time. Never remove food from your mouth, except bones, seeds, or pits.

Table Setting for an Elegant Dinner

1. Set your dinner plate in the center.

2. Place a folded napkin on top of the plate or next to the salad fork.

3. The dinner fork goes to the left of the plate.

4. The salad fork goes to the left of the dinner fork.

5. Place your knife to the right of the dinner plate with the blade facing inwards.

6. The dinner spoon goes directly to the right of the knife.

7. Place your soup spoon or iced tea spoon to the right of the dinner spoon.

8. A small bread plate should be placed at the eleven o'clock position, with respect to the dinner plate.

9. Position a small butter knife diagonally across the bread plate.

10. At the one o'clock position (again with respect to the dinner plate), set a water goblet or tumbler.

11. Place the iced tea/wine goblet to the right of the water goblet.

■ ■ ■ ■ ■ ■ ■

Etiquette Tip

When it comes to using your cell phone at work, you have to be mindful of your co-workers and your boss, not to mention your own ability to get your job done. Here are some rules you should follow if you have your personal cell phone at work.

- *Turn off your cell phone ringer*

- *Use your cell phone only for important calls*

- *Let your cell phone calls go to voice mail*

- *Don't bring your cell phone to meetings*

Cell Phone Etiquette

It is hard to imagine life without our cell phones. Cell phones have become a vital part of our lives. They help us save time and have been credited for saving lives during emergencies. However, there is still a right way and as well as a wrong way to use them. Read on to learn how to properly use your cell phone in public.

1. If you are with people and you're receiving a call, you should excuse yourself and take the call elsewhere. It is especially annoying if there are multiple people with whom you are trying to carry on conversations.

2. Let the people on the other end of the phone know what you are doing. No matter how important the phone call is, they may offer to talk later if you're in a situation that might be less than ideal for talking on the phone.

3. Technology is impressive when it comes to cell phones, but there is no need to shout over the phone. It is annoying and disruptive to the people around you as well as unnecessary and unattractive.

4. If you're texting, the same rules apply. Stay aware of people around you.

5. **Don't Bring Your Cell Phone Into the Restroom . . . Ever.** This rule should apply to using your cell phone at work or anywhere. Why? . . . Well, if you must ask—you never know who's in there; the person on the other end of the line will hear bathroom sounds, e.g., toilets flushing.

Decorative Napkin Folding—"Water Lily"

One of the best known folds, the "water lily" is equally suitable for both formal and informal occasions. To make a flat, open lily, use a napkin made of soft, unstarched fabric. Use a crisper fabric to make sharper edges and a tall bowl-shape.

1. To find the exact center of the napkin, fold it in half to form a rectangle and crease the fold with your thumb. Open the napkin and repeat the fold the other way. The point at which the folds meet is the center. Fold each of the corners of the napkin in so they meet at the center.

2. Fold one corner in again, making sure it is exactly in the center.

3. Fold the other three corners into the center to form a smaller square.

4. Carefully lift the napkin and turn it over, keeping all the folded corners tucked underneath. Fold one of the corners into the center.

5. Fold each of the other three corners into the center so that you once again form a smaller square.

6. Holding the points at the center with your fingers, gently pull out the flap from under one of the corners. Pull out each of the other corners to form the petals of the water lily.

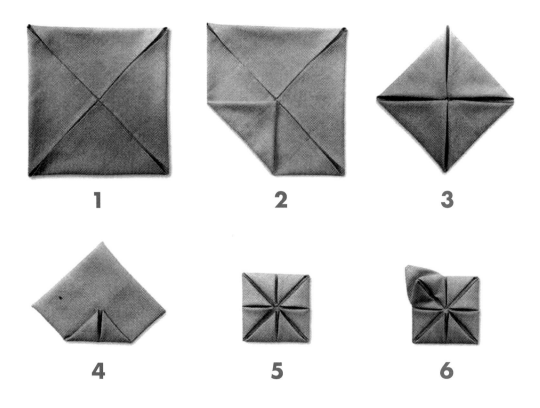

For more information, contact your local or state Cooperative Extension Service.

Dairy

Safe Homemade Ice Cream

Avoid homemade ice cream recipes that include uncooked eggs in the directions. Uncooked eggs may contain salmonella bacteria that are commonly found in nature. With proper care and handling, eggs pose no greater risk than any other perishable food.

Follow these simple steps for food safety when preparing homemade ice cream. Keep everything clean—freezer, dasher, storage container, and utensils. Cook the ice cream base over low heat until a candy thermometer registers 160 degrees. After cooking, chill the base immediately and thoroughly before freezing. Pasteurized egg products that are available in grocery stores can be substituted for uncooked eggs in homemade ice cream.

What Is Raw Milk?

Raw milk is milk from cows, sheep, or goats that has not been pasteurized to kill harmful bacteria. Raw milk can contain *Salmonella*, *E. coli*, and *Listeria*, all of which have been responsible for causing food-borne illness.

What Is Pasteurization?

Pasteurization is a process of heating milk to a specific temperature for a set period of time, to kill potentially harmful microorganisms. Microorganisms commonly found in raw milk can lead to diseases such as listeriosis, typhoid fever, tuberculosis, diphtheria, and brucellosis. Research shows that pasteurization does not significantly affect the nutritional quality of milk.

Dairy Pasteurization Table

TEMPERATURE	TIME	PASTEURIZATION
63°C (145°F)	30 Minutes	Vat Pasteurization
72°C (161°F)	15 Seconds	High Temperature Short Time Pasteurization (HTST)
89°C (191°F)	1.0 Second	Ultra Pasteurization

To Find Out If Milk and Dairy Products Have Been Pasteurized:

Read the label. Safe milk will have the word "pasteurized" on the label or package.

Ask your grocer or store clerk.

Don't buy milk or other dairy products from vendors at farmers' markets **unless you can confirm** that their products have been pasteurized.

FOOD EQUIVALENTS

Cottage Cheese
1 pound = 2 cups

Shredded Cheese
4 ounces = 1 cup

Cream Cheese
8 ounces = 16 tablespoons

Cream, Whipping
1 cup = 2 cups whipped

New Mexican Hot Chocolate Mix

Serves 16

Per serving
Calories 181
Protein 11 g
Carbohydrates 35 g
Total Fat 1 g
3% Calories from Fat
Cholesterol 4 mg
Fiber 2 g
Sodium 155 mg
Sugar 27 g

6¹/2 cups instant nonfat dry milk powder
1 cup sugar
³/4 cup baking cocoa

²/3 cup cornstarch
2 tablespoons cinnamon
2 teaspoons ground red chile

Sift the milk powder, sugar, baking cocoa, cornstarch, cinnamon and red chile into a large bowl. Store in an airtight container at room temperature.

For each serving, pour 1 cup water into a microwave-safe mug. Microwave on High until the water boils. Add ¹/2 cup of the chocolate mix and stir until dissolved. Microwave on High for 15 seconds or until the mixture thickens. Stir and serve.

Coffee Punch

Serves 20

Per serving
Calories 130
Protein 2 g
Carbohydrates 13 g
Total Fat 8 g
55% Calories from Fat
Cholesterol 31 mg
Fiber 0 g
Sodium 37 mg
Sugar 11 g

8 cups strong brewed coffee
2 cups milk
¹/2 cup sugar
1 teaspoon vanilla extract
1 cup heavy whipping cream, whipped

1 cup gold rum (optional)
1 quart vanilla ice cream or chocolate ice cream

Combine the coffee, milk, sugar and vanilla in a bowl and stir until the sugar dissolves. Chill, covered, in the refrigerator. To serve, stir the whipped cream and rum into the coffee mixture. Scoop the ice cream into a punch bowl. Pour the coffee mixture over the ice cream. Ladle into punch cups.

Listeria and Pregnancy
Pregnant women should take special care to avoid raw milk or raw milk products (including Mexican-style cheese like queso blanco or queso fresco) due to the risk of food-borne illness from listeria. Listeria is a harmful bacterium that can cause miscarriage, fetal death, and illness or death of a newborn.

Cheese Ring

Serves 10

Per serving
Calories 143
Protein 8 g
Carbohydrates 6 g
Total Fat 10 g
61% Calories from Fat
Cholesterol 69 mg
Fiber <1 g
Sodium 203 mg
Sugar 3 g

8   ounces sharp Cheddar cheese, shredded
1/2   cup crackers, crushed
1   (2-ounce) jar pimento, drained and chopped
1   cup milk

1/2   teaspoon celery seeds
1/4   teaspoon dry mustard
2   tablespoons vinegar
  Juice of 1/4 lemon
1   tablespoon sugar
2   eggs, beaten

Preheat the oven to 325 degrees. Grease an 8-inch oven-safe ring mold with butter or nonstick cooking spray. Mix the cheese, crackers and pimento in a large bowl. Add the milk, celery seeds, dry mustard, vinegar, lemon juice, sugar and eggs and mix well. Pour into the prepared mold. Bake for 1 hour. Unmold onto a serving platter.

Note: Fill the center of the cheese ring with peas, if desired.

Nutritional information does not include the butter or nonstick cooking spray used for greasing the ring mold.

American Cheese Ball

Serves 40

Per serving
Calories 63
Protein 2 g
Carbohydrates 1 g
Total Fat 6 g
82% Calories from Fat
Cholesterol 18 mg
Fiber 0 g
Sodium 78 mg
Sugar <1 g

16   ounces cream cheese, softened
2   cups (8 ounces) firmly packed finely shredded Cheddar cheese
1 1/2   tablespoons lemon juice
1   tablespoon (or more) hot pepper sauce
1 1/2   tablespoons freshly ground horseradish, or to taste

1   teaspoon finely grated sweet onion
  Salt and pepper to taste
  Chopped ham, chopped bell pepper, chopped pecans, chopped parsley or chopped olives to taste

Combine the cream cheese, Cheddar cheese, lemon juice, hot pepper sauce, horseradish, onion, salt and pepper in a bowl of an electric mixer fitted with a dough hook. Mix until well combined. Place on plastic wrap. Shape into a ball by pressing the outside of the plastic wrap. Remove the plastic wrap and roll in your choice of coating. Chill, wrapped in plastic wrap, for 24 to 48 hours before serving to enhance the flavor. Serve with assorted crackers.

Note: The cheese ball may be stored in the refrigerator for three to five days. For the holidays, coat the cheese ball with sliced pimento-stuffed olives. For a quicker festive coating, coat with a mixture of chopped olives and chopped pecans.

Fruity Cheese Ball

Serves 28

Per serving
Calories 137
Protein 2 g
Carbohydrates 8 g
Total Fat 12 g
72% Calories from Fat
Cholesterol 18 mg
Fiber 1 g
Sodium 96 mg
Sugar 4 g

1 (15-ounce) can fruit cocktail
1 (8-ounce) can crushed pineapple
16 ounces cream cheese, softened
1 (4-ounce) package vanilla instant
     pudding mix
2 cups chopped pecans

Drain the fruit cocktail and pineapple and pat dry. Combine the cream cheese, fruit cocktail and pineapple in a large mixing bowl and mix well. Add the pudding mix and mix well. Shape into a ball and wrap in plastic wrap. Chill for 8 to 10 hours. To serve, remove the plastic wrap and roll the cheese ball in the pecans to coat. Serve with graham crackers or gingersnaps.

Pineapple Cheese Ball

Serves 12

Per serving
Calories 158
Protein 5 g
Carbohydrates 9 g
Total Fat 13 g
68% Calories from Fat
Cholesterol 18 mg
Fiber 1 g
Sodium 528 mg
Sugar 7 g

16 ounces light cream cheese, softened
1 (15-ounce) can crushed
     pineapple, drained
2 tablespoons finely chopped
     green onions
2 to 3 teaspoons seasoned salt
1/2 to 1 cup chopped pecans

Combine the cream cheese, pineapple, green onions, seasoned salt and pecans in a large mixing bowl and beat well. Shape into a ball and wrap in plastic wrap. Chill for 8 to 10 hours to enhance the flavor. Serve with assorted crackers.

Milk in Your Diet

(Milk 8-ounce Serving Comparison)

Type of Milk	Calories	Grams of Fat
Whole	150	8
2%	120	5
1%	102	3
Skim	86	0

Low-fat milk products provide the calcium you need without the fat and calories. If your calcium is low, you have a higher risk for osteoporosis, colon cancer, high blood pressure, and kidney stones.

Wild Rice Soup

Serves 6 to 8

1 cup wild rice
3 cups water
1 onion, minced
2 or 3 carrots, minced
2 tablespoons butter
2 cups water
2 cups (1 pint) whipping cream
2 cups milk
2 (10-ounce) cans cream of potato soup or
    cream of chicken soup
1 pound processed cheese, cut into chunks
1 (4-ounce) can mushrooms, drained
10 slices bacon, crisp-fried and crumbled
1 (2-ounce) package slivered almonds

Bring the rice and 3 cups water to a boil in a saucepan. Reduce the heat and simmer, covered, for 1 hour. Sauté the onion and carrots in the butter in a skillet until tender. Combine the sautéed vegetables, 2 cups water, the cream, milk and canned soup in a large saucepan. Cook over medium heat until heated through, stirring constantly. Add the cheese, mushrooms, bacon and almonds. Cook until the cheese melts, stirring constantly. Stir in the hot rice. Ladle into soup bowls.

SIGNATURE RECIPE

Wild rice is a grain fundamental to Ojibwe culture. Historically, a dream about a gift of "food growing on water" resulted in families finding nourishment through difficult winters. Wild rice provided stability to a culture dependent on hunting, fishing, and fur trade. It is harvested by canoeing into a stand of plants, bending ripe grain heads with wooden sticks, and threshing seeds into a canoe. Wild rice continues to have special status and cultural importance.

Per serving
Calories 922
Protein 32 g
Carbohydrates 49 g
Total Fat 68 g
66% Calories from Fat
Cholesterol 208 mg
Fiber 5 g
Sodium 2268 mg
Sugar 15 g

Wisconsin Cheese Garden Lasagna

Serves 8

SIGNATURE RECIPE

Cheese is Wisconsin's pride and passion. When people think of cheese, they think of Wisconsin. The nation's top cheese producer, Wisconsin is home to classics such as Cheddar cheese and Colby cheese. Wisconsin is also America's leader in specialty and artisan cheese making, with more than six hundred varieties, types, and styles. With its rich heritage of cheese-making excellence, it's no surprise Wisconsin wins more awards for its cheeses than any other state or country.

Per serving
Calories 487
Protein 28 g
Carbohydrates 32 g
Total Fat 28 g
51% Calories from Fat
Cholesterol 117 mg
Fiber 3 g
Sodium 713 mg
Sugar 6 g

1/4 cup (1/2 stick) butter	1/4 cup balsamic vinegar
2 garlic cloves, minced	2 cups Wisconsin ricotta cheese
1 cup chopped asparagus	1 cup (4 ounces) grated Wisconsin Parmesan cheese
1 cup chopped zucchini	
1 cup chopped green onions	
1 cup chopped yellow squash	1 egg, beaten
1 cup chopped red bell pepper	1/2 teaspoon salt
	1/2 teaspoon pepper
6 ounces portobello mushrooms, chopped	12 no-cook lasagna noodles
2 cups chopped Roma tomatoes	2 cups (8 ounces) shredded Wisconsin mozzarella cheese
2 cups baby spinach leaves, chopped	1 cup (4 ounces) shredded Wisconsin smoked provolone cheese
1/4 cup fresh basil leaves, chopped	
1 tablespoon fresh oregano leaves, chopped	

Preheat the oven to 350 degrees. Melt the butter in a skillet over medium heat. Add the garlic and sauté for 1 to 2 minutes or until tender. Add the asparagus, zucchini, green onions, squash, bell pepper, mushrooms, tomatoes and spinach and sauté for 4 to 5 minutes or until tender. Stir in the basil, oregano and vinegar. Remove from the heat and set aside.

Combine the ricotta cheese, 1/2 cup of the Parmesan cheese, the egg, salt and pepper in a bowl and mix well.

Layer four of the noodles in a buttered 9×13-inch baking pan. Spread one-half of the ricotta cheese mixture over the noodles. Layer one-third of the vegetable mixture, 1/4 cup of the mozzarella cheese and 1/2 cup of the provolone cheese over the ricotta cheese mixture. Repeat the layers with four of the remaining noodles, the remaining ricotta cheese mixture, one-half of the remaining vegetable mixture, 3/4 cup of the remaining mozzarella cheese and the remaining provolone cheese. Continue layering with the remaining four noodles, remaining vegetable mixture, remaining 1 cup mozzarella cheese and remaining 1/2 cup Parmesan cheese. Bake for 35 to 45 minutes or until cooked through. Let stand for 5 to 10 minutes before serving.

Note: This recipe is provided compliments of the Wisconsin Milk Marketing Board.

Easy Cheesy Sauce

Serves 8

2 tablespoons butter or margarine
2 tablespoons all-purpose flour
1 cup milk
1/2 cup (2 ounces) shredded
    Cheddar cheese

Place the butter in a microwave-safe bowl or a 4-cup glass measure. Microwave on High for 30 to 60 seconds or until melted. Stir in the flour. Whisk in the milk until smooth. Microwave on High for 3 minutes. Remove from the microwave and mix well. Microwave for 1 minute longer or until thickened. Add the cheese and stir until melted. Serve over hot cooked vegetables.
Note: Other shredded cheeses may be used.

Per serving
Calories 79
Protein 3 g
Carbohydrates 3 g
Total Fat 6 g
70% Calories from Fat
Cholesterol 18 mg
Fiber <1 g
Sodium 77 mg
Sugar 1 g

Dairy Products
The recommended 1,300 milligrams of calcium daily can be obtained from three to four servings of dairy products, such as milk, yogurt, or cheeses. Choose low-fat dairy products for the needed nutrients with less fat.

Orange Creamsicle

Serves 9

2 cups nonfat vanilla yogurt
1 (6-ounce) can frozen orange
    juice concentrate
1 teaspoon vanilla extract

Combine the yogurt, orange juice concentrate and vanilla in a bowl and mix until smooth. Pour into ice cube trays or small paper or plastic cups with a spoon standing up inside. Freeze until firm. Store in a freezer bag or airtight freezer container.

Per serving
Calories 83
Protein 3 g
Carbohydrates 18 g
Total Fat <1 g
1% Calories from Fat
Cholesterol 1 mg
Fiber 0 g
Sodium 39 mg
Sugar 16 g

Breads & Grains

Tips for Breads

Storing bread in the refrigerator will extend its shelf life.

Use a serrated knife for easier slicing of bread.

If a casserole recipe calls for cooked rice, you can cook the rice the night before. Refrigerate the cooked rice until you are ready to put the casserole together.

Check yeast expiration dates before starting your recipe.

Add one teaspoon olive oil per one quart of water when cooking pasta.

Kids in the Kitchen

Kids love to help in the kitchen. It makes them feel important and needed. As children grow, teach them food preparation skills that will last a lifetime.

At a young age, children learn about the environment around them by using their senses. They learn through tasting, touching, smelling, and listening. The kitchen is a great place to learn.

Two-year-olds are learning to use their large body muscles. They will enjoy activities such as scrubbing vegetables and fruits, dipping vegetables and fruits, snapping fresh green beans, and tearing lettuce.

Three-year-olds are learning to use their hands. Try activities like pouring liquids, mixing batter for pancakes and waffles, spreading peanut butter on bread, and kneading bread or pizza dough.

Four- and five-year-olds are learning how to manage their fingers. Offer these young chefs tasks such as beating eggs with a whisk, measuring ingredients, mashing fruits, or juicing oranges.

Children love to eat what they make. Plan ahead when you want their young hands in your kitchen and it will be a fun and "stirring" experience for everyone.

GRAIN FOOD EQUIVALENTS

Macaroni
1 cup (3$^1/2$ ounces) uncooked = 2$^1/2$ cups cooked

Noodles, Medium
3 cups (4 ounces) uncooked = 4 cups cooked

Rice, Long Grain
1 cup uncooked = 3 cups cooked

Rice, Quick-Cooking
1 cup uncooked = 2 cups cooked

Spaghetti
8 ounces uncooked = 4 cups cooked

Crackers, Saltine
14 crackers = $^1/2$ cup finely crushed

Crackers, Graham
7 squares = $^1/2$ cup finely chopped

Braided Honey Wheat Bread   *Serves 24*

SIGNATURE RECIPE

A field of golden Kansas wheat, waving in the wind under the hot summer sun, will often leave visitors and natives alike speechless. It's a true sight to behold. Known as "The Wheat State" and "Breadbasket of the World," Kansas leads the nation in wheat production and flour milling science. Without a doubt, some of the best bread bakers come from sunny Kansas kitchens, using recipes that have been lovingly passed down from generation to generation.

Per serving
Calories 95
Protein 4 g
Carbohydrates 17 g
Total Fat 2 g
16% Calories from Fat
Cholesterol 11 mg
Fiber 2 g
Sodium 158 mg
Sugar 2 g

1^1/$_2$ cups water (80 degrees)
1   cup bread flour
3   cups whole wheat flour
2   tablespoons gluten
2   tablespoons dry
      milk powder
1^1/$_2$ teaspoons salt

2   tablespoons butter
2   tablespoons honey
1^1/$_2$ teaspoons bread
      machine yeast
1   egg, beaten
1   teaspoon poppy seeds

Preheat the oven to 375 degrees. Accurately measure the water, bread flour, whole wheat flour, gluten, milk powder, salt, butter, honey and yeast and add to the bread machine pan in the order recommended by the manufacturer. Set the machine on the dough mode, checking after 5 minutes to make sure the dough has formed a soft ball. If the dough is too dry, add an additional ^{1}/$_2$ to 1 tablespoon water. If the dough is too wet, add an additional 1 tablespoon bread flour at a time until of the desired consistency. Continue on the dough mode until the dough is mixed and risen. Remove the dough from the bread machine.

Divide the dough into six equal portions. Roll each portion into a uniform 15-inch rope. Wet your fingers and pinch three of the ropes together at one end. Braid the ropes together, sealing the ends together with a small amount of water and tucking the ends underneath. Repeat with the remaining three ropes.

Place the braids on greased baking sheets. Cover and let rise for 1 hour or until doubled in bulk. Brush with the egg and sprinkle with the poppy seeds. Bake for 25 minutes or until golden brown, tenting with foil after 15 minutes to prevent overbrowning. Remove from the baking sheets and cool on a wire rack.

Nutritional information does not include any additional bread flour or whole wheat flour that may be used.

Oatmeal Bread

Serves 24

Per serving
Calories 137
Protein 3 g
Carbohydrates 27 g
Total Fat 2 g
10% Calories from Fat
Cholesterol 3 mg
Fiber 1 g
Sodium 155 mg
Sugar 4 g

2 cups boiling water
1 cup rolled oats
2 tablespoons butter, softened
2 envelopes dry yeast
1/3 cup warm water
1 1/2 teaspoons salt
1/2 cup molasses
5 cups all-purpose flour

Preheat the oven to 325 degrees. Pour the boiling water over the oats in a large bowl. Add the butter and let stand until the mixture is cool. Dissolve the yeast in the warm water in a small bowl. Add to the cool oat mixture and mix well. Stir in the salt and molasses. Add 2 cups of the flour and mix well. Add 2 cups of the remaining flour and mix well. Knead on a lightly floured surface for 10 minutes or until the dough is smooth and elastic, adding the remaining 1 cup flour as needed if the dough becomes sticky. Let rise, covered, until doubled in bulk. Punch the dough down and divide into two equal portions. Shape into two loaves and place in two greased 5×8-inch loaf pans. Let rise, covered, until doubled in bulk. Bake for 50 minutes.

Note: You can add 1 cup raisins or 3/4 cup dried fruit and peels or 1/2 cup orange marmalade and reduce the molasses to 1/4 cup. The dough may also be shaped into thirty buns and baked for 20 to 25 minutes or until golden brown.

Dakota Bread

Serves 24

SIGNATURE RECIPE

Settlers coming to North Dakota established the fertile Red River Valley in the east with "Bonanza" farms and the vast grasslands of the west with large ranching operations, including ranches owned by Theodore Roosevelt. Agriculture continues to play a major role in the state's economy. North Dakota leads the nation in production of durum wheat, spring wheat, sunflowers, canola, and oats; it is second in honey and all wheat production and third in rye. Dakota Bread showcases these agricultural commodities.

Per serving
Calories 156
Protein 9 g
Carbohydrates 20 g
Total Fat 5 g
27% Calories from Fat
Cholesterol 17 mg
Fiber 1 g
Sodium 272 mg
Sugar 4 g

1	envelope active dry yeast
1/2	cup warm water (105 to 115 degrees)
2	tablespoons sunflower oil or canola oil
1	egg
1/2	cup cottage cheese
1/4	cup honey
1	teaspoon salt
2 to 21/2	cups bread flour
1/2	cup whole wheat flour
1/4	cup wheat germ
1/4	cup rye flour
1/4	cup rolled oats
1/4	cup cornmeal
1	egg white
1/4	cup sunflower seeds, wheat germ or rolled oats

Preheat the oven to 375 degrees. Sprinkle the yeast over the warm water in a bowl and stir to dissolve. Mix the sunflower oil, egg, cottage cheese, honey and salt in a large bowl. Add the yeast mixture and 2 cups of the bread flour and beat until the bread flour is moistened. Stir in the whole wheat flour, wheat germ, rye flour and oats gradually. Add enough of the remaining bread flour to form a soft dough. Knead on a floured surface for 10 minutes or until smooth and elastic. Place in a greased bowl, turning to coat the surface. Cover loosely with oiled plastic wrap. Let rise in a warm place for 30 minutes or until doubled in bulk. Uncover and punch the dough down. Shape the dough into a round loaf. Place in a greased glass pie plate sprinkled with the cornmeal. Cover with oiled plastic wrap and let rise for 1 hour or until doubled in bulk. Uncover and brush with the egg white. Sprinkle with the sunflower seeds. Bake for 30 to 40 minutes or until golden brown, covering loosely with foil during the last 10 to 15 minutes to prevent overbrowning. Remove from the pie plate and cool on a wire rack.

Note: You may add 1 cup cooked barley with the whole wheat flour. To make 1 cup of cooked barley, cook 1/2 cup quick pearl barley for 10 minutes.

All-Season Bread

Serves 16

Per serving
Calories 338
Protein 4 g
Carbohydrates 49 g
Total Fat 15 g
39% Calories from Fat
Cholesterol 35 mg
Fiber 1 g
Sodium 330 mg
Sugar 30 g

3	cups all-purpose flour
2	teaspoons baking soda
1	teaspoon salt
1/2	teaspoon baking powder
1 1/2	teaspoons cinnamon
3/4	cup finely chopped walnuts or pecans
3	medium eggs
2	cups sugar
3/4	cup vegetable oil
2	teaspoons vanilla extract
1	cup crushed pineapple
2	cups shredded peeled apples

Preheat the oven to 350 degrees. Mix the flour, baking soda, salt, baking powder, cinnamon and walnuts together. Beat the eggs lightly in a large mixing bowl. Add the sugar, oil and vanilla and beat until creamy. Stir in the pineapple and apples. Add the flour mixture and stir until moistened. Spoon into two well-greased and floured 5×9-inch loaf pans. Bake for 1 hour or until a wooden pick inserted near the center comes out clean. Cool in the pans for 10 minutes. Invert onto wire racks to cool completely.

Note: Just switch the apples with a different fruit or vegetable to get a differently flavored loaf for each season. The loaves may be baked in different-sized pans with slight baking time changes. For a 6-cup bundt pan, bake for 45 minutes. For two 3-pound shortening cans, bake for 1 1/4 hours. For eight 2×4-inch miniature loaf pans, bake for 30 to 35 minutes or until brown.

For **Sweet Potato Bread**, use 2 cups shredded peeled sweet potatoes and add 1 tablespoon pineapple juice.

For **Carrot Bread**, use 2 cups shredded peeled carrots and add 1 tablespoon pineapple juice.

For **Zucchini Bread**, use 2 cups shredded zucchini.

Chocolate Banana Bread

Serves 10

Per serving
Calories 288
Protein 5 g
Carbohydrates 45 g
Total Fat 11 g
33% Calories from Fat
Cholesterol 62 mg
Fiber 3 g
Sodium 314 mg
Sugar 24 g

1 1/4	cups all-purpose flour	2	medium eggs
3/4	cup whole wheat flour	1	cup mashed bananas
1/4	cup baking cocoa	1/4	cup milk
1	teaspoon salt	1	teaspoon vanilla extract
1/2	cup (1 stick) butter, softened	1/2	cup chopped pecans (optional)
1	cup sugar		

Preheat the oven to 350 degrees. Mix the all-purpose flour, whole wheat flour, baking cocoa and salt together. Cream the butter and sugar in a mixing bowl until light and fluffy. Add the eggs, bananas, milk and vanilla and mix well. Add the flour mixture and mix just until combined. Fold in the pecans. Spoon into a greased 5×9-inch loaf pan. Bake for 60 to 65 minutes or until a wooden pick inserted near the center comes out clean. Cool in the pan for 10 minutes. Invert onto a wire rack to cool completely.

Tropical Whole Wheat Banana Bread

Serves 12

Per serving
Calories 376
Protein 6 g
Carbohydrates 59 g
Total Fat 14 g
33% Calories from Fat
Cholesterol 53 mg
Fiber 3 g
Sodium 269 mg
Sugar 33 g

Whole Grain

Eat at least six ounces of grains daily. At least three ounces should consist of whole grains. Look for "whole" before grain in the list of ingredients. Using bran cereal in a recipe is a good method for adding more fiber to your diet.

1 1/2	cups whole wheat flour	3	eggs
1 1/2	cups all-purpose flour	2/3	cup canola oil
1 1/2	cups sugar	2	cups mashed bananas
1	teaspoon baking soda	1	(8-ounce) can crushed pineapple, drained
1	teaspoon cinnamon		
3/4	teaspoon salt		

Preheat the oven to 350 degrees. Mix the whole wheat flour, all-purpose flour, sugar, baking soda, cinnamon and salt in a large mixing bowl. Combine the eggs, canola oil, bananas and pineapple in a bowl and mix well. Add to the flour mixture and mix by hand until all of the ingredients are moistened. Pour into two greased and floured 4×8-inch loaf pans. Bake for 50 to 60 minutes or until a crack forms in the top of each loaf.

Note: If you use nonstick loaf pans, you do not have to grease and flour the pans.

Cranberry Nut Bread

Serves 12

Per serving
Calories 209
Protein 3 g
Carbohydrates 32 g
Total Fat 8 g
34% Calories from Fat
Cholesterol 16 mg
Fiber 1 g
Sodium 370 mg
Sugar 15 g

2   cups all-purpose flour
3/4   cup sugar
3/4   teaspoon salt
1 1/2 teaspoons baking powder
1 1/2 teaspoons baking soda
1   cup fresh cranberries, chopped
1/2   cup walnuts, chopped
1   medium egg
1/4   cup vegetable oil
3/4   cup orange juice
1   tablespoon orange zest

Preheat the oven to 350 degrees. Mix the flour, sugar, salt, baking powder and baking soda in a large bowl. Add the cranberries and walnuts and stir to coat. Combine the egg, oil, orange juice and orange zest in a bowl and mix well. Pour into the flour mixture and stir until blended. Spoon into a greased 5×9-inch loaf pan. Bake for 50 minutes or until a wooden pick inserted near the center comes out clean. Cool in the pan for 10 minutes. Invert onto a wire rack to cool completely.

Barley Corn Bread

Serves 12

Per serving
Calories 158
Protein 4 g
Carbohydrates 22 g
Total Fat 6 g
35% Calories from Fat
Cholesterol 49 mg
Fiber 2 g
Sodium 172 mg
Sugar 5 g

1   cup barley flour (Alaskan Hulless)
1   cup cornmeal
1/4   cup sugar
1/2   teaspoon baking soda
1/4   teaspoon salt
1   cup buttermilk
2   eggs
5   tablespoons butter, melted

Preheat the oven to 375 degrees. Grease an 8×8-inch baking dish or muffin cups with nonstick cooking spray, butter or vegetable oil. Mix the barley flour, cornmeal, sugar, baking soda and salt in a 2- or 3-quart mixing bowl. Beat the buttermilk, eggs and butter in a 2-quart mixing bowl until smooth. Pour into the flour mixture and stir until combined. Pour into the prepared baking dish and spread evenly. Bake for 30 minutes or until a wooden pick inserted near the center comes out clean and the bread has pulled away from the sides of the pan. Remove from the oven and serve hot.

SIGNATURE RECIPE

*Corn bread is an all-
American quick bread that
substitutes cornmeal for
most (or all) of the flour.
Real Tennessee corn bread
uses white cornmeal—
and no sugar—and is
baked in Lodge cast iron.
The oldest family-owned
cookware foundry in
America, Lodge is located
in South Pittsburg,
Tennessee, a tiny
community on the
Cumberland Plateau
of the Appalachian
Mountains, where the
National Corn Bread
Festival is held each
year on the last weekend
in April.*

Per serving
Calories 146
Protein 3 g
Carbohydrates 23 g
Total Fat 5 g
30% Calories from Fat
Cholesterol 19 mg
Fiber 2 g
Sodium 508 mg
Sugar 2 g

Tennessee Corn Bread

Serves 12

2   cups self-rising white cornmeal
1/2 teaspoon baking soda
1 1/2 cups buttermilk
1   egg
3   tablespoons vegetable oil

Preheat the oven to 450 degrees. Grease cast-iron muffin cups and preheat in the oven until the pan begins to smoke. Mix the cornmeal and baking soda in a bowl. Add the buttermilk, egg and oil and mix well. Pour into the hot muffin cups, filling two-thirds full. Bake for 20 to 25 minutes or until golden brown.

Note: The corn bread may be baked in a cast-iron cornstick mold to make sixteen cornsticks or in an 8- or 9-inch cast-iron skillet to make twelve wedges. This recipe makes an excellent corn bread for serving with a steaming bowl of chili in winter or with a plate of fresh summertime garden vegetables. It is also perfect for making corn bread dressing, another Southern favorite.

Butterhorn Rolls

Serves 32

1/4	ounce dry yeast	1/2	cup (1 stick) butter, softened
1	tablespoon sugar	4 1/2	cups all-purpose flour
1	cup warm water (115 degrees)	1	teaspoon salt
3	medium eggs, well beaten	2	tablespoons butter, melted
1/2	cup sugar		

Preheat the oven to 375 degrees. Dissolve the yeast and 1 tablespoon sugar in the warm water in a small bowl. Combine the eggs, 1/2 cup sugar and 1/2 cup butter in a large bowl and beat well. Add the yeast mixture and mix well. Add 3 cups of the flour and the salt and beat with a wooden spoon. Add the remaining 1 1/2 cups flour quickly and beat well. The dough will be very soft. Cover the bowl with plastic wrap and chill for 8 to 10 hours.

Divide the dough into four equal portions. Roll each portion into a 12- to 14-inch circle on a lightly greased and floured surface. Brush each circle with 1/2 tablespoon of the melted butter. Cut each circle into eight wedges. Roll up beginning at the large end and shape into crescents. Place on two greased baking sheets and cover with plastic wrap. Let rise in a warm place for 2 hours or until doubled in bulk. Remove the plastic wrap. Bake for 10 to 12 minutes or until light golden brown. Serve warm.

Per serving
Calories 116
Protein 2 g
Carbohydrates 17 g
Total Fat 4 g
33% Calories from Fat
Cholesterol 27 mg
Fiber 1 g
Sodium 104 mg
Sugar 4 g

Whole Wheat Rolls

Serves 48

2 to 2 1/2	cups whole wheat flour	2 1/4	cups warm water (105 to 115 degrees)
2 to 2 1/2	cups all-purpose flour	1/4	cup shortening
1	cup graham flour or bread flour	2	eggs
2	envelopes dry yeast	1/2	cup sugar
		2	teaspoons salt

Preheat the oven to 375 degrees. Mix the whole wheat flour, all-purpose flour and graham flour together. Dissolve the yeast in the warm water in a large bowl. Let stand for 5 minutes. Add the shortening, eggs, sugar and salt and beat at medium speed until blended. Stir in enough of the flour mixture to form a soft dough. Knead on a well-floured surface until smooth and elastic. Place in a greased bowl, turning to coat the surface. Cover with plastic wrap or a clean towel. Let rise in a warm place free from drafts for 1 hour or until doubled in bulk.

Punch the dough down. Divide the dough into four equal portions. Shape each portion into twelve balls. Place 2 inches apart on greased baking sheets. Cover and let rise in a warm place free from drafts for 30 minutes or until doubled in bulk. Uncover and bake for 15 minutes.

Per serving
Calories 74
Protein 2 g
Carbohydrates 14 g
Total Fat 2 g
18% Calories from Fat
Cholesterol 9 mg
Fiber 1 g
Sodium 100 mg
Sugar 2 g

Bread Machine Adaptation
To adapt the flour for coarser bread, use one cup bread flour and two cups whole wheat flour. Increase the water to allow for the denseness and dryness of the wheat flour during the dough mode in a bread machine.

Cinnamon Rolls

Serves 32

Per serving
Calories 205
Protein 3 g
Carbohydrates 37 g
Total Fat 5 g
23% Calories from Fat
Cholesterol 4 mg
Fiber 1 g
Sodium 85 mg
Sugar 15 g

1/4   ounce dry yeast
31/4   cups warm water
1/2   cup vegetable oil or butter
1/4   cup granulated sugar
1   teaspoon salt
7   cups all-purpose flour
1   cup granulated sugar
1/4   cup (1/2 stick) butter, chilled
        and grated
1 to 2 tablespoons cinnamon
2   cups confectioners' sugar
4 to 5 tablespoons milk
1/4   teaspoon almond extract

Preheat the oven to 350 degrees. Dissolve the yeast in 1/4 cup of the warm water in a large bowl. Let stand for 5 minutes to proof. Add the remaining 3 cups water, the oil, 1/4 cup granulated sugar, the salt and flour and mix well. Let rise, covered, in a warm place for 2 hours or until doubled in bulk. Punch the dough down. Roll on a lightly floured surface into a rectangle 1 inch thick. Sprinkle the rectangle with 1 cup granulated sugar, the butter and cinnamon. Roll up as for a jelly roll and press the seam to seal. Cut into slices and place in two greased 9×13-inch baking pans. Let rise, covered, in a warm place until doubled in bulk. Bake for 30 minutes or until golden brown.

Combine the confectioners' sugar, milk and almond extract in a bowl and mix until smooth. Pour over the warm rolls.

Buttermilk Bran Muffins

Serves 12

Per serving
Calories 188
Protein 3 g
Carbohydrates 19 g
Total Fat 12 g
56% Calories from Fat
Cholesterol 32 mg
Fiber 2 g
Sodium 221 mg
Sugar 5 g

3/4	cup bran	1/2	cup raisins
1	cup buttermilk	1/2	cup shredded carrots
1	egg, or an equivalent amount of egg substitute	1 1/4	cups all-purpose flour
		1	teaspoon baking soda
1/3	cup honey	1/4	teaspoon salt
1/3	cup vegetable oil	1	teaspoon nutmeg

Preheat the oven to 425 degrees. Mix the bran, buttermilk, egg, honey, oil, raisins and carrots in a bowl. Let stand for 10 minutes. Sift the flour, baking soda, salt and nutmeg into a large bowl. Make a well in the center and add the bran mixture. Stir just enough to moisten the flour mixture. The batter should be lumpy. Do not overmix. Spoon into lightly greased muffin cups, filling three-fourths full. Bake for 15 to 20 minutes or until a tester comes out clean when inserted into the center of a muffin.

Note: Do not use bran flakes or bran cereal in this recipe. Use only raw bran. You may substitute 1/3 cup applesauce for the vegetable oil. For extra flavor and protein, add 1/3 cup chopped nuts.

Wild Blueberry Corn Muffins

Serves 12

Per serving
Calories 284
Protein 3 g
Carbohydrates 26 g
Total Fat 19 g
59% Calories from Fat
Cholesterol 29 mg
Fiber 2 g
Sodium 262 mg
Sugar 8 g

1 1/4	cups cornmeal	1	egg
1	cup all-purpose flour	1	cup buttermilk
1/4	cup granulated sugar	3/4	cup canola oil
1	teaspoon baking soda	1 1/2	cups fresh or frozen wild blueberries
1/2	teaspoon salt		
1/4	cup packed brown sugar		

Preheat the oven to 450 degrees. Mix the cornmeal, flour, granulated sugar, baking soda, salt and brown sugar in a large bowl. Whisk the egg, buttermilk and canola oil in a bowl. Add to the cornmeal mixture all at once and stir until combined. Fold in the blueberries. Spoon into well-greased muffin cups, filling three-fourths full. Bake for 20 minutes or until golden brown.

Raspberry Lemon Muffins

Serves 12

Per serving
Calories 259
Protein 6 g
Carbohydrates 43 g
Total Fat 8 g
26% Calories from Fat
Cholesterol 1 mg
Fiber 2 g
Sodium 320 mg
Sugar 20 g

2	cups all-purpose flour	1/2	teaspoon salt
1	cup quick-cooking oats	1/2	cup egg substitute
1	cup packed brown sugar	1 1/2	cups buttermilk
1	tablespoon grated lemon zest	1/3	cup vegetable oil
1 1/2	teaspoons baking powder	1	teaspoon vanilla extract
1	teaspoon baking soda	3/4	cup crushed or frozen raspberries

Preheat the oven to 375 degrees. Mix the flour, oats, brown sugar, lemon zest, baking powder, baking soda and salt in a large bowl. Blend the egg substitute, buttermilk, oil and vanilla in a bowl. Add to the dry ingredients. Spread the raspberries over the top. Stir just until the dry ingredients are moistened. Spoon into greased or paper-lined muffin cups, filling three-fourths full. Bake for 20 to 25 minutes or until the top is firm to the touch.

Note: Crushed or frozen strawberries can be substituted for the raspberries. Almond extract can be used instead of vanilla extract.

Lemon Zest

Use a citrus zester or a vegetable peeler to remove the zest from a lemon. Be sure to remove only the outermost colored portion, leaving the white pith.

Ployes (Acadian Buckwheat Pancakes)

Serves 6

Per serving
Calories 72
Protein 2 g
Carbohydrates 16 g
Total Fat <1 g
5% Calories from Fat
Cholesterol 0 mg
Fiber 1 g
Sodium 301 mg
Sugar <1 g

1/2	cup buckwheat flour	1/4	teaspoon salt
1/2	cup all-purpose flour	1 1/3	cups cold water
2 1/2	teaspoons baking powder		

Combine the buckwheat flour, all-purpose flour, baking powder, salt and water in a bowl and mix well. Let stand for 5 minutes. Heat a nonstick griddle until hot. Spoon about 2 tablespoons of the batter onto the hot griddle and spread evenly. Cook the ployes (rhymes with boys) on one side only until the batter bubbles have popped, the pancake is not wet and the underside is light brown. Remove from the griddle. Repeat the process with the remaining batter.

Blueberry Buckle Coffee Cake   *Serves 12*

2   cups all-purpose flour
3/4   cup sugar
2 1/2 teaspoons baking powder
3/4   teaspoon salt
1/4   cup shortening
3/4   cup milk
1   egg
2   cups canned or fresh blueberries, drained
1/2   cup sugar
1/3   cup all-purpose flour
1/2   teaspoon cinnamon
1/4   cup (1/2 stick) margarine, softened

Preheat the oven to 350 degrees. Combine 2 cups flour, 3/4 cup sugar, the baking powder, salt, shortening, milk and egg in a bowl and mix well. Fold in the blueberries. Spread in a greased 9×13-inch baking dish. Mix 1/2 cup sugar, 1/3 cup flour, the cinnamon and margarine in a bowl. Sprinkle over the batter. Bake for 45 to 50 minutes or until golden brown.

Per serving
Calories 262
Protein 3 g
Carbohydrates 43 g
Total Fat 9 g
30% Calories from Fat
Cholesterol 18 mg
Fiber 1 g
Sodium 298 mg
Sugar 24 g

Traditional Lefse

Per serving
Calories 256
Protein 4 g
Carbohydrates 31 g
Total Fat 13 g
46% Calories from Fat
Cholesterol 25 mg
Fiber 1 g
Sodium 764 mg
Sugar 5 g

3   cups riced or mashed cooked potatoes
1/2 cup cream
1/4 cup (1/2 stick) butter, softened
1   tablespoon salt
1/4 cup sugar
1/4 cup vegetable oil
2   cups all-purpose flour

Combine the potatoes, cream, butter, salt, sugar and oil in a bowl and mix well. Let stand until cool or chill for 3 to 10 hours. Add the flour and mix well using your hands. Shape the dough into golf ball–size portions. Roll each portion on a lightly floured pastry cloth with a lightly floured rolling pin until thin. Cook on a hot dry lefse griddle or nonstick skillet until golden brown on each side, turning once.

Baked Apple Raisin Oatmeal

Serves 6

Per serving
Calories 481
Protein 11 g
Carbohydrates 69 g
Total Fat 19 g
35% Calories from Fat
Cholesterol 75 mg
Fiber 7 g
Sodium 468 mg
Sugar 28 g

1/4 cup vegetable oil
1/4 cup applesauce
1/2 cup packed brown sugar
2   eggs
3 1/2 cups quick-cooking oats
2   teaspoons baking powder
1   cup milk
1   teaspoon cinnamon
1/2 cup raisins
1/4 cup pecans

Preheat the oven to 350 degrees. Combine the oil, applesauce, brown sugar and eggs in a bowl and mix well. Add the oats, baking powder, milk and cinnamon and mix well. Stir in the raisins and pecans. Spoon into an 8×8-inch baking pan sprayed with nonstick cooking spray. Bake for 30 minutes.

Anne's Banana Breakfast Bars   *Serves 12*

3/4 cup unsweetened
    applesauce
3/4 cup packed brown sugar
1   egg, beaten
1   teaspoon cinnamon
1/4 teaspoon baking soda

1 1/2 cups ripe bananas, mashed
4   cups rolled oats
1/2 cup dried cranberries
1/2 cup walnuts or pecans,
    chopped

Preheat the oven to 350 degrees. Combine the applesauce, brown sugar, egg, cinnamon, baking soda, bananas, oats, cranberries and walnuts in a large bowl and mix well. The batter will be very stiff. Spread the batter evenly in a 9×13-inch baking pan lightly coated with nonstick cooking spray. Bake for 30 to 35 minutes or until golden brown and a wooden pick inserted into the center comes out clean. Remove from the oven to cool completely. Cut into bars. Store in an airtight container or freeze in single resealable freezer bags.

Per serving
Calories 209
Protein 5 g
Carbohydrates 38 g
Total Fat 5 g
22% Calories from Fat
Cholesterol 18 mg
Fiber 4 g
Sodium 37 mg
Sugar 19 g

How to Measure
When measuring flour or granulated sugar, do not tap the measuring cup or pack the ingredients with the back of a spoon. However, brown sugar should be packed into a dry measuring cup.

Measure teaspoonfuls or tablespoonfuls of dry ingredients by dipping out a heaping spoonful and passing the straight edge of a knife across the top to level.

Per serving
Calories 238
Protein 5 g
Carbohydrates 42 g
Total Fat 7 g
24% Calories from Fat
Cholesterol 0 mg
Fiber 5 g
Sodium 8 mg
Sugar 16 g

Quinoa Salad

Serves 6 to 8

1	cup quinoa	3/4	cup sliced green onions
2	cups water	2	teaspoons finely shredded
1	cup finely shredded		orange zest
	red cabbage	1/2	cup orange juice
1	cup mixed dried	1/4	cup chopped fresh mint
	fruit pieces	2	tablespoons olive oil

Bring the quinoa and water to a boil in a large saucepan. Cover and reduce the heat. Simmer for 10 to 15 minutes or until all of the water is absorbed. Stir in the cabbage, dried fruit, green onions, orange zest, orange juice, mint and olive oil. Cook over medium heat until heated through, stirring constantly. Serve warm or at room temperature.

Per serving
Calories 131
Protein 7 g
Carbohydrates 19 g
Total Fat 3 g
20% Calories from Fat
Cholesterol 40 mg
Fiber 1 g
Sodium 120 mg
Sugar 2 g

Fried Rice

Serves 12

1	tablespoon vegetable oil
1	onion, chopped
2	medium eggs, beaten
1	cup chopped cooked chicken
4	cups cooked rice
2	cups frozen peas or mixed vegetables
2	teaspoons soy sauce

Heat the oil in a skillet or wok. Add the onion and eggs. Cook until the eggs are scrambled, stirring constantly. Add the chicken and cook until heated through. Add the rice and cook until heated through, stirring gently. Add the peas and soy sauce and mix well. Cook until the vegetables are heated through.

Fried Rice

Fried rice can be made with any available cooked meat or vegetables you have on hand. Use cooked brown rice for a hearty flavor and an even brown color. Try adding chopped green onions and using oyster sauce instead of soy sauce.

Easy Homemade Whole Grain Pizza Crust

Serves 12

Per serving
Calories 140
Protein 3 g
Carbohydrates 16 g
Total Fat 7 g
47% Calories from Fat
Cholesterol 1 mg
Fiber 2 g
Sodium 283 mg
Sugar 1 g

1	cup all-purpose flour	2/3	cup low-fat milk
1	cup whole wheat flour	1/4	cup canola oil
2	teaspoons baking powder	2	tablespoons olive oil
1	teaspoon salt		

Combine the all-purpose flour, whole wheat flour, baking powder, salt, milk and canola oil in a bowl and mix vigorously to form a ball. Place on a floured surface and knead ten times. Place between two sheets of waxed paper and roll into a circle. Remove the waxed paper and brush the circle with the olive oil.

To use, preheat the oven to 425 degrees. Spread purchased pizza sauce over the pizza dough. Sprinkle with your choice of fresh vegetables and mozzarella cheese. Bake for 20 minutes or until the toppings are hot and the cheese melts.

The nutritional information includes only the pizza crust.

Holiday Snack Mix

Serves 32

Per serving
Calories 128
Protein 3 g
Carbohydrates 10 g
Total Fat 9 g
61% Calories from Fat
Cholesterol 4 mg
Fiber 2 g
Sodium 47 mg
Sugar 6 g

2	cups honey nut Chex cereal	1/4	cup (1/2 stick) butter, melted
2	cups honey nut Cheerios	1	tablespoon cinnamon
1 1/2	cups peanuts or cashews	1	teaspoon chili powder
1 1/2	cups chopped pecans	1 1/2	cups dried cranberries

Preheat the oven to 350 degrees. Mix the cereals, peanuts and pecans in a 9×13-inch baking pan. Pour the butter over the cereal mixture. Stir in the cinnamon and chili powder. Bake for 20 minutes, stirring every 5 to 8 minutes. Remove from the oven. Stir in the dried cranberries. Cool and store in an airtight container.

Note: Do not add the dried cranberries before baking. This delicious and appetizing snack is full of nutrients.

Vegetables

Ground herbs are stronger than dried, which are stronger than fresh. If a recipe calls for 1/4 teaspoon of ground herbs, use 3/4 to 1 teaspoon of dried or 2 teaspoons of fresh herbs.

SPICE AND HERB CHART	
Dried Beans	Cumin, cayenne, chili, parsley, pepper, sage, savory, thyme
Beef	Basil, bay, chili, cilantro, curry, cumin, garlic, marjoram, mustard, oregano, parsley, pepper, rosemary, sage, savory, tarragon, thyme
Breads	Anise, basil, caraway, cardamom, cinnamon, coriander, cumin, dill, garlic, lemon peel, orange peel, oregano, poppy seeds, rosemary, saffron, sage, thyme
Cheese	Basil, caraway, celery seeds, chervil, chili, chives, coriander, cumin, dill, garlic, horseradish, lemon peel, marjoram, mint, mustard, nutmeg, paprika, parsley, pepper, sage, tarragon, thyme
Chicken	Allspice, basil, bay, cinnamon, curry, dill, fennel, garlic, ginger, mustard, paprika, rosemary, saffron, sage, savory, tarragon, thyme
Eggs	Basil, chervil, chili, chives, curry, dill, fennel, ginger, lemon peel, marjoram, oregano, paprika, parsley, pepper, sage, tarragon, thyme
Fish	Anise, basil, bay, cayenne, celery seeds, chives, curry, dill, fennel, garlic, ginger, lemon peel, marjoram, mustard, oregano, parsley, rosemary, saffron, sage, savory, tarragon, thyme
Lamb	Basil, bay, cinnamon, coriander, cumin, curry, dill, garlic, marjoram, mint, mustard, oregano, parsley, rosemary, savory, tarragon, thyme
Potatoes	Basil, caraway, celery seeds, chervil, chives, coriander, dill, marjoram, oregano, paprika, parsley, poppy seeds, rosemary, tarragon, thyme
Salad Dressings	Basil, celery seeds, chives, dill, fennel, garlic, horseradish, marjoram, mustard, oregano, paprika, parsley, pepper, rosemary, saffron, tarragon, thyme
Salads	Basil, caraway, chives, dill, garlic, lemon peel, marjoram, parsley, pepper, rosemary, sage, savory, thyme
Soups	Basil, bay, chervil, chili, chives, cumin, dill, fennel, garlic, marjoram, parsley, pepper, rosemary, sage, savory, thyme
Sweets	Allspice, angelica, anise, cardamom, cinnamon, cloves, fennel, ginger, lemon peel, nutmeg, mint, orange peel, rosemary
Tomatoes	Basil, bay, celery seeds, cinnamon, chili, curry, dill, fennel, garlic, ginger, marjoram, oregano, parsley, rosemary, savory, tarragon, thyme

SIGNATURE RECIPE

Michigan is known as the second most diverse agriculture state in the country. Michigan is number one in asparagus, blueberry, dried beans, pickles, and tart cherry production. Because of its diversity, Michigan is also becoming known for its wine production. Spring is beautiful in Michigan, with asparagus stands popping up all over the countryside. Asparagus has been grown, eaten, and cultivated for more than two thousand years. This healthy vegetable is very diverse as it can be cooked, steamed, or grilled and eaten hot, warm, or chilled.

Per serving
Calories 81
Protein 5 g
Carbohydrates 5 g
Total Fat 5 g
56% Calories from Fat
Cholesterol 6 mg
Fiber 2 g
Sodium 250 mg
Sugar 2 g

Roasted Asparagus with Parmesan Cheese

Serves 4

1	pound asparagus, trimmed
1	tablespoon olive oil
1/4	teaspoon salt
1/4	teaspoon pepper
1/3	cup grated Parmesan cheese

Preheat the oven to 450 degrees. Place the asparagus in a single layer on a rimmed baking sheet. Drizzle with the olive oil. Sprinkle with the salt and pepper. Roll the asparagus spears to lightly coat. Roast medium-thick spears for 15 minutes or thin spears for 10 minutes or until tender, testing with a fork to determine doneness. Remove from the oven and sprinkle with the cheese. Return to the oven and bake until the cheese melts. Serve hot.

Note: The asparagus may be seasoned with salt-free herb blends.

Roasted Asparagus

Serves 8

2 pounds asparagus, trimmed
1/4 cup olive oil
1/2 teaspoon pepper

Preheat the oven to 450 degrees. Toss the asparagus in the olive oil in a large bowl. Place in a single layer on a rimmed baking sheet. Sprinkle with the pepper. Roast for 5 minutes or until tender-crisp, shaking the baking sheet once or twice to turn the asparagus spears.

Per serving
Calories 82
Protein 2 g
Carbohydrates 4 g
Total Fat 7 g
69% Calories from Fat
Cholesterol 0 mg
Fiber 2 g
Sodium 2 mg
Sugar 2 g

Black Bean Salsa

Serves 12

2 (16-ounce) cans black beans
2 (12-ounce) cans yellow and white corn
1/2 cup fresh cilantro, chopped
1 cup chopped green bell pepper
2 purple onions, chopped
8 Roma tomatoes, chopped
2 jalapeño chiles, chopped
2 tablespoons canola oil
6 tablespoons lime juice or lemon juice
2 teaspoons salt
2 teaspoons garlic powder

Rinse the beans and corn; drain. Place the beans and corn in a bowl. Add the cilantro, bell pepper, onions, tomatoes and jalapeño chiles and mix well. Combine the canola oil, lime juice, salt and garlic powder in a bowl and mix well. Stir into the bean mixture. Chill, covered, for 2 to 10 hours. Serve with tortilla chips.

Per serving
Calories 128
Protein 5 g
Carbohydrates 27 g
Total Fat 4 g
20% Calories from Fat
Cholesterol 0 mg
Fiber 6 g
Sodium 918 mg
Sugar 5 g

Farmers' Market Black Bean Salsa

Serves 12

Per serving
Calories 63
Protein 3 g
Carbohydrates 16 g
Total Fat 1 g
7% Calories from Fat
Cholesterol 0 mg
Fiber 4 g
Sodium 361 mg
Sugar 4 g

Stock the Pantry

Keep a supply of canned vegetables in the pantry for the family meal. Fresh vegetables and dip make a quick and nutritious snack or appetizer before a meal, or they go great with sandwiches or on a picnic. Dried beans and peas are easy to store and prepare.

1   (15-ounce) can black beans, drained and rinsed
1   (15-ounce) can whole kernel corn, drained
1   (15-ounce) can petite diced tomatoes, drained
1/2   cup chopped onion
1/2   cup chopped green bell pepper
2   tablespoons lime juice
1   garlic clove, pressed or minced
1/2   cup bottled salsa

Combine the beans, corn, tomatoes, onion, bell pepper, lime juice, garlic and salsa in a bowl and mix well. Chill until serving time. Serve with tortilla chips.

Note: Instead of the canned tomatoes, use one or two fresh large tomatoes, chopped. Instead of the canned corn, use 1 1/2 cups frozen corn kernels or fresh corn kernels, cooked and cut from the cob.

Bean and Corn Dip

Serves 12

Per serving
Calories 104
Protein 3 g
Carbohydrates 19 g
Total Fat 3 g
23% Calories from Fat
Cholesterol 0 mg
Fiber 3 g
Sodium 640 mg
Sugar 4 g

2   tablespoons olive oil
1/2   teaspoon garlic powder
1   (5-ounce) bottle green pepper sauce
2   (11-ounce) cans white Shoe Peg corn, drained
1   (15-ounce) can black beans, drained
1   large tomato, finely chopped
1   cup finely chopped purple onion

Mix the olive oil, garlic powder and green pepper sauce in a medium bowl. Stir in the corn, beans, tomato and onion. Chill, covered, for 2 to 10 hours before serving. Serve with corn chips.

Note: It is important to use green pepper sauce for the flavors it offers.

Bean and Corn Salad

Serves 12

2	cups frozen corn kernels	1/2	cup sliced green onions
1	red bell pepper, chopped	1/4	cup balsamic vinegar
1	tomato, chopped	2	tablespoons lemon juice
1	(15-ounce) can chick-peas, drained and rinsed	1/4	cup olive oil
1	(15-ounce) can black beans, drained and rinsed	2	tablespoons chopped parsley
		1/2	teaspoon ground cumin
1	(15-ounce) can pinto beans, drained and rinsed	1/2	teaspoon pepper
		1	teaspoon minced garlic

Per serving
Calories 169
Protein 6 g
Carbohydrates 27 g
Total Fat 6 g
28% Calories from Fat
Cholesterol 0 mg
Fiber 6 g
Sodium 390 mg
Sugar 3 g

Combine the corn, bell pepper, tomato, chick-peas, black beans, pinto beans, green onions, vinegar, lemon juice, olive oil, parsley, cumin, pepper and garlic in a large bowl and mix well. Chill, covered, until serving time.

Note: You may also serve this as a dip with tortilla chips.

Bean and Rice Salad

Serves 10

1	(16-ounce) can kidney beans, drained and rinsed	1/2	cup picante sauce
		1/2	cup sliced green onions
		1/2	teaspoon ground cumin
1	(16-ounce) can corn, drained	2	cups chilled cooked whole grain rice
1/4	cup fat-free Italian salad dressing		

Per serving
Calories 126
Protein 5 g
Carbohydrates 26 g
Total Fat 1 g
8% Calories from Fat
Cholesterol <1 mg
Fiber 4 g
Sodium 397 mg
Sugar 4 g

Combine the beans, corn, salad dressing, picante sauce, green onions, cumin and rice in a bowl and mix well. Chill, covered, until serving time.

Black-Eyed Pea Salad

Serves 8

Per serving
Calories 219
Protein 8 g
Carbohydrates 30 g
Total Fat 8 g
32% Calories from Fat
Cholesterol 0 mg
Fiber 6 g
Sodium 613 mg
Sugar 7 g

3	(15-ounce) cans black-eyed peas	1/4	cup sugar
1	large green bell pepper, chopped	1/4	cup vinegar
1	small onion, chopped	2	drops of hot pepper sauce
1	(3-ounce) can pimentos	1/2	teaspoon garlic salt
1/4	cup vegetable oil	1/4	teaspoon salt
		1/8	teaspoon pepper

Mix the peas, bell pepper, onion and pimentos in a 2-quart bowl. Combine the oil, sugar, vinegar, hot sauce, garlic salt, salt and pepper in a bowl and mix well. Stir into the salad. Chill, covered, for 8 to 10 hours.

Black-Eyes and Corn Salad

Serves 6

Per serving
Calories 229
Protein 9 g
Carbohydrates 34 g
Total Fat 8 g
30% Calories from Fat
Cholesterol 0 mg
Fiber 8 g
Sodium 112 mg
Sugar 6 g

3	cups cooked black-eyed peas	3	tablespoons olive oil
2	cups cooked whole kernel corn	1	teaspoon chili powder
1	cup chopped tomatoes	1/4	teaspoon sugar
2	teaspoons cilantro	1/4	teaspoon salt
1/4	cup lime juice	1/4	teaspoon pepper
		1/8	teaspoon garlic powder

Combine the peas, corn, tomatoes and cilantro in a large bowl and mix gently. Mix the lime juice, olive oil, chili powder, sugar, salt, pepper and garlic powder in a small bowl. Add to the salad and mix well. Chill, covered, until serving time.

Hoppin' John Salad

Serves 10

1	onion, chopped	4	cups cooked white rice
1/4	cup olive oil	1/2	cup olive oil
2	cups fresh black-eyed peas	1/4	cup white wine vinegar
2	cups fresh corn kernels	1 1/2	teaspoons seasoned salt
2	cups fresh baby lima beans	1	teaspoon pepper
2	cups chicken broth	1/4	cup bacon bits

Sauté the onion in 1/4 cup olive oil in a skillet for 3 to 5 minutes or until tender. Add the peas, corn, beans and broth. Bring to a boil. Cover and reduce the heat. Simmer for 30 minutes or until the vegetables are tender. Drain and place in a large bowl. Stir in the rice. Chill, covered, for 4 hours. Just before serving, mix 1/2 cup olive oil, the vinegar, seasoned salt and pepper in a bowl. Add the dressing and bacon bits to the vegetable mixture and toss to coat.

Per serving
Calories 511
Protein 20 g
Carbohydrates 71 g
Total Fat 18 g
31% Calories from Fat
Cholesterol 1 mg
Fiber 13 g
Sodium 322 mg
Sugar 7 g

Vegetable Varieties
The USDA recommends eating a variety of vegetables. Include both dark green leafy vegetables and yellow-orange vegetables in the daily diet. Eat more dried beans and peas. These can be included in soups.

Best-Ever Black-Eyed Peas

Serves 12

2	cups dried black-eyed peas	2	teaspoons Worcestershire sauce
1	cup chopped celery	3	tablespoons molasses
1	onion, chopped	8	cups water
1	envelope dry onion soup mix	1/2	teaspoon sugar
2	teaspoons beef bouillon granules	1/16	teaspoon paprika
		1	large smoked turkey wing

Drain and rinse the peas. Combine the peas, celery, onion, onion soup mix, bouillon granules, Worcestershire sauce, molasses, water, sugar and paprika in a 4-quart saucepan and mix well. Add the turkey wing. Bring to a boil; reduce the heat. Simmer, covered, for 8 to 10 hours, stirring and adding additional water as needed. Discard the bones before serving.

Per serving
Calories 128
Protein 9 g
Carbohydrates 22 g
Total Fat 1 g
5% Calories from Fat
Cholesterol 6 mg
Fiber 3 g
Sodium 180 mg
Sugar 6 g

Tennessee Caviar

Serves 30

Per serving
Calories 86
Protein 4 g
Carbohydrates 11 g
Total Fat 4 g
37% Calories from Fat
Cholesterol 0 mg
Fiber 3 g
Sodium 183 mg
Sugar 3 g

3	(15-ounce) cans black-eyed peas, drained	1/2	cup hot salsa
1	large green bell pepper, chopped	1/4	cup cider vinegar
1	large onion, chopped	3/4	cup sliced green olives
1/2	cup chopped jalapeño chiles	3/4	cup Italian salad dressing
		2	small bay leaves
		1/16	teaspoon salt

Combine the peas, bell pepper, onion, jalapeño chiles, salsa, vinegar, green olives and salad dressing in a bowl and mix well. Stir in the bay leaves and salt. Chill, covered, for 8 to 10 hours. Discard the bay leaves. Serve with corn chips.

Note: For those who prefer mild flavors, omit the jalapeño chiles and use mild salsa.

Texas Caviar

Serves 20

Per serving
Calories 115
Protein 3 g
Carbohydrates 13 g
Total Fat 6 g
47% Calories from Fat
Cholesterol 0 mg
Fiber 3 g
Sodium 463 mg
Sugar 2 g

1	(16-ounce) can pinto beans, drained	2	(4-ounce) jars sliced jalapeño chiles, or to taste
1	(16-ounce) can black-eyed peas, drained	1/2	cup chopped green onion tops
1	(16-ounce) can white hominy, drained	1/2	cup chopped fresh parsley
2	tomatoes, chopped	1	(8-ounce) bottle Italian salad dressing
1	green bell pepper, chopped		
2	garlic cloves, chopped		

Combine the beans, peas, hominy, tomatoes, bell pepper, garlic, jalapeño chiles, green onions and parsley in a large bowl and mix well. Add the salad dressing and mix well. Chill, covered, for 2 hours or longer. Drain before serving. Serve with tortilla chips.

Delaware's Best Beans

Serves 20

SIGNATURE RECIPE

1   (20-ounce) package Italian turkey
      sausage links
1   (28-ounce) can baked beans
1   (10-ounce) package frozen lima
      beans, thawed
1   (16-ounce) can kidney beans, drained
1   (8-ounce) can tomato sauce
2   tablespoons mustard
1   cup brown sugar blend (sucralose base)
1   small onion, chopped
1   (6-ounce) package sliced
      turkey pepperoni

Preheat the oven to 350 degrees. Place the sausage in a glass dish. Microwave on High for 8 minutes. Cut the sausage into slices. Combine with the baked beans, lima beans, kidney beans, tomato sauce, mustard, brown sugar blend, onion and pepperoni in a bowl and mix well. Spoon into a greased large baking dish. Bake, covered, for 1¹/₄ hours, stirring every 20 minutes.

Note: Using turkey sausage and turkey pepperoni considerably reduces the calories and fat in this recipe. Regular brown sugar can be used instead of the brown sugar blend.

With twenty-five hundred farms and five hundred thousand acres in production, Delaware has more than a $1 billion agricultural industry. Lima beans are an important crop in Delaware. Of the forty thousand acres of lima beans grown throughout the United States, Delaware annually plants ten to twelve thousand acres of them for commercial processing purposes. Also, Delaware was ranked eighth among the states in the pounds of broiler chickens raised with 76 percent of farm cash income coming from this commodity (2007).

Per serving
Calories 144
Protein 10 g
Carbohydrates 20 g
Total Fat 3 g
16% Calories from Fat
Cholesterol 19 mg
Fiber 4 g
Sodium 560 mg
Sugar 6 g

Marinated Green Beans

Serves 12

Per serving
Calories 126
Protein <1 g
Carbohydrates 7 g
Total Fat 11 g
77% Calories from Fat
Cholesterol 0 mg
Fiber 1 g
Sodium 457 mg
Sugar 4 g

1   (29-ounce) can green beans, drained
1   (16-ounce) bottle balsamic
      vinaigrette
1   (4-ounce) jar pimentos, chopped

Place the beans and vinaigrette in a large sealable plastic bag and seal the bag. Marinate in the refrigerator for 2 to 10 hours. To serve, place the marinated beans in a serving bowl and add the pimentos. Serve cold as a salad or side dish.

Lima Bean Salad

Serves 8

Per serving
Calories 196
Protein 9 g
Carbohydrates 29 g
Total Fat 6 g
25% Calories from Fat
Cholesterol 0 mg
Fiber 9 g
Sodium 223 mg
Sugar 1 g

5   cups hot cooked baby lima beans, drained
3   tablespoons olive oil
3   tablespoons lemon juice
1/8   teaspoon garlic powder
1   teaspoon dried basil
3/4   teaspoon salt
1/4   teaspoon white pepper
1   cup chopped tomato
1/3   cup chopped red onion

Combine the beans, olive oil, lemon juice, garlic powder, basil, salt and white pepper in a large bowl and mix well. Let stand for 10 to 15 minutes to cool, stirring frequently. Add the tomato and onion. Marinate at room temperature for 1 to 2 hours before serving.

Easy Black Bean Lasagna

Serves 10

Per serving
Calories 236
Protein 14 g
Carbohydrates 32 g
Total Fat 8 g
27% Calories from Fat
Cholesterol 41 mg
Fiber 5 g
Sodium 642 mg
Sugar 3 g

1   (15-ounce) can black beans
1   (28-ounce) can crushed tomatoes
1   cup chopped onion
1/2 cup chopped green bell pepper
3/4 cup salsa
1   teaspoon chili powder
1/2 teaspoon ground cumin
1   cup reduced-fat cottage cheese
1/4 teaspoon garlic powder
1   egg
8   ounces lasagna noodles, cooked
1 1/2 cups (6 ounces) shredded Cheddar cheese
        or mozzarella cheese

Preheat the oven to 350 degrees. Mash the beans slightly in a large bowl. Stir in the undrained tomatoes, onion, bell pepper, salsa, chili powder and cumin. Combine the cottage cheese, garlic powder and egg in a small bowl and mix well.

Spread 1 cup of the tomato mixture in a 9×13-inch baking dish sprayed with nonstick cooking spray. Arrange one-half of the noodles over the tomato mixture, overlapping slightly. Spread one-half of the remaining tomato mixture over the noodles. Spread the cottage cheese mixture carefully over the tomato mixture. Continue layering with one-half of the Cheddar cheese, the remaining noodles, the remaining tomato mixture and the remaining Cheddar cheese. Cover with a sheet of foil sprayed with nonstick cooking spray. Bake for 40 to 45 minutes or until heated through. Uncover and let stand for 15 minutes before serving.

Note: Other varieties of beans may be used.

Wheat Berry Broccoli Salad

Serves 8

Per serving
Calories 278
Protein 6 g
Carbohydrates 43 g
Total Fat 11 g
33% Calories from Fat
Cholesterol 10 mg
Fiber 6 g
Sodium 284 mg
Sugar 26 g

1/2 cup wheat berries	1/2 cup raisins
2 bunches broccoli, cut into florets	1/4 cup chopped purple onion
2 cups seedless grapes, cut into halves	1 cup light mayonnaise
2 tablespoons bacon bits	1/2 cup sugar
	2 tablespoons vinegar

Bring water to a boil in a saucepan. Add the wheat berries and reduce the heat. Simmer, uncovered, for 1 hour or until cooked through. The wheat berries will retain a firm chewy texture when cooked. Drain and set aside to cool.

Combine the wheat berries, broccoli, grapes, bacon bits, raisins and onion in a large bowl. Mix the mayonnaise, sugar and vinegar in a small bowl. Add to the broccoli mixture just before serving and toss to coat.

Note: The dressing may be made a day ahead and chilled until serving time. One bunch broccoli and one head cauliflower or dried cranberries may be used.

Broccoli and Grape Salad

Serves 25

Per serving
Calories 219
Protein 4 g
Carbohydrates 11 g
Total Fat 18 g
74% Calories from Fat
Cholesterol 13 mg
Fiber 1 g
Sodium 247 mg
Sugar 9 g

6 cups chopped fresh broccoli	2/3 cup slivered almonds
2 cups chopped celery	1 1/2 cups seedless green grapes
1/2 cup chopped green onions	1 1/2 cups seedless red grapes
1 pound bacon, crisp-cooked and crumbled	2/3 cup sugar
	2 cups mayonnaise
	2 tablespoons vinegar

Combine the broccoli, celery, green onions, bacon, almonds, green grapes and red grapes in a 4-quart serving bowl. Mix the sugar, mayonnaise and vinegar in a bowl. Pour over the broccoli mixture and stir gently until evenly coated. Chill, covered, for 8 to 10 hours before serving to enhance the flavors.

Broccoli Orange Salad with Poppy Seed Dressing

Serves 4

Per serving
Calories 192
Protein 3 g
Carbohydrates 19 g
Total Fat 13 g
57% Calories from Fat
Cholesterol 0 mg
Fiber 5 g
Sodium 35 mg
Sugar 13 g

2   cups bite-size orange pieces
2   cups bite-size broccoli florets
1/4 cup thinly sliced red onion
4   cups torn romaine
1/4 cup Poppy Seed Dressing (below)
1/4 cup pecans

Combine the oranges, broccoli, onion and romaine in a salad bowl and toss to mix. Add the dressing and toss to coat. Sprinkle with the pecans and serve.

Poppy Seed Dressing

Makes 1³/4 cups

Per serving
Calories 344
Protein <1 g
Carbohydrates 15 g
Total Fat 33 g
83% Calories from Fat
Cholesterol 0 mg
Fiber <1 g
Sodium 84 mg
Sugar 14 g

1   cup vegetable oil
1/3 cup cider vinegar
1/2 cup sugar
1   teaspoon dry mustard
1/4 teaspoon salt
1¹/2 tablespoons poppy seeds

Combine the oil, vinegar, sugar, dry mustard, salt and poppy seeds in a jar with a tight-fitting lid. Seal the jar and shake until blended. Store any unused portion in the refrigerator.

Broccoli Pasta Delight

Per serving
Calories 235
Protein 9 g
Carbohydrates 45 g
Total Fat 2 g
9% Calories from Fat
Cholesterol 0 mg
Fiber 3 g
Sodium 31 mg
Sugar 2 g

1/4	cup water	1	small zucchini, thinly sliced
1	tablespoon margarine		Salt to taste
1/4	teaspoon garlic powder	16	ounces spaghetti or angel hair pasta, cooked and drained
1/4	teaspoon dried dill weed		
1/4	teaspoon pepper		
3	cups bite-size broccoli florets		

Heat the water, margarine, garlic powder, dill weed and pepper in a skillet until the margarine melts. Add the broccoli and sauté for 5 minutes. Add the zucchini and sauté for 3 minutes or until tender-crisp. Sprinkle with salt to taste. Place the hot pasta on a serving platter. Arrange the hot vegetables around the edge and serve.

Note: Other vegetables may be used in combination or alone.

Cabbage Soup

Per serving
Calories 189
Protein 10 g
Carbohydrates 22 g
Total Fat 7 g
32% Calories from Fat
Cholesterol 19 mg
Fiber 7 g
Sodium 472 mg
Sugar 9 g

1	onion, chopped	1	(14-ounce) can no-salt-added diced tomatoes
1 or 2	garlic cloves, minced	1/4	cup chopped red or green bell pepper
8	ounces sweet or hot Italian turkey sausage	1	tablespoon brown sugar
2	tablespoons olive oil	1	(15-ounce) can white kidney beans, drained and rinsed
2	carrots, cut into halves and thinly sliced	1	tablespoon white vinegar
1	rib celery, thinly sliced	1/16	teaspoon salt, or to taste
1	teaspoon caraway seeds	1/8	teaspoon pepper
2	cups low-fat low-sodium chicken broth		
2	cups chopped cabbage		

Sauté the onion, garlic and sausage in the olive oil in a 4-quart saucepan until tender. Add the carrots and celery. Sauté for several minutes or until tender. Add the caraway seeds and sauté for 1 minute. Add the broth, cabbage, tomatoes, bell pepper and brown sugar. Bring to a boil; reduce the heat. Simmer, covered, for 15 to 20 minutes or until the vegetables are tender. Add the beans, vinegar, salt and pepper. Simmer, uncovered, for 5 to 10 minutes or until heated through. Ladle into soup bowls.

Note: Instead of using sweet or hot Italian turkey sausage, try using half sweet and half hot sausage for a flavorful soup. Red kidney beans, garbanzo beans, or black beans may be substituted for the white kidney beans. This soup freezes well, so make a double batch and freeze in meal-sized portions for a quick meal on a busy day.

Mexican Coleslaw

Serves 8

Per serving
Calories 63
Protein 1 g
Carbohydrates 10 g
Total Fat 3 g
34% Calories from Fat
Cholesterol 0 mg
Fiber 2 g
Sodium 155 mg
Sugar 4 g

4   cups finely shredded green cabbage
1   cup chopped green onions
1   cup thinly sliced red bell pepper
1   cup cooked whole kernel yellow corn
2¹/₂ tablespoons cider vinegar
1   tablespoon water
¹/₂ teaspoon garlic powder
¹/₂ teaspoon ground cumin
¹/₂ teaspoon crumbled dry leaf oregano
¹/₄ cup chopped fresh cilantro
¹/₂ to 1 jalapeño chile, seeded and
        chopped (optional)
4   teaspoons olive oil
2   teaspoons sugar
¹/₂ teaspoon salt

Combine the cabbage, green onions, bell pepper and corn in a large bowl and toss to mix. Mix the vinegar, water, garlic powder, cumin, oregano, cilantro, jalapeño chile, olive oil, sugar and salt in a small bowl. Pour over the cabbage mixture and toss to coat. Chill, covered, for 1 hour before serving.

Favorite Coleslaw

Serves 8

Per serving
Calories 71
Protein 1 g
Carbohydrates 13 g
Total Fat 2 g
23% Calories from Fat
Cholesterol 0 mg
Fiber 1 g
Sodium 105 mg
Sugar 2 g

2 tablespoons white vinegar	3 cups shredded cabbage
1 tablespoon vegetable oil	1 1/2 cups shredded carrots
1 1/2 teaspoons mustard	1/4 cup chopped onion
1/2 cup sugar substitute	1/4 cup chopped green
1/4 teaspoon salt	bell pepper
1/4 teaspoon celery seeds	

Mix the vinegar, oil, mustard, sugar substitute, salt and celery seeds in a jar with a tight-fitting lid. Seal the jar and shake well. Combine the cabbage, carrots, onion and bell pepper in a 4-cup container. Add the dressing and toss to coat. Chill, covered, until serving time.

Cabbage Supreme

Serves 8

Per serving
Calories 212
Protein 7 g
Carbohydrates 14 g
Total Fat 15 g
61% Calories from Fat
Cholesterol 18 mg
Fiber 3 g
Sodium 575 mg
Sugar 6 g

3 slices bread, toasted	2 tablespoons all-purpose
1/4 cup (1/2 stick) margarine	flour
1 small head cabbage, rinsed	1 cup milk
1/4 cup water	1 teaspoon salt
2 tablespoons margarine	1 cup (4 ounces) shredded sharp Cheddar cheese

Preheat the oven to 250 degrees. Cut the toasted bread into 1/2-inch cubes. Melt 1/4 cup margarine in an ovenproof skillet. Add the bread cubes and toss to coat. Bake for 5 minutes or until brown. Remove from the oven. Increase the oven temperature to 350 degrees.

Cut the cabbage into 1-inch squares. Steam the cabbage in the water in a heavy saucepan for 5 to 10 minutes or until tender. Melt 2 tablespoons margarine in a saucepan. Stir in the flour. Add the milk. Cook until thickened and smooth, stirring constantly. Stir in the salt.

Place one-third of the cabbage in a greased 1 1/2-quart baking dish. Layer with 1/3 cup of the white sauce and 1/3 cup of the cheese. Continue layering with the remaining cabbage, remaining white sauce and remaining cheese. Top with the toasted bread cubes. Bake for 20 minutes or until bubbly.

Crisp Red Cabbage

Serves 6

4   cups shredded red cabbage
2   apples, peeled and cut into thin wedges
1/4   cup (or more) water
1/4   cup red wine vinegar or apple
        cider vinegar
2   tablespoons brown sugar
1/2   teaspoon salt
1/4   teaspoon nutmeg

Per serving
Calories 67
Protein 1 g
Carbohydrates 17 g
Total Fat <1 g
2% Calories from Fat
Cholesterol 0 mg
Fiber 2 g
Sodium 209 mg
Sugar 13 g

Spray a medium saucepan with nonstick cooking spray. Place the cabbage, apples, water, vinegar and brown sugar in the prepared saucepan and mix well. Simmer, covered, over medium heat for 10 minutes or until the cabbage is tender-crisp, turning the cabbage several times and adding additional water if needed to prevent sticking. Add the salt and nutmeg. Serve warm.

Apple-Glazed Baby Carrots

Serves 6

3   cups baby carrots
1   tablespoon lemon juice concentrate
1   tablespoon low-calorie margarine
3   tablespoons apple juice concentrate
2/3   cup low-fat low-sodium chicken broth
1   teaspoon cinnamon
2   teaspoons cornstarch
1   teaspoon water

Per serving
Calories 53
Protein 1 g
Carbohydrates 10 g
Total Fat 1 g
19% Calories from Fat
Cholesterol 3 mg
Fiber 1 g
Sodium 48 mg
Sugar 6 g

Steam the carrots, covered, over 2 inches of boiling water in a saucepan for 3 minutes. Sprinkle with the lemon juice concentrate. Melt the margarine in a 10-inch skillet over medium heat. Add the apple juice concentrate and heat until melted. Add the broth and cinnamon. Bring to a boil. Mix the cornstarch with 1 teaspoon water in a bowl and add to the skillet. Reduce the heat. Cook until thickened, stirring constantly. Add the carrots and toss to coat.

Roasted Ginger Carrot Soup *Serves 8 to 10*

Per serving
Calories 157
Protein 2 g
Carbohydrates 21 g
Total Fat 8 g
42% Calories from Fat
Cholesterol 22 mg
Fiber 3 g
Sodium 886 mg
Sugar 9 g

1¹/2 pounds carrots, peeled and
        cut into halves lengthwise
1   pound parsnips, peeled and
        cut into quarters lengthwise
1   large onion, sliced
1   (3-inch) piece of fresh ginger,
        peeled and chopped
6   tablespoons butter
3   tablespoons dark brown sugar
8   cups (or more) chicken broth or
        vegetable broth
       Salt to taste
1/16   teaspoon cayenne pepper
1/4   cup crème fraîche for garnish
1/4   cup minced fresh chives for garnish

Preheat the oven to 350 degrees. Combine the carrots, parsnips, onion and ginger in a shallow roasting pan. Dot with the butter and sprinkle with the brown sugar. Pour 2 cups of the broth over the vegetables. Bake, covered with foil, for 2 hours or until the vegetables are very tender. Place in a large stockpot. Add the remaining 6 cups broth, salt and cayenne pepper. Bring to a boil. Reduce the heat and simmer, partially covered, for 10 minutes. Purée the soup in batches in a blender or food processor, adding additional broth if needed. Return the soup to the stockpot. Adjust the seasonings to taste. Cook until heated through. Ladle into soup bowls. Garnish each with a dollop of the crème fraîche and sprinkle with the chives.

Note: For a vegetarian soup, use vegetable broth instead of the chicken broth. Winter squash or pumpkin can be substituted for the carrots. This soup makes a large quantity, is easy to prepare, and freezes well.

Jack Rabbit Carrot Cake

Serves 16

Cake

2 cups all-purpose flour
1/2 cup granulated sugar
1/2 cup packed brown sugar
2 teaspoons baking soda
2 teaspoons cinnamon
1 teaspoon salt
1/2 cup apple butter
1/2 cup canola oil
1 tablespoon vanilla extract
2 eggs
2 egg whites
3 cups shredded carrots

Cream Cheese Frosting

1/2 cup cream cheese,
softened
1/4 cup (1/2 stick)
butter, softened
3 1/2 cups confectioners' sugar
1 teaspoon vanilla extract

Per serving
Calories 385
Protein 4 g
Carbohydrates 51 g
Total Fat 19 g
44% Calories from Fat
Cholesterol 57 mg
Fiber 1 g
Sodium 419 mg
Sugar 36 g

Reduced Fat

Substituting reduced-fat ingredients is an easy change to make recipes lower in fat. You can also substitute an equal amount of applesauce for the oil in a recipe. Replacing 1/2 cup oil and 2 eggs in packaged baking mixes with 1/2 cup nonfat yogurt is also a great fat-reducing option.

To prepare the cake, preheat the oven to 350 degrees. Mix the flour, granulated sugar, brown sugar, baking soda, cinnamon and salt in a large bowl and make a well in the center. Whisk the apple butter, canola oil, vanilla, eggs and egg whites in a bowl. Add to the flour mixture, stirring just until moistened. Fold in the carrots. Pour into three 8-inch cake pans coated with nonstick cooking spray. Bake for 15 minutes or until a wooden pick inserted into the center comes out clean. Cool in the pans for 10 minutes. Invert onto wire racks to cool completely.

To prepare the frosting, beat the cream cheese and butter in a mixing bowl until smooth. Add the confectioners' sugar gradually, beating constantly. Add the vanilla and mix well. Spread between the layers and over the top and side of the cake.

Zesty Mexican Cauliflower

Serves 6

Per serving
Calories 90
Protein 4 g
Carbohydrates 16 g
Total Fat 2 g
21% Calories from Fat
Cholesterol 8 mg
Fiber 2 g
Sodium 227 mg
Sugar 4 g

1½	cups cauliflower florets	¼	cup (1 ounce) low-fat shredded Cheddar cheese
½	cup low-fat sour cream		
1	tablespoon low-fat mayonnaise	1½	cups cooked fresh corn kernels
1	teaspoon hot pepper sauce		
½	cup salsa		

Steam the cauliflower over boiling water in a saucepan for 5 minutes or until tender. Drain and set aside. Combine the sour cream, mayonnaise, hot sauce and salsa in a large saucepan. Cook over medium heat until bubbly, stirring constantly. Add the cauliflower, cheese and corn and toss well.

New Mexico Green Chile Rellenos

Serves 12

Per serving
Calories 294
Protein 19 g
Carbohydrates 9 g
Total Fat 21 g
63% Calories from Fat
Cholesterol 144 mg
Fiber 1 g
Sodium 461 mg
Sugar 5 g

12	large whole green chiles	5	eggs
1	pound Monterey Jack cheese, cut into 12 strips	¼	cup all-purpose flour
		1¼	cups milk
8	ounces Cheddar cheese, shredded	½	teaspoon salt
		½	teaspoon pepper
½	teaspoon paprika	⅛	teaspoon Tabasco sauce

Preheat the oven to 350 degrees. Remove the seeds from the green chiles. Insert a Monterey Jack cheese strip into each green chile. Arrange in a single layer in a greased 9×13-inch baking dish. Sprinkle with the Cheddar cheese and paprika. Beat the eggs in a bowl. Add the flour and beat until smooth. Add the milk, salt, pepper and Tabasco sauce and mix well. Pour over the green chiles. Bake for 45 minutes or until set.

Note: Add browned ground beef or chopped cooked chicken for variety of flavor and nutritional value.

Corn Salad

Serves 8

1 (15-ounce) can white Shoe Peg corn
1/2 cup finely chopped bell pepper
1/2 onion, finely chopped
1 large tomato, chopped
1 tablespoon mayonnaise
Salt and pepper to taste

Combine the corn, bell pepper, onion and tomato in a bowl and mix well. Stir in the mayonnaise, salt and pepper. Chill, covered, until serving time.

Per serving
Calories 75
Protein 2 g
Carbohydrates 13 g
Total Fat 2 g
23% Calories from Fat
Cholesterol 1 mg
Fiber 1 g
Sodium 239 mg
Sugar 3 g

Corn and Black Bean Salad

Serves 14

1 (15-ounce) can black soybeans or
    black beans, drained and rinsed
2 cups frozen or fresh corn kernels
1 small tomato, chopped
1/4 cup minced purple onion
1/2 zucchini, chopped
1/2 cucumber, peeled and chopped
1/2 large red or green bell
    pepper, chopped
1/4 cup light Italian salad dressing

Combine the soybeans, corn, tomato, onion, zucchini, cucumber, bell pepper and salad dressing in a bowl and mix well. Chill, covered, for 30 minutes or longer. Serve with tortilla chips or pita chips.

Note: Add grilled chicken and place on a bed of fresh greens to serve as a main dish or serve in a pita pocket.

Per serving
Calories 65
Protein 4 g
Carbohydrates 9 g
Total Fat 2 g
29% Calories from Fat
Cholesterol <1 mg
Fiber 3 g
Sodium 42 mg
Sugar 1 g

Corn Pudding

Serves 12

Per serving
Calories 258
Protein 5 g
Carbohydrates 28 g
Total Fat 15 g
50% Calories from Fat
Cholesterol 63 mg
Fiber 3 g
Sodium 498 mg
Sugar 8 g

1/2 cup (1 stick) butter, melted
1 (14-ounce) can cream-style corn
1 (15-ounce) can whole kernel corn, drained
2 eggs, beaten
1 cup sour cream
1 (8-ounce) package corn muffin mix

Preheat the oven to 375 degrees. Combine the butter, cream-style corn and whole kernel corn in a bowl and mix well. Add the eggs and sour cream and mix well. Stir in the corn muffin mix. Pour into a greased 9×13-inch glass baking dish. Bake for 35 to 40 minutes or until set.

Note: Corn and pork are two Hoosier favorites. Indiana ranks fifth in the production of seed corn, fifteenth in the production of sweet corn, and second in the production of popcorn. In 1908 Nick Freinstein created the first pork tenderloin sandwich when he placed pork schnitzel on a bun and sold it from his streetcar.

Tropical Cucumber Tomato Salsa

Serves 48

Per serving
Calories 4
Protein <1 g
Carbohydrates 1 g
Total Fat <1 g
7% Calories from Fat
Cholesterol 0 mg
Fiber <1 g
Sodium 49 mg
Sugar <1 g

1 large cucumber, peeled and seeded
1 small onion
2 garlic cloves
1 cup fresh mango chunks
4 tomatoes, seeded
2 small jalapeño chiles or
   serrano chiles, seeded
1/4 cup fresh cilantro
3 tablespoons fresh lime juice
1/16 teaspoon Tabasco sauce
1 teaspoon sea salt
1/2 teaspoon freshly ground pepper

Pulse the cucumber, onion, garlic, mango, tomatoes, jalapeño chiles, cilantro, lime juice and Tabasco sauce twelve times in a food processor or until the cucumbers, mango and onion are chopped. Do not overprocess. Spoon into a serving bowl. Stir in the salt and pepper. Serve with tortilla chips, pita chips or toasted French baguette slices. Store in an airtight container in the refrigerator for up to 1 week.

Cucumber Salad

Serves 12

Per serving
Calories 471
Protein 10 g
Carbohydrates 21 g
Total Fat 38 g
73% Calories from Fat
Cholesterol 29 mg
Fiber <1 g
Sodium 491 mg
Sugar 16 g

3	(3-ounce) packages lime gelatin
8	ounces fat-free cream cheese
3	cups boiling water
2	cups cold water
1	cup evaporated skim milk or fat-free evaporated milk
2	cups mayonnaise
2	cups fat-free sour cream
2	cups chopped seeded peeled cucumbers
1	cup chopped celery
	Salt to taste
2	cups drained low-fat yogurt
1/2	cup mayonnaise
1/2	cup evaporated skim milk or fat-free evaporated milk
	Pepper to taste
	Cucumber slices for garnish

Combine the gelatin, cream cheese and boiling water in a bowl and stir until the gelatin dissolves and the cream cheese melts. Add the cold water and let stand until cool. Combine 1 cup evaporated milk, 2 cups mayonnaise, the sour cream, chopped cucumbers, celery and salt in a bowl and mix well. Fold into the gelatin mixture. Pour into a 3-quart mold or loaf pans that have been rinsed in cold water or into a 9×13-inch pan. Chill for 8 to 10 hours or until set. Unmold onto a serving plate. Combine the yogurt, 1/2 cup mayonnaise, 1/2 cup evaporated milk, salt and pepper in a bowl. Pour over each serving and garnish with cucumber slices.

Eggplant with Garlic Sauce

Serves 4

Per serving
Calories 350
Protein 25 g
Carbohydrates 26 g
Total Fat 17 g
43% Calories from Fat
Cholesterol 76 mg
Fiber 10 g
Sodium 1392 mg
Sugar 13 g

1	tablespoon sugar
1	tablespoon cornstarch
1/4	cup soy sauce
1	tablespoon vinegar
1	pound ground pork
1	garlic clove, minced
1	(2-inch) piece of ginger, minced
1	carrot, peeled and sliced
1	bell pepper, sliced
2	eggplant, sliced
	Chili powder to taste

Combine the sugar, cornstarch, soy sauce and vinegar in a small bowl and mix well. Brown the ground pork with the garlic and ginger in a large saucepan, stirring until the pork is crumbly. Add the carrot, bell pepper and eggplant and stir-fry until almost tender. Add the soy sauce mixture. Cook until thickened, stirring constantly. Stir in chili powder.

Note: Other vegetables and meats can be used with the same sauce.

Almond Bibb Salad

Serves 6

1 head Bibb lettuce, torn
1/4 head iceberg lettuce, torn
1/2 cup thinly sliced celery
2 green onions, thinly sliced
1/4 cup vegetable oil
2 tablespoons sugar, or an equivalent amount of sugar substitute
2 tablespoons wine vinegar
1 tablespoon minced fresh parsley
1/2 teaspoon salt
1/8 teaspoon hot red pepper sauce
1 (11-ounce) can mandarin oranges, drained
1/2 cup sliced almonds, toasted
1 purple onion, sliced (optional)

Per serving
Calories 191
Protein 3 g
Carbohydrates 18 g
Total Fat 13 g
59% Calories from Fat
Cholesterol 0 mg
Fiber 2 g
Sodium 210 mg
Sugar 14 g

Place the Bibb lettuce, iceberg lettuce, celery and green onions in a large sealable plastic bag and seal the bag. Store in the refrigerator until serving time. Mix the oil, sugar, vinegar, parsley, salt and hot sauce in a jar with a tight-fitting lid. Chill, covered, until serving time.

To serve, shake the dressing until combined. Pour over the lettuce mixture in the bag. Seal the bag and shake to coat. Place the salad on individual salad plates. Top with the mandarin oranges, almonds and purple onion.

Wilted Garden Leaf Lettuce

Serves 4

1 bunch leaf lettuce
6 to 8 radishes, sliced
4 to 6 green onions, sliced
5 slices bacon, crisp-cooked and crumbled
1/4 cup white vinegar
1 tablespoon sugar
2 tablespoons water
1/2 teaspoon salt
1/4 teaspoon dry mustard
1/8 teaspoon pepper

Per serving
Calories 88
Protein 5 g
Carbohydrates 7 g
Total Fat 4 g
45% Calories from Fat
Cholesterol 011 mg
Fiber 1 g
Sodium 548 mg
Sugar 4 g

Rinse the lettuce and spin dry in a salad spinner. Place the lettuce in a large bowl. Add the radishes, green onions and bacon. Bring the vinegar, sugar, water, salt, dry mustard and pepper to a simmer in a saucepan. Pour over the lettuce mixture and toss to wilt. Serve immediately.

French Onion Soup

Serves 4

Per serving
Calories 449
Protein 22 g
Carbohydrates 24 g
Total Fat 28 g
55% Calories from Fat
Cholesterol 83 mg
Fiber 2 g
Sodium 1345 mg
Sugar 09 g

1	large loaf French bread	1/2	cup dry red wine
1/4	cup (1/2 stick) butter	2	(10-ounce) cans
1	teaspoon sugar		condensed beef broth
3	large onions, thinly sliced	8	ounces Emmentaler
1	tablespoon all-purpose		cheese or other Swiss
	flour		cheese, sliced
2 1/2	cups water		

Preheat the oven to 325 degrees. Cut four 1-inch-thick slices from the bread loaf and place on a baking sheet. Reserve the remaining bread for serving. Bake the bread slices for 10 minutes or just until brown and toasted. Remove from the oven. Increase the oven temperature to 425 degrees.

Melt the butter in a 4-quart saucepan. Stir in the sugar. Add the onions and mix well. Cook over medium heat for 10 minutes or until the onions are golden brown. Stir in the flour until well combined. Add the water, wine and broth. Bring to a boil. Reduce the heat and simmer, covered, for 10 minutes.

Ladle the soup into four 12-ounce ovenproof soup bowls. Place one slice of toasted bread on top of each. Fold the cheese slices and arrange to fit on top of the bread. Place the bowls on a baking sheet for easier handling. Bake for 10 minutes or until the cheese melts. Serve with the remaining bread on the side.

Note: To give the soup a French effect, use Le Creuset or other cast-iron soup pots instead of the ovenproof bowls. Shredded cheese may be used instead of sliced cheese.

Cheesy Potato Soup

Serves 8

Per serving
Calories 396
Protein 16 g
Carbohydrates 43 g
Total Fat 19 g
42% Calories from Fat
Cholesterol 51 mg
Fiber 3 g
Sodium 1679 mg
Sugar 8 g

4	chicken bouillon cubes	1	(20-ounce) can cream of
5	cups water		chicken soup
1	cup sliced carrots	12 to 16	ounces American
1	cup sliced celery		cheese, cut into cubes
1	cup minced onion		Crumbled cooked bacon
6	potatoes, cut into chunks		for garnish

Dissolve the bouillon cubes in the water in a large heavy stockpot. Add the carrots, celery, onion and potatoes. Cook until the vegetables are tender. Add the soup and cheese. Reduce the heat to low. Simmer until the cheese melts. Ladle into soup bowls. Garnish with bacon.

Note: For a plan-ahead meal, combine the bouillon cubes, water, carrots, celery, onion and potatoes in a slow cooker. Cook on Low for 6 to 8 hours. Add the soup and cheese 30 minutes before serving.

Potato Onion Soup

Serves 12

5 slices bacon	2¹/₂ cups chopped
1 to 2 cups thinly sliced onions	peeled potatoes
1 (12-ounce) can	1 teaspoon salt
evaporated milk	1 teaspoon curry powder
1¹/₂ cups water	¹/₄ cup parsley leaves
1¹/₂ cups chicken broth	

Fry the bacon in a skillet until crisp. Remove the bacon to paper towels to drain and cool, reserving the drippings in the skillet. Crumble the bacon. Sauté the onions in the reserved drippings until translucent. Combine with the evaporated milk, water, broth, potatoes, salt and curry powder in a saucepan and mix well. Bring to a boil; reduce the heat. Simmer for 20 minutes or until the potatoes are tender. Ladle into soup bowls. Sprinkle with the parsley and crumbled bacon.

Nutritional analysis includes the entire amount of bacon drippings.

Per serving
Calories 102
Protein 5 g
Carbohydrates 13 g
Total Fat 4 g
32% Calories from Fat
Cholesterol 12 mg
Fiber 1 g
Sodium 350 mg
Sugar 5 g

Plan Ahead
When you are preparing food, make enough extra for two meals. Store half in the refrigerator to eat in a day or two, or store it, clearly labeled, in the freezer to eat later in the month. This works well with chili, casseroles, soups, and stews.

Best Twice-Baked Potatoes

Serves 8

4 (8-ounce) russet potatoes	¹/₂ cup low-fat buttermilk
2 tablespoons butter or	3 small green onions, thinly
margarine	sliced or chopped
¹/₂ cup low-fat sour cream	Salt and pepper to taste
²/₃ cup shredded sharp	Paprika to taste
Cheddar cheese	

Preheat the oven to 400 degrees. Wrap the potatoes in foil. Bake for 1 hour. Let stand until cool enough to handle. Preheat the broiler. Unwrap the potatoes and cut into halves lengthwise. Scoop out the potatoes into a bowl, leaving a ¹/₈- to ¹/₄-inch shell. Arrange the potato shells on a baking sheet. Add the butter, sour cream, cheese, buttermilk, green onions, salt and pepper to the potatoes and mash well. Mound into the potato shells. Sprinkle with paprika. Broil for 10 to 15 minutes or until light brown and heated through. Cool for 10 minutes.

Note: These may be prepared in advance and frozen. Prepare the filled potato shells and place on a baking sheet. Cover lightly and freeze until firm. Remove the frozen potatoes from the baking sheet and place in a freezer bag or container and seal tightly. Store in the freezer. To serve, place the potatoes on a microwave-safe plate. Microwave on High for 2 to 3 minutes per potato or until heated through.

Per serving
Calories 233
Protein 7 g
Carbohydrates 35 g
Total Fat 07 g
28% Calories from Fat
Cholesterol 23 mg
Fiber 3 g
Sodium 131 mg
Sugar 3 g

Twice-Baked Potatoes

Serves 8

SIGNATURE RECIPE

Idaho is the powerhouse for potatoes. Although many varieties are grown in Idaho, the Russet Burbank is by far the most popular and produced potato. Idaho has perfect conditions for growing potatoes. Its mild growing season in the summer paired with rich, light soil and high elevations create an ideal potato growing environment. Although the potato can be prepared in many ways, we have chosen a baked potato variation for our recipe.

Per serving
Calories 361
Protein 12 g
Carbohydrates 35 g
Total Fat 20 g
48% Calories from Fat
Cholesterol 51 mg
Fiber 4 g
Sodium 501 mg
Sugar 3 g

4	large Idaho russet potatoes
8	slices bacon
1	cup sour cream
1/2	cup milk
1/4	cup (1/2 stick) butter
1/2	teaspoon salt
1/4	teaspoon pepper
1	cup (4 ounces) shredded Cheddar cheese
8	green onions, sliced

Preheat the oven to 350 degrees. Scrub the potatoes and wrap in foil. Bake for 1 hour. Remove from the oven and cool for 10 minutes. Maintain the oven temperature. Fry the bacon in a large skillet over medium-high heat until evenly brown and crisp. Remove to paper towels to drain and cool. Crumble the bacon.

Unwrap the potatoes and cut into halves lengthwise. Scoop the potatoes into a large bowl, reserving the potato shells. Add the sour cream, milk, butter, salt, pepper, one-half of the cheese and one-half of the green onions to the potatoes and mix well. Spoon into the reserved potato shells and place in a baking dish. Top each with the remaining cheese, remaining green onions and the bacon. Bake for 15 minutes.

West Virginia Fried Potato Stew with Ramps

Serves 10

5 pounds potatoes
1 pound ramps
1 pound salt pork

Scrub the potatoes; peel, if desired. Cut the potatoes into paper-thin slices. Soak the ramps, including the leaves. Drain the ramps and cut into 1-inch round pieces. Cut the salt pork into paper-thin slices. Combine the potatoes, ramps and salt pork in a 10-inch skillet. Fry over low heat until tender and cooked through.

SIGNATURE RECIPE

Ramps are celebrated across Appalachia. Shady coves reaching about three thousand feet provide near-perfect growing conditions. Ramps are similar to wild green onions, although leafier, and their smell can most charitably be described as horrible. Many ramp devotees claim they possess magical healing powers from prevention of colds to cleansing of the blood. They may be right, for the ramp's European cousin, the ramson, has recently been found to have antibiotic properties.

Per serving
Calories 536
Protein 8 g
Carbohydrates 46 g
Total Fat 37 g
61% Calories from Fat
Cholesterol 39 mg
Fiber 4 g
Sodium 655 mg
Sugar 3 g

Sinless Potato Casserole

Per serving
Calories 176
Protein 10 g
Carbohydrates 25 g
Total Fat 9 g
38% Calories from Fat
Cholesterol 15 mg
Fiber 1 g
Sodium 648 mg
Sugar 2 g

1	cup low-fat sour cream
3	tablespoons ranch salad dressing mix
1	(10-ounce) can 98% fat-free cream of chicken soup
10	ounces low-fat Cheddar cheese, shredded
1	(32-ounce) package shredded hash brown potatoes, thawed

Preheat the oven to 350 degrees. Mix the sour cream and salad dressing mix in a bowl. Add the soup and cheese and mix well. Combine with the hash brown potatoes in a large bowl and mix well. Spoon into an 11×14-inch baking pan sprayed with nonstick cooking spray. Bake for 45 minutes.

Golden Sweet Potato Nuggets

Serves 6

Per serving
Calories 141
Protein 2 g
Carbohydrates 28 g
Total Fat 3 g
17% Calories from Fat
Cholesterol 0 mg
Fiber 1 g
Sodium 121 mg
Sugar 0 g

2	teaspoons ground cumin
1	teaspoon chili powder
1/2	teaspoon paprika
1/4	teaspoon salt
1/2	teaspoon garlic powder (optional)
1	tablespoon olive oil
1 1/2	pounds sweet potatoes, cut into small pieces

Preheat the oven to 425 degrees. Mix the cumin, chili powder, paprika, salt, garlic powder and olive oil in a sealable plastic bag. Add the sweet potatoes and seal the bag. Shake the bag to coat well. Spread on a lightly oiled baking sheet. Bake for 8 minutes. Turn the sweet potato pieces. Bake for 5 to 10 minutes longer or until tender. Serve warm.

Grilled Sweet Potatoes

Serves 5

4   large sweet potatoes
1/4   cup (1/2 stick) light butter, melted
1   teaspoon pepper

Preheat the grill for 20 minutes or until all coals are uniformly ashy gray in color. Scrub the sweet potatoes under running water with a vegetable brush. Cut into 1/2-inch slices. Brush one side with the butter and sprinkle with the pepper.

Arrange brushed side down on a grill rack and repeat the process on the remaining side. Grill for 20 minutes, turning and brushing with the remaining butter until the sweet potatoes are soft when pricked with a fork.

SIGNATURE RECIPE

The Mississippi sweet potato industry began in 1915 when Tennessee farmers moved to Vardaman. Today approximately twenty thousand acres of sweet potatoes are grown there. An excellent source of vitamins A and C, sweet potatoes are also cholesterol free, fat free, a good source of dietary fiber, contain potassium and vitamin B-6, and are full of beta carotene. With the versatility of sweet potatoes, they can be used to make muffins, cheesecakes, and the traditional casserole.

Per serving
Calories 177
Protein 2 g
Carbohydrates 32 g
Total Fat 5 g
24% Calories from Fat
Cholesterol 16 mg
Fiber 1 g
Sodium 73 mg
Sugar 0 g

Sweet Potato Casserole

Serves 10

Per serving
Calories 112
Protein 1 g
Carbohydrates 22 g
Total Fat 3 g
22% Calories from Fat
Cholesterol 0 mg
Fiber 2 g
Sodium 71 mg
Sugar 14 g

4	yams or sweet potatoes
1/2	cup packed brown sugar
1/4	cup (1/2 stick) low-fat margarine
	Nutmeg to taste

Preheat the oven to 350 degrees. Peel the yams and cut into chunks. Cook in boiling water in a saucepan just until tender; drain. Place in a shallow baking dish sprayed with nonstick cooking spray. Sprinkle with the brown sugar and dot with the margarine. Sprinkle with nutmeg. Bake for 30 minutes or until cooked through.

Note: Brown sugar substitute may be used for those following a diabetic diet.

Sweet Potato Casserole with Coconut-Walnut Topping

Serves 12

Per serving
Calories 378
Protein 5 g
Carbohydrates 48 g
Total Fat 20 g
46% Calories from Fat
Cholesterol 32 mg
Fiber 3 g
Sodium 191 mg
Sugar 31 g

1	(29-ounce) can sweet potatoes, drained
1/2	cup granulated sugar
1/2	cup milk
1/3	cup margarine, melted
2	eggs, lightly beaten
1	teaspoon vanilla extract
1	cup shredded coconut
1	cup packed light brown sugar
1	cup chopped walnuts
1/3	cup all-purpose flour
1/3	cup margarine, melted

Preheat the oven to 375 degrees. Mash the sweet potatoes in a bowl. Add the granulated sugar, milk, 1/3 cup margarine, the eggs and vanilla and mix well. Pour into a 9×13-inch baking dish sprayed with nonstick cooking spray. Mix the coconut, brown sugar, walnuts and flour in a bowl. Stir in 1/3 cup margarine. Sprinkle over the sweet potato mixture. Bake for 20 minutes.

Sweet Potato Casserole with Cranberry Topping

Serves 8

Per serving
Calories 312
Protein 3 g
Carbohydrates 50 g
Total Fat 12 g
34% Calories from Fat
Cholesterol 19 mg
Fiber 3 g
Sodium 135 mg
Sugar 28 g

1   (29-ounce) can sweet potatoes or
       yams, drained
2   cups fresh or frozen cranberries
1/2 cup packed light brown sugar
2   tablespoons butter or margarine, melted
1/2 cup orange juice
1/2 cup chopped walnuts
1/4 cup packed light brown sugar
1/2 teaspoon cinnamon
3   tablespoons butter or margarine, chilled

Preheat the oven to 350 degrees. Cut the sweet potatoes into
1/4-inch slices. Place in a greased 2 1/2-quart baking dish. Top with
the cranberries, 1/2 cup brown sugar and the melted butter. Pour the
orange juice over the top. Bake, covered, for 30 minutes.

Mix the walnuts, 1/4 cup brown sugar and the cinnamon in a bowl.
Cut in the chilled butter until crumbly. Sprinkle over the sweet potato
mixture. Bake, uncovered, for 10 minutes or until the topping is
golden brown.

Mama's Sweet Potato Casserole *Serves 12*

SIGNATURE RECIPE

North Carolina ranks first in the production of the nutritious sweet potato. Approximately thirty-six thousand acres of sweet potatoes are grown in North Carolina—nearly 40 percent of the total United States production. Many sweet potatoes are marketed as yams, but are actually sweet potatoes with a vivid orange color, a soft moist consistency when cooked, and a uniquely sweet flavor. The term "yam" has been used ever since slaves from West Africa mistook the sweet potato for their native "nyami."

6	large sweet potatoes
1/2	cup (1 stick) butter
1	cup all-purpose flour
1	cup packed dark brown sugar
4	teaspoons baking powder
1	teaspoon salt
1	teaspoon cinnamon
1/2	teaspoon nutmeg
1	teaspoon ground allspice
1	(15-ounce) can crushed pineapple, drained
16	large marshmallows (optional)

Preheat the oven to 350 degrees. Peel the sweet potatoes and cut into chunks. Cook the sweet potatoes in boiling water in a saucepan until soft; drain. Mash the sweet potatoes with the butter in a large bowl. Add the flour, brown sugar, baking powder, salt, cinnamon, nutmeg and allspice and mix well. Fold in the pineapple. Pour into a buttered 9×12-inch baking dish. Bake for 30 minutes or until brown on top. Remove from the oven. Preheat the broiler. Press the marshmallows into the surface. Broil until the marshmallows are brown.

Note: Two 29-ounce cans of sweet potatoes may be used.

Per serving
Calories 280
Protein 3 g
Carbohydrates 51 g
Total Fat 8 g
25% Calories from Fat
Cholesterol 20 mg
Fiber 1 g
Sodium 427 mg
Sugar 23 g

Sweet Potato Pie

Serves 6

2 cups mashed boiled
    sweet potatoes
2 eggs
2 tablespoons margarine
1 cup sugar
1/3 cup milk
1/2 teaspoon vanilla extract
1/4 teaspoon cinnamon
1/4 teaspoon nutmeg
1 baked (9-inch) pie shell

Per serving
Calories 415
Protein 6 g
Carbohydrates 63 g
Total Fat 16 g
35% Calories from Fat
Cholesterol 63 mg
Fiber 3 g
Sodium 260 mg
Sugar 39 g

Preheat the oven to 400 degrees. Combine the sweet potatoes, eggs, margarine, sugar, milk, vanilla, cinnamon and nutmeg in a mixing bowl and mix well. Pour into the pie shell. Bake for 10 minutes. Reduce the oven temperature to 350 degrees. Bake until the center is firm. Cool on a wire rack.

Note: Two cups of canned sweet potatoes may be used.

Pumpkin Delight

Serves 12 to 15

2 cups pumpkin
3/4 cup sugar
3 eggs
8 ounces evaporated milk
1 (2-layer) package spice cake mix
1 cup (2 sticks) margarine, melted
1 cup pecans, chopped
8 ounces whipped topping

Per serving
Calories 430
Protein 5 g
Carbohydrates 42 g
Total Fat 27 g
56% Calories from Fat
Cholesterol 47 mg
Fiber 2 g
Sodium 409 mg
Sugar 30 g

Preheat the oven to 350 degrees. Beat the pumpkin, sugar, eggs and evaporated milk in a mixing bowl. Pour into a greased 9×13-inch baking pan. Sprinkle with the cake mix. Drizzle the margarine over the cake mix. Top with the pecans. Bake for 1 hour. Cut into squares and top with the whipped topping. Serve cool or warm.

Pumpkin Whoopie Pies

Serves 12 to 16

SIGNATURE RECIPE

As part of a school-year-long adventure in civics, Wells Memorial Elementary School in Harrisville got the pumpkin named as New Hampshire's official state fruit by the General Court in 2006. Since 1991 Keene has held an annual pumpkin festival that celebrates community. The Guinness World Record for most Jack-o'lanterns in one place was set in 2003 with 28,592 pumpkins. Boston held a pumpkin fest in 2006 and took the lead with a total of 30,128.

Per serving
Calories 463
Protein 5 g
Carbohydrates 69 g
Total Fat 19 g
36% Calories from Fat
Cholesterol 84 mg
Fiber 1 g
Sodium 393 mg
Sugar 48 g

1/2	cup water
1/2	cup corn oil, vegetable oil or canola oil
1	(15-ounce) can pure pumpkin
1	teaspoon vanilla extract
4	eggs
1 1/2	cups granulated sugar
1 1/2	teaspoons cinnamon
1	teaspoon ground cloves
1	teaspoon nutmeg
3	cups all-purpose flour
2	teaspoons baking powder
2	teaspoons baking soda
1/2	teaspoon salt
8	ounces cream cheese, softened
1/2	cup (1 stick) butter, softened
2	teaspoons vanilla extract
4	cups confectioners' sugar

Preheat the oven to 350 degrees. Combine the water, corn oil, pumpkin, 1 teaspoon vanilla and the eggs in a bowl and mix well. Add the granulated sugar, cinnamon, cloves, nutmeg, flour, baking powder, baking soda and salt and mix well. Drop by spoonfuls onto a lightly greased or baking parchment–lined cookie sheet and spread slightly to make sure they are round. Allow only six cookies per cookie sheet as the cookies will spread while baking. Bake for 12 to 14 minutes or until brown. Remove to wire racks to cool.

Beat the cream cheese, butter and 2 teaspoons vanilla in a mixing bowl until light and fluffy. Add the confectioners' sugar and beat until smooth. Spread on one-half of the cookies. Top with the remaining cookies.

Note: You may substitute 3 1/2 teaspoons pumpkin pie spice for the three spices used in the recipe with very similar results.

Rhubarb Crunch

Serves 9

Per serving
Calories 371
Protein 3 g
Carbohydrates 67 g
Total Fat 11 g
26% Calories from Fat
Cholesterol 0 mg
Fiber 3 g
Sodium 129 mg
Sugar 48 g

6	cups sliced rhubarb
1	cup granulated sugar
2	teaspoons cinnamon
1	cup all-purpose flour
1	cup packed brown sugar
1	cup rolled oats
1/2	cup (1 stick) margarine or butter

Preheat the oven to 375 degrees. Toss the rhubarb with the granulated sugar and cinnamon in a bowl. Mix the flour, brown sugar and oats in a bowl. Cut in the margarine until crumbly. Place one-half of the oat mixture in a 9×9-inch baking pan sprayed with oil. Cover with the rhubarb mixture. Top with the remaining oat mixture. Bake for 45 to 60 minutes or until golden brown and bubbly in the center. Serve warm with ice cream.

Spinach Pie with a Potato Crust

Serves 8

Per serving
Calories 165
Protein 9 g
Carbohydrates 14 g
Total Fat 9 g
45% Calories from Fat
Cholesterol 39 mg
Fiber 2 g
Sodium 192 mg
Sugar 2 g

2	large potatoes, peeled and sliced 1/4 inch thick
1	egg
1/2	cup egg substitute
4	ounces Neufchâtel cheese, softened
4	ounces fat-free cottage cheese
2	tablespoons grated Parmesan cheese
2	tablespoons olive oil
1/8	teaspoons pepper
1	(10-ounce) package frozen spinach, cooked and squeezed dry

Preheat the oven to 350 degrees. Spray a 9-inch pie plate with nonstick cooking spray. Arrange the potatoes over the bottom and up the side of the pie plate. Beat the egg in a bowl. Add the egg substitute, Neufchâtel cheese, cottage cheese, Parmesan cheese, olive oil and pepper and mix well. Fold in the spinach. Pour over the potatoes. Bake for 35 to 40 minutes or until set.

A weekly meal plan will assist in preparing nutritious meals for the family. Follow daily servings or portion-based nutrition recommendations. Time is a family's most important resource. Use preparation or shopping time as "together time." Dividing tasks among family members reduces preparation time.

Southwest Squash

Serves 6

Per serving
Calories 104
Protein 1 g
Carbohydrates 5 g
Total Fat 9 g
76% Calories from Fat
Cholesterol 0 mg
Fiber 1 g
Sodium 39 mg
Sugar 3 g

4   cups chopped summer squash
1/4 cup olive oil
1/2 cup chopped onion
1/2 teaspoon minced garlic
1   cup chopped tomato
2   tablespoons canned chopped
     green chiles
1/4 teaspoon chili powder
1/8 teaspoon ground cumin
1/8 teaspoon red pepper, or to taste

Preheat the oven to 450 degrees. Toss the squash in the olive oil in a bowl to coat. Place in a shallow baking dish. Roast for 10 to 20 minutes or until tender. Sauté the onion and garlic in a hot skillet for 3 to 5 minutes or until tender. Stir in the tomato, green chiles, chili powder, cumin and red pepper. Cook until heated through. Stir in the roasted squash. Serve immediately.

Zucchini Italian Style

Serves 8

Per serving
Calories 156
Protein 11 g
Carbohydrates 7 g
Total Fat 10 g
55% Calories from Fat
Cholesterol 34 mg
Fiber 2 g
Sodium 442 mg
Sugar 4 g

2   zucchini, sliced
1   (16-ounce) can stewed or
     Italian tomatoes
1   small onion, sliced
1   (3-ounce) can sliced mushrooms
12   ounces mozzarella cheese,
     shredded

Preheat the oven to 350 degrees. Layer the zucchini, tomatoes, onion and mushrooms in a 9×13-inch baking dish. Bake for 30 to 45 minutes or until the zucchini is tender. Sprinkle with the cheese. Bake for 10 to 15 minutes or until the cheese melts.

Fried Green Tomatoes

Serves 8

4   large green tomatoes
1¹/2 cups buttermilk
1   tablespoon salt
1   teaspoon pepper
1   cup self-rising flour
1   cup cornmeal
3   cups peanut oil
     Salt to taste

Cut the tomatoes into sixteen slices ¹/4 to ¹/3 inch thick. Place in a shallow dish. Pour the buttermilk over the tomatoes. Sprinkle with 1 tablespoon salt and the pepper. Mix the self-rising flour and cornmeal in a shallow dish. Dredge the tomato slices in the flour mixture. Fry the tomatoes a few at a time in the hot oil in a large cast-iron skillet over medium heat for 3 minutes on each side or until golden brown. Drain on paper towels. Sprinkle with salt to taste. Serve warm.

SIGNATURE RECIPE

In Alabama, we love our tomatoes. From red to purple to green, tomatoes are a cornerstone of our diet, and we love growing our own. Sometimes we can't wait until those tomatoes growing everywhere from our kitchen windows to our gardens ripen. So we pick 'em green and fry 'em up! Fried green tomatoes epitomize Alabama cuisine, and when shared with family, friends, and neighbors, they embody the Southern hospitality that defines us.

Per serving
Calories 866
Protein 5 g
Carbohydrates 30 g
Total Fat 82 g
84% Calories from Fat
Cholesterol 2 mg
Fiber 3 g
Sodium 1136 mg
Sugar 6 g

Farmers' Market Salsa

Serves 8

Per serving
Calories 35
Protein 1 g
Carbohydrates 5 g
Total Fat 2 g
44% Calories from Fat
Cholesterol 0 mg
Fiber 1 g
Sodium 5 mg
Sugar 3 g

4	large ripe tomatoes
1/4	cup chopped onion
1/4	cup chopped cilantro
1	tablespoon chopped fresh oregano
2	garlic cloves, minced
1	teaspoon minced jalapeño chile, or to taste
1	tablespoon olive oil
2	teaspoons lime juice
	Salt and pepper to taste

Cut the tomatoes into quarters and remove the seeds. Chop the tomatoes and place in a medium bowl. Add the onion, cilantro, oregano, garlic, jalapeño chile, olive oil, lime juice, salt and pepper and mix well. Let stand, loosely covered, at room temperature for 10 to 15 minutes for the flavors to blend. Serve immediately or store in the refrigerator for later use.

Greek Salad Salsa

Serves 4

3   tablespoons olive oil
1^1/$_2$ tablespoons lemon juice
1^1/$_2$ teaspoons chopped fresh oregano, or
          ^{1}/$_2$ teaspoon dried oregano
1   teaspoon sugar
^{1}/$_2$ teaspoon salt
1   pound fresh tomatoes, chopped
^{2}/$_3$ cup chopped peeled cucumber
^{1}/$_3$ cup chopped green bell pepper
^{1}/$_4$ cup chopped black olives
2   tablespoons chopped red onion
2   ounces feta cheese, crumbled

Whisk the olive oil, lemon juice, oregano, sugar and salt in a bowl. Add the tomatoes, cucumber, bell pepper, olives, onion and cheese and stir until coated. Serve immediately with pita chips.

Per serving
Calories 170
Protein 3 g
Carbohydrates 9 g
Total Fat 14 g
73% Calories from Fat
Cholesterol 13 mg
Fiber 2 g
Sodium 529 mg
Sugar 6 g

SIGNATURE RECIPE

Arizona, the Grand Canyon State and sixth-largest state, has a diverse population including Hispanic and Native American Indians. Southwestern culture means all types of salsas, gazpacho, quesadillas, and burritos.

Arizona is the winter vegetable capital with lettuce leading the way, plus broccoli, cauliflower, chiles, and tomatoes. Its vegetable and fruit production includes citrus and melons. Almost 50 percent of our nation's fresh produce enters the border at Nogales, Arizona.

Per serving
Calories 87
Protein 3 g
Carbohydrates 15 g
Total Fat 3 g
27% Calories from Fat
Cholesterol 0 mg
Fiber 4 g
Sodium 16 mg
Sugar 9 g

Gazpacho

Serves 10

6   tomatoes
4   large cucumbers
2   large white onions
2   green chiles
2   bunches cilantro
2   (8-ounce) cans salsa verde
1   (64-ounce) can vegetable juice cocktail

Chop the tomatoes, cucumbers, onions, green chiles and cilantro into small pieces. Combine with the salsa verde and vegetable juice cocktail in a large bowl. Marinate in the refrigerator for 2 hours or longer. Serve cold. Store in the refrigerator.

Note: Adjust the "heat" by the type of chiles you add. Anaheim chiles are milder; jalapeño chiles and serrano chiles are hotter. Cold gazpacho is a refreshing summer lunch or healthy appetizer.

Corn Bread Salad

Serves 16

Per serving
Calories 356
Protein 12 g
Carbohydrates 34 g
Total Fat 20 g
50% Calories from Fat
Cholesterol 18 mg
Fiber 5 g
Sodium 990 mg
Sugar 7 g

2   (6-ounce) packages sweet yellow corn bread mix
1   cup sour cream
1   cup mayonnaise
1   envelope ranch salad dressing mix
2   (15-ounce) cans light kidney beans, drained and rinsed
2   (11-ounce) cans sweet niblet corn, drained
1   bell pepper, chopped
2   large tomatoes, chopped
10 slices bacon, crisp-cooked and crumbled
2   cups (8 ounces) shredded Mexican cheese
1   cup chopped green onions
    Chopped tomatoes for garnish

Prepare and bake the corn bread mix using the package directions. Let stand until cool. Crumble the corn bread. Mix the sour cream, mayonnaise and ranch salad dressing mix in a bowl. Layer the corn bread, beans, corn, bell pepper, tomatoes and bacon one-half at a time in a large serving bowl. Spread the sour cream mixture over the layers. Sprinkle with the cheese and green onions. Garnish with chopped tomatoes.

Pasta Salad

Serves 5

Per serving
Calories 243
Protein 11 g
Carbohydrates 40 g
Total Fat 6 g
21% Calories from Fat
Cholesterol 5 mg
Fiber 7 g
Sodium 410 mg
Sugar 7 g

6   ounces whole wheat pasta
2   cups chopped tomatoes
4   green onions, chopped
1   bell pepper, chopped
1   (4-ounce) can sliced or whole black olives, drained
8   ounces frozen peas, thawed
1   tablespoon garlic powder
2   tablespoons light Italian salad dressing
1/3 cup shredded Parmesan cheese

Prepare the pasta using the package directions; drain. Combine the tomatoes, green onions, bell pepper, olives, peas, garlic powder, salad dressing and cheese in a large bowl or storage container and mix well. Add the pasta and toss to mix. Chill until serving time.

Note: Whole wheat pasta is recommended in this recipe because it contains a higher fiber content. Half whole wheat pasta and half regular pasta can be used, if desired. For quick thawing of the frozen peas, place them in a colander and drain the pasta over them. Other vegetables such as cucumber, zucchini, and carrots can be used. To serve hot, sauté a few servings of cold pasta salad in a skillet sprayed with nonstick cooking spray over medium heat for a few minutes or until heated through.

Curry Rice Salad

Serves 8

Per serving
Calories 201
Protein 5 g
Carbohydrates 33 g
Total Fat 7 g
30% Calories from Fat
Cholesterol 0 mg
Fiber 4 g
Sodium 1128 mg
Sugar 1 g

1   (7-ounce) package chicken-flavored
      rice vermicelli mix
1   (14-ounce) can marinated artichoke hearts
5   green onions, chopped
6   large stuffed green olives, sliced
1/3 cup low-fat mayonnaise
1   teaspoon curry powder

Prepare the rice mix using the package directions. Let stand until cool. Drain the artichoke hearts, reserving the marinade. Slice the artichoke hearts. Combine the artichoke hearts, green onions, green olives and rice in a bowl and mix well. Mix the reserved marinade, mayonnaise and curry powder in a small bowl. Add to the rice mixture and mix well. Serve at room temperature or chilled.

Note: To serve as a main dish, add 2 cups chopped cooked chicken.

Oklahoma Rice Salad

Serves 8

Per serving
Calories 106
Protein 2 g
Carbohydrates 6 g
Total Fat 4 g
31% Calories from Fat
Cholesterol 2 mg
Fiber 2 g
Sodium 105 mg
Sugar 2 g

2   cups cooked brown rice
2   tablespoons light French salad dressing
1/2 cup steamed frozen green peas
1/4 cup reduced-fat mayonnaise-style
      salad dressing
1   teaspoon curry powder
1   cup cauliflower florets, sliced
1/4 cup radishes, sliced
1/4 cup celery, sliced
      Salt and pepper to taste

Combine the rice and French salad dressing in an 8-cup bowl and mix well. Fold in the peas. Chill, covered with plastic wrap, for 30 minutes. Mix the mayonnaise-style salad dressing and curry powder in a small bowl. Stir into the chilled rice mixture. Fold in the cauliflower, radishes and celery. Sprinkle with salt and pepper.

Note: The flavor of this salad may be enhanced by the addition of 1 teaspoon chopped garlic and 1/4 cup minced onion to the mayonnaise-style salad dressing mixture before the vegetables are combined with the rice mixture.

Pine Nut Salad

Serves 8

3   large cucumbers, chopped
1   cup finely sliced celery
1   bunch parsley, finely chopped
1   cup black olives, coarsely chopped
2   cups fresh spinach, shredded
1   cup pine nuts
$1/2$ cup olive oil
$1/4$ cup vinegar
$1/16$ teaspoon oregano
     Salt and pepper to taste

Mix the cucumbers, celery, parsley, black olives, spinach and pine nuts in a large bowl. Whisk the olive oil, vinegar, oregano, salt and pepper in a small bowl. Pour over the vegetable mixture and toss to coat.

SIGNATURE RECIPE

Nevada has many thousands of native piñon nut trees that bear an abundant crop of sweet pine nuts. Many years ago, numerous tribes of Washoes, Paiutes, and Shoshones roamed all over Nevada in search of food. One food they harvested was pine nuts, which they considered a life-sustaining gift from the gods. Today pine nuts are used in a variety of dishes from salads to desserts. Toasting pine nuts brings out their sweet flavor.

Per serving
Calories 279
Protein 4 g
Carbohydrates 8 g
Total Fat 27 g
84% Calories from Fat
Cholesterol 0 mg
Fiber 3 g
Sodium 174 mg
Sugar 3 g

Hazelnut Quinoa Salad

Serves 6

SIGNATURE RECIPE

There are more than one hundred varieties of hazelnuts grown throughout the world. In the United States, the majority of hazelnuts are grown in Oregon. More than 99 percent of domestic hazelnuts are grown near Portland, Oregon, in the Willamette Valley. The sweet, exotic flavor and distinctive texture of hazelnuts make them perfect for a wide variety of dishes. But it's also a nut with nutritional substance. Hazelnuts are ideal for a healthy snacks or meals.

$1/2$ cup hazelnuts, toasted
$1/2$ cup quinoa
1 cup water
$1/2$ cup Italian salad dressing
1 cup frozen petite peas, thawed and drained
$1^1/2$ cups chopped seeded peeled cucumbers
1 cup cherry tomatoes, cut into halves
$1/2$ cup chopped yellow or orange bell pepper
$1/4$ teaspoon pepper

Remove the skins from the hazelnuts. Chop the hazelnuts coarsely. Rinse the quinoa under running water for 1 minute. Place the quinoa and 1 cup water in a medium saucepan. Bring to a boil over high heat. Cover and reduce the heat to low. Simmer for 15 to 20 minutes or until all of the water is absorbed. Fluff with a fork. Cool completely.

Process the salad dressing and $1/4$ cup of the hazelnuts in a food processor or blender until smooth. Combine the cooled quinoa, peas, cucumbers, tomatoes and bell pepper in a large bowl and mix well. Add the salad dressing mixture and toss to coat. Sprinkle with the pepper and the remaining hazelnuts. Serve immediately.

Note: You may substitute 2 cups cooked couscous for the quinoa. If preparing in advance, add the peas just before serving.

Per serving
Calories 244
Protein 5 g
Carbohydrates 19 g
Total Fat 17 g
62% Calories from Fat
Cholesterol 0 mg
Fiber 4 g
Sodium 207 mg
Sugar 4 g

Marinated Vegetable Salad

Serves 10

Per serving
Calories 235
Protein 3 g
Carbohydrates 30 g
Total Fat 12 g
44% Calories from Fat
Cholesterol 0 mg
Fiber 3 g
Sodium 384 mg
Sugar 18 g

2/3   cup sugar
3/4   cup cider vinegar
1/2   cup canola oil
      Salt and pepper to taste
1   (15-ounce) can
         French-style green
         beans, drained
1   (15-ounce) can peas with
         diced carrots, drained

1   (15-ounce) can Shoe Peg
         corn or white whole
         kernel corn, drained
1   cup chopped onion
1   cup chopped celery
1   cup chopped green
         bell pepper

Bring the sugar, vinegar, canola oil, salt and pepper to a boil in a saucepan. Boil until the sugar is dissolved. Remove from the heat to cool. Combine the green beans, peas with diced carrots, corn, onion, celery and bell pepper in a large bowl and mix well. Pour the cooled marinade over the vegetables. Marinate, covered, in the refrigerator for 24 hours to allow the flavors to blend.

Note: This salad may be stored in the refrigerator for a week.

Shopping

Displays and packages are tempting and cause shoppers to buy unneeded items. Make a grocery list at home before shopping. Check to see what foods are on hand, those used frequently, and those needed for the week's meal plan. Stick to the list.

Garden Platter

Serves 8

Per serving
Calories 88
Protein 3 g
Carbohydrates 5 g
Total Fat 7 g
63% Calories from Fat
Cholesterol 17 mg
Fiber 2 g
Sodium 127 mg
Sugar 1 g

1 3/4 cups broccoli florets
3/4   cup cauliflower florets
1   zucchini, sliced
1   yellow squash, sliced
12   cherry tomatoes

8   ounces mushrooms
1/4   cup (1/2 stick) butter
1/4   teaspoon garlic salt
1/4   cup (1 ounce) grated
          Parmesan cheese

Cut the broccoli and cauliflower into pieces about 2 1/4 inches long. Arrange the broccoli around the edge of a 12-inch microwave-safe serving plate with the stems pointing toward the center. Place the cauliflower between the broccoli. Place the zucchini and yellow squash in the center of the plate. Microwave on High for 5 to 8 minutes or until the vegetables are tender-crisp. Drain if needed. Add the tomatoes and mushrooms to the vegetables. Place the butter and garlic salt in a 2-cup glass measure. Microwave on High until melted. Drizzle over the vegetables and sprinkle with the cheese. Microwave, uncovered, on High for 1 to 2 minutes or until the tomatoes and mushrooms are heated through.

Note: You may add 1/4 teaspoon dried thyme. Other vegetables may be substituted.

Tofu Tacos

Serves 8

Per serving
Calories 182
Protein 9 g
Carbohydrates 26 g
Total Fat 7 g
32% Calories from Fat
Cholesterol 0 mg
Fiber 6 g
Sodium 453 mg
Sugar 4 g

8	ounces firm tofu fortified with calcium	1/2	large red bell pepper, finely chopped
2	tablespoons canola oil		Juice of 1/2 lemon or lime
1	(15-ounce) can whole kernel corn, drained	1/4	teaspoon garlic powder
1	(15-ounce) can black beans, drained	1/2	teaspoon chili powder
		8	corn tortillas

Cut the tofu into 1/4-inch cubes. Heat the canola oil in a medium skillet. Add the tofu and stir-fry for 15 to 20 minutes or until light brown. Add the corn, beans, bell pepper, lemon juice, garlic powder and chili powder. Cook over low heat for 5 to 10 minutes or until heated through. Spoon into the tortillas.

Note: The mixture may be used for a tofu taco salad. There is no need to heat the mixture after the tofu is cooked. Just spoon the mixture over cold salad greens and drizzle with salsa. The spices can be adjusted to taste.

Types of Tofu

Firm tofu is dense and solid and holds up very well in stir-fry dishes, soups, or on the grill—anywhere that you want the tofu to maintain its shape. Firm tofu is also higher in protein, fat, and calcium than other forms of tofu. Soft tofu is a good choice for recipes that call for blended tofu or in Oriental soups. Silken tofu is a creamy, custard-like product that works well in puréed or blended dishes.

Summer Vegetable Dish

Serves 4

Per serving
Calories 144
Protein 6 g
Carbohydrates 24 g
Total Fat 6 g
30% Calories from Fat
Cholesterol 0 mg
Fiber 4 g
Sodium 189 mg
Sugar 9 g

1	tablespoon margarine	1/4	teaspoon salt
2	cups fresh corn kernels (about 4 ears of corn)	1/2	teaspoon sugar
2	cups chopped fresh tomatoes	1/2	teaspoon ground cumin
		1/8	teaspoon black pepper or white pepper
2	cups sliced zucchini		

Melt the margarine in a 9- or 10-inch nonstick skillet. Add the corn, tomatoes, zucchini, salt, sugar, cumin and pepper. Cook, covered, over low heat for 6 minutes or until the vegetables are tender. Serve hot.

Roasted Root Vegetables

Serves 16

2 cups frozen pearl onions
1 large rutabaga, peeled and cut into 3/4-inch pieces
1 pound carrots, peeled and cut into 1/2-inch pieces
1 pound parsnips, peeled and cut into 1/2-inch pieces
1 pound turnips, peeled and cut into 3/4-inch pieces

3 tablespoons butter, melted
3 tablespoons olive oil
1 1/2 tablespoons dried thyme
1 1/2 teaspoons salt
3/4 teaspoon pepper
2 (10-ounce) packages frozen brussels sprouts
3 or 4 garlic cloves, minced

Preheat the oven to 425 degrees. Combine the onions, rutabaga, carrots, parsnips and turnips in an 8-quart roasting pan. Drizzle with the butter and olive oil. Sprinkle with the thyme, salt and pepper and toss to coat. Bake, covered, for 30 minutes. Stir in the brussels sprouts and garlic. Bake, loosely covered, for 50 to 60 minutes or until the vegetables are tender and beginning to brown, stirring occasionally.

Per serving
Calories 121
Protein 3 g
Carbohydrates 18 g
Total Fat 5 g
36% Calories from Fat
Cholesterol 6 mg
Fiber 5 g
Sodium 290 mg
Sugar 5 g

Clean Up
During food preparation, cleaning as you go will reduce time and make it possible for everyone to eat together. Make after-dinner clean-up a family affair. Children learn many life skills as they work around the house.

Vegetable Namul

Serves 4

1 bunch watercress
1 1/2 cups boiling water
1 garlic clove, minced
1 teaspoon sesame oil
1/4 teaspoon sugar
3 tablespoons soy sauce

1 carrot, grated
1/8 teaspoon cayenne pepper or red pepper (optional)
1 teaspoon sesame seeds, toasted

Rinse the watercress. Remove any undesirable leaves and tough stems. Cut the watercress into 1-inch lengths. Place the watercress in the boiling water in a bowl. Let stand for 3 minutes; drain thoroughly. Mix the garlic, sesame oil, sugar and soy sauce in a large bowl. Add the watercress and carrot. Sprinkle with the cayenne pepper and sesame seeds.

Note: You may use a package of bean sprouts, a package of chop suey mix, or chopped cabbage instead of the watercress.

Per serving
Calories 33
Protein 2 g
Carbohydrates 4 g
Total Fat 1 g
34% Calories from Fat
Cholesterol 0 mg
Fiber 1 g
Sodium 1009 mg
Sugar 2 g

Poultry & Eggs

Chickens and Turkeys and Ducks . . . oh, my!
Keeping Poultry Safe from the Store to the Table

1. When shopping for food, pick up raw poultry and other cold items last. This will eliminate the amount of time that raw poultry is not being refrigerated and that potentially harmful bacteria are able to grow and multiply.

2. In your grocery cart, place raw poultry away from ready-to-eat foods like fruit, vegetables, and prepared foods, and keep an eye out for dripping juices. This will help to prevent cross-contamination. **Cross-contamination** is when a potentially hazardous food comes into contact with a food that will not be cooked any more before it is served. Therefore, harmful bacteria can be transferred from the raw food to the ready-to-eat food.

3. Raw poultry should be stored promptly in a freezer or refrigerator at 40°F (5°C) or below.

4. When preparing raw poultry, it's a good idea to use **separate equipment**, including cutting boards and knives, that will not be used for other food items. After preparation, all equipment should be washed thoroughly with soap and hot water, preferably in a dishwasher. Also, be sure to **wash your hands** before and after handling raw poultry. Equipment and hands can both be sources of cross-contamination.

5. Finally, cook all poultry to an **internal temperature of 165°F (74°C) for 15 seconds**. This includes whole or ground chicken, turkey, duck, and others.

6. Leftovers should be stored in a refrigerator for no more than three to four days or in a freezer for two to three months.

Safe Cooking Temperatures–as measured with a meat thermometer

PRODUCT	INTERNAL COOKED TEMPERATURE (F)
Poultry	
Chicken and Turkey, whole	165°F
Poultry parts	165°F
Duck and Goose	165°F
Stuffing (cooked alone or in bird)	165°F

Chicken Dip

Per serving
Calories 244
Protein 11 g
Carbohydrates 3 g
Total Fat 21 g
77% Calories from Fat
Cholesterol 56 mg
Fiber <1 g
Sodium 511 mg
Sugar 1 g

Serves 20

1	(29-ounce) can chicken
16	ounces cream cheese
1	(10-ounce) can cream of chicken soup
1	cup mayonnaise
1	cup salsa

Combine the chicken, cream cheese, soup, mayonnaise and salsa in a slow cooker. Cook on Medium for 1 hour or until the cream cheese melts and the temperature is 165 degrees. Reduce the slow cooker setting to Low. Serve warm with taco chips.

Greek Chicken Salad

Per serving
Calories 372
Protein 24 g
Carbohydrates 9 g
Total Fat 26 g
65% Calories from Fat
Cholesterol 96 mg
Fiber 1 g
Sodium 867 mg
Sugar 5 g

Serves 6

3	cups chopped cooked chicken
2	cucumbers, peeled, seeded and chopped
1 1/4	cups crumbled feta cheese or chopped Swiss cheese
2/3	cup sliced black olives
1/4	cup chopped fresh parsley, or 1 to 2 tablespoons dried parsley
1	cup light mayonnaise
1/2	cup plain low-fat yogurt
1	garlic clove, minced
1 1/2	teaspoons dried crushed oregano

Combine the chicken, cucumbers, cheese, olives and parsley in a large bowl and mix well. Mix the mayonnaise, yogurt, garlic and oregano in a small bowl. Add to the chicken mixture and toss lightly to coat. Chill until serving time. Serve on lettuce leaves or in pita bread or tortilla wraps.

Oriental Chicken Salad

Serves 8

3   tablespoons sugar
2   tablespoons water
1/4   cup vinegar
1   tablespoon sesame oil
    Salt and pepper to taste
2 or 3 chicken pieces, cooked
        and shredded
1   head iceberg lettuce, torn into
        bite-size pieces
1   head Manoa lettuce, torn into
        bite-size pieces
1   rib celery, sliced
1   carrot, sliced
1 or 2 green onions, cut into 1¹/2-inch
        lengths (optional)
1   bunch Chinese parsley or cilantro,
        cut into 1¹/2-inch lengths (optional)
3   ounces won ton strips or chips,
        crushed (optional)
1   tablespoon toasted sesame seeds

Combine the sugar, water, vinegar, sesame oil, salt and pepper in a medium jar with a tight-fitting lid. Seal the jar and shake well. Chill until serving time.

Combine the chicken, iceberg lettuce, Manoa lettuce, celery, carrot, green onions, Chinese parsley, won ton strips and sesame seeds in a large bowl and toss to mix. Add the dressing just before serving and toss to coat.

Note: Other types of leafy greens may be used. Substitute chicken with other low-fat protein sources such as imitation crab meat, fish, turkey, and so forth.

Per serving
Calories 189
Protein 13 g
Carbohydrates 17 g
Total Fat 9 g
40% Calories from Fat
Cholesterol 33 mg
Fiber 3 g
Sodium 78 mg
Sugar 07 g

Egg Safety

To prepare safe eggs, cook to 160 degrees, until the yolks and whites are firm.

Even clean, whole eggs can be contaminated with bacteria called Salmonella, which is often associated with chicken and other types of poultry. To prevent illness from Salmonella, be sure to take the following steps:

- *Refrigerate eggs promptly.*
- *Store eggs in their original carton and use them within three weeks.*
- *Cook eggs until the yolk and the white are firm. To be safe, do not serve runny scrambled eggs.*
- *Casseroles and other dishes containing eggs should be cooked to 160 degrees (72 degrees C). A food thermometer is the only way to be sure!*
- *Serve eggs and dishes that contain eggs immediately after cooking. They should not be left at room temperature for more than two hours. After two hours they need to be reheated to 160 degrees or refrigerated.*

Chicken Barley Vegetable Chili *Serves 12*

SIGNATURE RECIPE

The Golden State of California continues to rank number one nationally in agriculture production. Its seventy-five thousand farms produce a veritable bounty of products, with 84 percent being family-owned. This recipe heralds the variety of California agricultural products and incorporates healthful whole grain, vegetables, and lean protein, featuring barley, dried beans, chicken and turkey, vegetables (garlic, kale, onions, peppers, and tomatoes), and herbs (basil, cumin seeds, and oregano). This recipe makes good eating taste delicious.

Per serving
Calories 391
Protein 34 g
Carbohydrates 54 g
Total Fat 5 g
12% Calories from Fat
Cholesterol 37 mg
Fiber 26 g
Sodium 157 mg
Sugar 3 g

1 tablespoon olive oil	2 cups diced tomatoes, or
1 large bell pepper, chopped	1 (15-ounce)
1 large onion, chopped	can diced tomatoes
2 garlic cloves, chopped	6 cups low-sodium
2 tablespoons cumin seeds	chicken broth
8 ounces turkey breakfast	1 bunch kale, chopped
sausage patties, or other	(about 8 cups)
low-fat sausage	1 teaspoon dried basil leaves
3 cups chopped	1 teaspoon dried
cooked chicken	oregano leaves
1/2 cup uncooked pearl barley	1/4 cup finely chopped
4 cups navy beans, or	fresh cilantro
2 (15-ounce) cans navy	2 tablespoons lime juice
beans, drained	Salt and pepper to taste

Heat the olive oil in a 6- to 8-quart saucepan. Add the bell pepper, onion, garlic and cumin seeds and sauté until slightly cooked. Brown the sausage in a skillet, breaking the sausage into pieces; drain. Stir the sausage and chicken into the vegetable mixture. Add the barley, beans, tomatoes, broth, kale, basil and oregano and mix well. Bring to a boil; reduce the heat. Simmer for 40 minutes or until the barley is tender. To serve, stir in the cilantro and lime juice. Sprinkle with salt and pepper. Ladle into soup bowls.

Note: Sprinkle with grated cheese at serving time, if desired. This soup freezes well, but may need additional broth or water added when reheating.

Wild Rice Chicken Soup

Serves 6

Per serving
Calories 270
Protein 21 g
Carbohydrates 36 g
Total Fat 5 g
16% Calories from Fat
Cholesterol 29 mg
Fiber 2 g
Sodium 1016 mg
Sugar 5 g

- 5   cups water
- 1   (6-ounce) package long grain and wild rice mix
- 1   (10-ounce) can reduced-fat reduced-sodium cream of chicken soup
- 1¹/2   cups 1% or skim milk
- 8   ounces fat-free cream cheese, cut into cubes
- ¹/4   teaspoon salt, or to taste
- 2   (4-ounce) chicken breasts, baked and chopped
- 1   (10-ounce) package frozen chopped broccoli (optional)
- 1   large carrot, shredded
- ¹/4   cup sliced almonds, toasted

Bring the water, rice mix and the contents of the rice mix seasoning packet to a boil in a large saucepan. Cover and reduce the heat. Simmer for 20 minutes, stirring occasionally. Add the soup, milk, cream cheese and salt. Cook until the cream cheese melts, stirring constantly. Add the chicken, broccoli and carrot. Cook over medium-low heat for 5 to 6 minutes or until the vegetables and rice are tender. Ladle into soup bowls and sprinkle with the almonds.

Note: To shorten the cooking time, microwave the vegetables on High for 2 to 3 minutes or until tender before adding to the soup. The soup may be made without the chicken, or with the chicken and without the vegetables. When chicken breasts are on sale, bake and freeze them, making this recipe a quick and hearty meal. Enjoy using the base recipe and substituting seafood or other vegetables.

Chicken and Dumplings

Per serving
Calories 596
Protein 46 g
Carbohydrates 26 g
Total Fat 34 g
51% Calories from Fat
Cholesterol 228 mg
Fiber 2 g
Sodium 848 mg
Sugar 3 g

1	(4-pound) chicken	1	cup all-purpose flour
2	carrots, peeled and cut into large pieces	2	teaspoons baking powder
1	small onion, cut into quarters	1/2	teaspoon salt
		1/4	teaspoon parsley flakes
2	ribs celery, cut into large pieces	1/8	teaspoon poultry seasoning
1/4	teaspoon pepper	1	egg, well beaten
1/2	teaspoon salt	1 1/2	tablespoons shortening, melted
2	bay leaves	1/3	cup milk
12	cups (about) water	1	cup cream

Discard the chicken parts inserted in the chicken cavity. Place the chicken in a 6-quart or larger stockpot. Add the carrots, onion, celery, pepper, salt and bay leaves. Add enough of the water to cover the chicken. Bring to a boil; reduce the heat to low. Simmer, covered, for 1 1/2 hours or until the chicken pulls away easily from the bones. Remove the chicken from the stockpot. Let the chicken stand until cool enough to handle. Chop the chicken, discarding the skin and bones. Strain the stock, discarding the solids. Return 8 cups of the stock to the stockpot, reserving the remaining stock for another purpose. Add the chopped chicken.

Mix the flour, baking powder, salt, parsley flakes and poultry seasoning in a bowl. Add the egg, shortening and milk and mix to form a stiff batter. Stir the cream into the chicken mixture. Bring to a rolling boil. Drop the dough by teaspoonfuls into the boiling mixture. Reduce the heat to low. Cook, covered, for 15 minutes. Do not remove the lid while the dumplings are cooking. Gently remove the dumplings from the stock with a slotted spoon and set aside. Ladle the chicken and gravy into serving bowls and place the dumplings on top.

Note: Frozen green peas and/or carrots can be added with the cream to add color. This is an excellent way to add vegetables and make this a one-pot meal. Cook and chop the chicken the night before serving. Store the chicken in the refrigerator in the measured chicken stock. Before heating the chicken and stock, any fat can be easily removed by skimming off the top. After measuring the stock needed to complete the recipe, any extra stock can be reserved for other recipes such as soups or rice. The extra stock can be frozen until needed.

Brunswick Stew

Serves 8

3 1/2   pounds chicken parts, or
      1 (3 1/2-pound) broiler chicken
1 1/2   teaspoons salt
1 1/2   cups chopped potatoes
1   (15-ounce) can tomato purée
2   cups fresh or canned chopped tomatoes
1 1/2   cups fresh or frozen lima beans
3/4   cup chopped onion
1   cup white corn kernels
1   cup yellow corn kernels
1   teaspoon sugar
1/4   teaspoon salt
1/4   teaspoon black pepper
1/8   teaspoon red pepper

Place the chicken and 1 1/2 teaspoons salt in a large Dutch oven or stockpot. Add enough water to cover the chicken. Bring to a boil; reduce the heat. Simmer, covered, for 2 hours or until the chicken is cooked through and falling off the bones. Drain the chicken, reserving the broth. Let the chicken stand until cool enough to handle. Chop the chicken, discarding the skin and bones. Skim any fat from the reserved broth. Return the broth to the Dutch oven. Bring to a boil. Reduce the heat and simmer until the broth is reduced to 2 cups. Add the potatoes. Simmer for 10 minutes. Add the tomato purée, tomatoes, beans and onion. Simmer for 20 minutes. Stir in the chicken, white corn, yellow corn and sugar. Simmer for 10 to 15 minutes or until the vegetables are tender and the stew thickens. Stir in 1/4 teaspoon salt, the black pepper and red pepper. Ladle into soup bowls.

SIGNATURE RECIPE

Virginia is known for many culinary firsts. It is believed that Brunswick Stew was first prepared in Brunswick County, Virginia, in 1828. The stew was originally made with squirrel. Today chicken is often the meat of choice and is complemented by a mixture that has come to include tomatoes, potatoes, corn, and lima beans. Since agriculture is Virginia's largest industry and broiler chickens are the number-one farm enterprise, locally grown ingredients are abundant for this Virginia favorite.

Per serving
Calories 363
Protein 33 g
Carbohydrates 45 g
Total Fat 7 g
16% Calories from Fat
Cholesterol 68 mg
Fiber 11 g
Sodium 801 mg
Sugar 10 g

Easy Sweet-and-Sour Chicken   *Serves 6*

Per serving
Calories 427
Protein 41 g
Carbohydrates 26 g
Total Fat 17 g
37% Calories from Fat
Cholesterol 119 mg
Fiber 2 g
Sodium 550 mg
Sugar 19 g

2¹/₂ pounds boneless
    skinless chicken
1 (20-ounce) can
    pineapple chunks
1 (8-ounce) bottle low-fat
    creamy French
    salad dressing
1 envelope dry onion
    soup mix

2 green bell peppers, cut
    into thin strips
1 tablespoon cornstarch
    (optional)
1 tablespoon water
    (optional)

Place the chicken in a slow cooker. Drain the pineapple, reserving the juice. Combine the reserved pineapple juice, salad dressing and onion soup mix in a bowl and mix well. Pour over the chicken. Cook, covered, on Low for 6 to 7 hours or on High for 3 to 4 hours. Add the pineapple and bell peppers. Cook for 20 minutes or until heated through. Arrange the chicken, pineapple and bell peppers on a large platter. Dissolve the cornstarch in the water in a small bowl. Stir into the juices in the slow cooker. Cook until slightly thickened, stirring constantly. Pour over the chicken.

Note: Red or yellow bell peppers may be used instead of green bell peppers, or try a combination of each.

Holding Food for Service

When holding foods for service, be sure to keep hot foods at 140 degrees or above and cold foods at 40 degrees or below.

Chicken and Garden Greens   *Serves 4*

Per serving
Calories 343
Protein 35 g
Carbohydrates 35 g
Total Fat 7 g
19% Calories from Fat
Cholesterol 63 mg
Fiber 3 g
Sodium 204 mg
Sugar 2 g

1 tablespoon olive oil
4 garlic cloves, finely chopped
1 pound skinless chicken breast strips
2 (14-ounce) cans no-fat low-sodium
    chicken broth
6 ounces angel hair pasta
9 ounces fresh spinach
¹/₂ teaspoon pepper

Heat the olive oil in a large skillet over medium-low heat. Add the garlic and sauté until golden brown. Add the chicken strips and cook to 165 degrees on a meat thermometer. Remove the chicken and set aside. Add the broth to the pan drippings and bring to a boil. Add the pasta. Boil, covered, for 6 minutes or until the pasta is al dente. Return the chicken to the skillet. Add the spinach. Cook, covered, for 5 minutes over medium heat until the spinach is tender. Sprinkle with the pepper. Serve in pasta bowls.

Note: Other greens or vegetables can be substituted for the spinach.

Arkansas Chicken and Dressing *Serves 20*

1   (8-pound) hen
1   cup chopped onion
4   ribs celery
1/2   cup (1 stick) butter
6   tablespoons chicken soup base
6   eggs, beaten
1   tablespoon sage
1   teaspoon pepper
21   slices bread heels, crumbled
3   quarts crumbled corn bread
        (about 12 cups)

Preheat the oven to 350 degrees. Cook the chicken in water to cover in a large saucepan until tender. Remove the chicken and let stand until cool enough to handle, reserving the broth in the saucepan. Chop the chicken, discarding the skin and bones. Add the onion and celery to the broth and cook until tender. Stir in the butter and soup base. Remove from the heat to cool. Stir in the eggs, sage and pepper.

Mix the bread crumbs and corn bread crumbs in a large bowl. Stir in the broth mixture until very soupy, adding water if needed. Pour one-half of the dressing into a greased roasting pan. Layer the chicken over the dressing. Cover the chicken with the remaining dressing. Bake for 1 hour or until set and 165 degrees on a meat thermometer in the center.

SIGNATURE RECIPE

In earlier times, Arkansans had access to chicken and eggs. A pen of chickens carried to a celebrated harvest meeting in the community became available for the meal. Corn bread or any leftover bread combined with vegetables from the garden (such as onion and celery) and the broth from cooking the chicken created Arkansas Chicken and Dressing. The dish made the holiday menu and Sunday lunch, as it fed large numbers of multiple generations of the family.

Per serving
Calories 460
Protein 29 g
Carbohydrates 45 g
Total Fat 17 g
34% Calories from Fat
Cholesterol 165 mg
Fiber 3 g
Sodium 1197 mg
Sugar 6 g

Cheesy Oven-Fried Chicken

Serves 4

Per serving
Calories 270
Protein 26 g
Carbohydrates 21 g
Total Fat 8 g
27% Calories from Fat
Cholesterol 68 mg
Fiber 1 g
Sodium 390 mg
Sugar <1 g

2	cups (bite-size) low-fat Cheddar-flavored crackers	1/8	teaspoon black pepper
1/2 to 3/4 teaspoon basil		1	pound boneless skinless chicken breasts
		2	tablespoons skim milk

Preheat the oven to 400 degrees. Place the crackers, basil and pepper in a large sealable plastic bag. Crush the crackers with a rolling pin, leaving the end open so the air can escape. Remove all visible fat from the chicken. Cut the chicken into sixteen strips about 1×3 inches each. Dip the chicken strips in the milk. Add a few strips at a time to the cracker mixture. Seal the bag and shake to coat. Place in a single layer in a shallow baking pan sprayed with nonstick cooking spray. Bake for 5 to 7 minutes or until the chicken is tender and registers 165 degrees on a meat thermometer.

Note: Turkey breast tenderloins may be used instead of the chicken. The crackers, basil and pepper may be processed finely in a food processor before placing in the bag.

For **Cheesy Chicken Nuggets**, prepare the recipe as above except cut the chicken into bite-size pieces. Bake for 5 minutes or until tender and the juices run clear.

Muenster Cheese Chicken

Serves 4

Per serving
Calories 523
Protein 39 g
Carbohydrates 23 g
Total Fat 31 g
53% Calories from Fat
Cholesterol 285 mg
Fiber 2 g
Sodium 1121 mg
Sugar 3 g

4	(4-ounce) boneless skinless chicken breasts	3	tablespoons butter
3	eggs, beaten	1	(14-ounce) can fat-free reduced-sodium chicken broth
8	ounces sliced fresh mushrooms	2	teaspoons lemon juice
3	tablespoons butter	4	(2/3-ounce) slices Muenster cheese
1	cup Italian-style bread crumbs		

Preheat the oven to 350 degrees. Flatten the chicken breasts with a meat mallet. Place the chicken and eggs in a large sealable plastic bag. Soak in the refrigerator for 3 to 10 hours. Sauté the mushrooms in 3 tablespoons butter in a skillet until tender. Place in a 9×13-inch baking dish. Roll the chicken in the bread crumbs. Melt 3 tablespoons butter in a skillet. Add the chicken. Brown on both sides, turning once. Arrange over the mushrooms. Pour the broth over the chicken and sprinkle with the lemon juice. Bake for 35 to 45 minutes or until the chicken registers 165 degrees on a meat thermometer. Top the chicken with the cheese. Bake for 3 to 5 minutes or until the cheese melts.

Note: Sauté chopped chicken breasts with the mushrooms as an alternative.

Balsamic-Glazed Chicken Breasts

Serves 12

Per serving
Calories 225
Protein 25 g
Carbohydrates 6 g
Total Fat 7 g
30% Calories from Fat
Cholesterol 70 mg
Fiber 1 g
Sodium 460 mg
Sugar 3 g

3	tablespoons vegetable oil
1	tablespoon butter
12	(6-ounce) chicken breasts
1	Spanish onion, thinly sliced
4	garlic cloves, chopped
2	pints cherry tomatoes, cut into quarters
6	tablespoons balsamic vinegar
2	cups red wine
2	teaspoons salt
	Freshly ground pepper to taste
3	tablespoons chopped fresh parsley for garnish

Preheat the oven to 350 degrees. Heat the oil and butter in a large skillet over high heat until bubbly. Add the chicken breasts four at a time to the skillet. Sear on each side for 1 to 2 minutes or until golden brown. Remove to a large baking dish. Add the onion and garlic to the drippings in the skillet. Cook for 5 minutes or until the onion is soft, stirring occasionally. Add the tomatoes and toss to combine. Add the vinegar, wine, salt and pepper. Bring to a boil; reduce the heat. Simmer for 10 minutes. Pour over the chicken. Bake on the top oven rack for 20 minutes or until the chicken registers 165 degrees on a meat thermometer. Remove from the oven and garnish with the parsley.

Egg Safety

Why is the yolk of a hard-boiled egg sometimes green?

The green ring around the yolk of a hard-boiled egg happens because hydrogen in the egg white combines with sulfur in the yolk. The cause is most often related to boiling the eggs too hard for too long. The green ring can also be caused by a high amount of iron in the cooking water. The green ring is harmless and safe to eat.

To avoid green eggs, hard-cook instead of hard-boiling eggs:

- *Place the eggs in a single layer in the saucepan. Add cold water to a depth of one inch above the eggs.*
- *Cover the pan and bring to a boil; remove from the heat.*
- *Let stand for fifteen minutes for large eggs, twelve minutes for medium eggs, and eighteen minutes for extra-large eggs; drain.*
- *Run cold water over the eggs.*
- *Store in the refrigerator for up to one week.*

Mushroom Chicken Piccata

Serves 4

Per serving
Calories 210
Protein 26 g
Carbohydrates 7 g
Total Fat 7 g
32% Calories from Fat
Cholesterol 63 mg
Fiber 1 g
Sodium 228 mg
Sugar 2 g

4   (4-ounce) chicken cutlets
    Salt and freshly ground
        pepper to taste
4   teaspoons olive oil
12 ounces cremini
        mushrooms,
        cut into quarters
2   teaspoons minced garlic

1/4 cup dry white wine
1/2 cup low-sodium
        chicken broth
4   thin lemon slices
    Juice of 1/2 lemon
2   tablespoons
        undrained capers

Sprinkle the chicken with salt and pepper. Heat a large sauté pan over medium heat. Add 2 teaspoons of the olive oil and heat briefly. Add the chicken. Cook for 2 minutes on each side or to 165 degrees on a meat thermometer. Remove the chicken to a plate and cover.

Add the remaining 2 teaspoons olive oil to the pan drippings and heat over medium-high heat. Add the mushrooms in a single layer. Cook for 5 minutes or until the mushrooms are red-brown on one side. Turn the mushrooms and add the garlic. Cook for 2 minutes. Add the wine, stirring to scrape up the brown bits from the bottom of the skillet. Bring to a boil. Add the broth and bring to a simmer. Add the lemon slices and lemon juice. Add the capers. Cook for 2 minutes or until a glaze forms. Return the chicken to the skillet. Cook until heated through.

Southwest Chicken Rolls

Serves 8

Per serving
Calories 270
Protein 28 g
Carbohydrates 14 g
Total Fat 11 g
37% Calories from Fat
Cholesterol 77 mg
Fiber 1 g
Sodium 857 mg
Sugar 2 g

8   (4-ounce) boneless
        skinless chicken breasts
4   ounces Monterey Jack
        cheese, cut into 8 slices
1   (4-ounce) can chopped
        green chiles

2   cups Cheddar cheese
        crackers, crushed
1   envelope taco
        seasoning mix

Preheat the oven to 350 degrees. Place the chicken between two sheets of waxed paper. Pound with a meat mallet or rolling pin to flatten. Place one cheese slice and a few green chiles on each chicken breast. Wrap the chicken around the filling and secure with wooden picks. Mix the crackers and taco seasoning mix in a shallow dish. Add the chicken roll-ups and press with the crumbs to coat. Place the roll-ups in a 9×9-inch baking dish sprayed with nonstick cooking spray. Bake for 20 to 30 minutes or until the chicken is tender and registers 165 degrees on a meat thermometer.

Note: The roll-ups may be microwaved on Medium-High power until the chicken is tender and the juices run clear.

Chicken Asparagus Casserole
Serves 12

Per serving
Calories 397
Protein 26 g
Carbohydrates 11 g
Total Fat 28 g
63% Calories from Fat
Cholesterol 100 mg
Fiber 2 g
Sodium 1225 mg
Sugar 3 g

6	(6-ounce) chicken breasts	16	oounces sharp Cheddar cheese, shredded
1	large onion, chopped	1	teaspoon hot pepper sauce
1/2	cup (1 stick) butter	1	teaspoon soy sauce
8	ounces sliced mushrooms	1	teaspoon salt
1	(4-ounce) jar chopped pimentos	1/2	teaspoon black pepper
1	(10-ounce) can cream of mushroom soup		Salt and red pepper to taste
1	(10-ounce) can cream of chicken soup	2	(15-ounce) cans asparagus tips, drained
1	(5-ounce) can evaporated milk	1/2	cup slivered or sliced almonds

Preheat the oven to 350 degrees. Cook the chicken in water to cover in a saucepan until tender or to 165 degrees on a meat thermometer. Drain the chicken and cool. Chop the chicken into bite-size pieces, discarding the skin and bones. Sauté the onion in the butter in a skillet until translucent. Add the mushrooms, pimentos, mushroom soup, chicken soup, evaporated milk, cheese, hot sauce, soy sauce, 1 teaspoon salt and the black pepper. Simmer until the cheese melts. Add salt and red pepper to taste.

Place the chicken in a well-buttered 9×12-inch baking dish. Layer the asparagus and sauce one-half at a time over the chicken. Sprinkle with the almonds. Bake until the chicken registers 165 degrees on a meat thermometer. Do not add any additional liquid even if it looks dry.

Wrapped Chicken Tenderloins
Serves 4

Per serving
Calories 220
Protein 29 g
Carbohydrates 7 g
Total Fat 8 g
34% Calories from Fat
Cholesterol 79 mg
Fiber <1 g
Sodium 640 mg
Sugar 5 g

1/4	cup mustard	8	boneless chicken tenderloins (1 pound)
1/4	cup pineapple juice or orange juice	8	slices very lean bacon or turkey bacon (8 ounces)
1	tablespoon brown sugar		

Preheat the grill. Mix the mustard, pineapple juice and brown sugar in a sealable plastic bag until the brown sugar dissolves. Add the chicken and seal the bag. Marinate in the refrigerator for 3 to 10 hours. Remove the chicken and discard the marinade. Wrap each piece of chicken with a slice of bacon and secure with wooden picks. Place on a grill rack. Grill for 10 minutes or to 165 degrees on a meat thermometer, turning frequently to prevent burning. Remove the wooden picks and serve.

Nutritional information includes the entire amount of marinade.

Cornell Barbecued Chicken

Serves 10

SIGNATURE RECIPE

The Cornell Chicken Barbecue Sauce was developed by Cornell University professor Dr. Robert C. Baker to help New York poultry farmers sell more birds. Today it's often referred to as State Fair Barbecue because it's used by a large chicken barbecue food vendor at the New York State Fair, where thousands of people experience its delectable taste each year. Several restaurants in New York State also use this sauce for their barbecued chicken.

1	extra-large egg
1	cup vegetable oil
2	cups cider vinegar
2	tablespoons salt
1	tablespoon poultry seasoning
1	teaspoon pepper
10	chicken breasts

Preheat a gas grill to medium or a charcoal grill until the charcoal burns down to glowing embers. Beat the egg in a bowl. Add the oil gradually, beating constantly. Add the vinegar, salt, poultry seasoning and pepper and mix well. Place the chicken on a grill rack. Grill for 1 hour or to 165 degrees on a meat thermometer, basting with the sauce during the last 15 to 30 minutes.

Note: The sauce can be stored in a glass jar in the refrigerator for no more than two weeks.

Per serving
Calories 353
Protein 27 g
Carbohydrates 1 g
Total Fat 26 g
68% Calories from Fat
Cholesterol 97 mg
Fiber <1 g
Sodium 1469 mg
Sugar <1 g

Chinese Chicken with Peppers and Onions

Serves 6

Per serving
Calories 203
Protein 14 g
Carbohydrates 10 g
Total Fat 12 g
49% Calories from Fat
Cholesterol 34 mg
Fiber 2 g
Sodium 272 mg
Sugar 4 g

3	(6-ounce) chicken breasts, split and skinned
2	tablespoons canola oil
4	(nickel-size) pieces of ginger
3	small hot red chiles, or $1/8$ teaspoon cayenne pepper
2	tablespoons canola oil
2	onions, cut into quarters and thinly sliced
3	green or red bell peppers, cut into 1-inch pieces
2	tablespoons low-sodium soy sauce
1/4	cup cooking sherry
1	teaspoon hot sesame oil

Cut the chicken into $1/2$-inch pieces. Heat 2 tablespoons canola oil in a wok or large skillet. Add the ginger, hot chiles and chicken. Stir-fry for 3 to 4 minutes or until the chicken is cooked through. Remove the chicken to a serving dish.

Heat 2 tablespoons canola oil in the drippings in the wok. Add the onions and bell peppers. Stir-fry until the onions are translucent. Return the chicken to the wok. Add the soy sauce and sherry. Stir-fry for 1 minute. Sprinkle with the sesame oil. Serve with brown rice.

Note: Mix green and red bell peppers for color variety. If yellow bell peppers are available and reasonably priced, use them as well.

Food Safety

Keep uncooked meats from coming into contact with other foods during preparation. Use a separate cutting board for the sole preparation of uncooked meat, poultry, and fish.

To sanitize cutting boards after cutting up uncooked meat, poultry, and other potentially hazardous foods, soak them in a solution of one tablespoon bleach to one gallon of room temperature water.

Hawaiian Stack-Ups

Serves 10 to 12

Per serving
Calories 568
Protein 19 g
Carbohydrates 80 g
Total Fat 19 g
31% Calories from Fat
Cholesterol 35 mg
Fiber 4 g
Sodium 607 mg
Sugar 11 g

2	(10-ounce) cans cream of chicken soup
1	cup chicken broth
2	cups (bite-size) pieces cooked chicken
4	cups cooked rice
1	(9-ounce) can chow mein noodles
3	tomatoes, cut into chunks
1	cup chopped celery
1/2	cup chopped green bell pepper
1	cup chopped green onions
1	(20-ounce) can pineapple chunks
1	cup (4 ounces) shredded Cheddar cheese
1/2	cup slivered almonds
1/2	cup shredded coconut
1	(4-ounce) jar pimentos

Combine the soup and broth in a medium saucepan and mix well. Add the chicken. Simmer for 8 to 10 minutes. Place the rice, chow mein noodles, chicken sauce, tomatoes, celery, bell pepper, green onions, pineapple, cheese, almonds, coconut and pimentos on twelve individual serving plates in the order listed in a row for stacking.

To serve, stack the rice, chow mein noodles and chicken sauce on individual serving plates. Continue stacking with the tomatoes, celery, bell pepper and green onions. Continue stacking with the pineapple, cheese and more chicken sauce, if desired. Top with the almonds, coconut and pimentos.

Note: You may substitute turkey for the chicken. This is a great dish for parties. The host provides the chicken sauce and asks each guest to bring one of the ingredients for the stack-ups.

Chicken Lū'au

Serves 5

2   pounds taro leaves
3   cups water
1/2   teaspoon Hawaiian salt or rock salt
1   tablespoon vegetable oil
2   garlic cloves, minced
1   pound boneless skinless chicken thighs,
           cut into 1-inch pieces
1/2   teaspoon Hawaiian salt or rock salt
1   cup water
1   cup skim milk

Discard the tough stems and ribs of the taro leaves and rinse the leaves under cold water. Place the leaves in a medium saucepan with 3 cups water and 1/2 teaspoon Hawaiian salt. Simmer, partially covered, for 1 hour. Drain and squeeze out the water. Heat the oil in a medium saucepan. Add the garlic and chicken. Cook until the chicken is brown. Sprinkle with 1/2 teaspoon Hawaiian salt and add 1 cup water. Simmer until the chicken is tender and registers 165 degrees on a meat thermometer. Drain the chicken and add the taro leaves. Stir in the milk. Bring to a boil. Serve immediately.

Note: Fresh spinach leaves may be substituted for taro leaves. Cook until the spinach is tender. Chopped cooked squid or octopus can be substituted for the chicken.

SIGNATURE RECIPE

Traditional Hawaiian foods combined what Polynesian voyagers brought with them and what the islands and ocean produced. Hawaii remains a crossroad for travelers going to Pacific Rim nations, the Americas, and Europe. Hawaiian food today reflects the many cultures that were brought to work on plantations, passed through, or made Hawaii home. Chicken Lū'au is an Island favorite served at gatherings, featuring the traditional taro leaves.

Per serving
Calories 193
Protein 20 g
Carbohydrates 7 g
Total Fat 10 g
45% Calories from Fat
Cholesterol 60 mg
Fiber <1 g
Sodium 314 mg
Sugar 2 g

Chicken Breasts and Vegetables

Per serving
Calories 285
Protein 38 g
Carbohydrates 17 g
Total Fat 7 g
21% Calories from Fat
Cholesterol 94 mg
Fiber 4 g
Sodium 608 mg
Sugar 8 g

6   (6-ounce) boneless skinless
      chicken breasts
2   teaspoons chicken bouillon granules
1   cup boiling water
1   tablespoon low-sodium soy sauce
1   tablespoon extra-virgin olive oil
1   pound baby carrots
8   ounces fresh mushrooms,
      sliced or cut into halves
1 or 2 red bell peppers, cut into strips
1 or 2 green bell peppers, cut into strips
1   onion, sliced
5   ribs celery, cut into diagonal slices

Cut each chicken breast into three or four pieces. Dissolve the bouillon granules in the boiling water. Stir in the soy sauce. Heat the olive oil in a large skillet over medium-high heat. Add the chicken and carrots. Cook until the chicken is light brown on all sides and the carrots are partially cooked, stirring occasionally. Reduce the heat to medium-low. Place the mushrooms, bell peppers, onion and celery on top of the chicken and carrots. Pour the bouillon mixture over the top. Cook, covered with a tight-fitting lid, for 10 minutes or until the chicken registers 165 degrees on a meat thermometer. Serve immediately.

Note: The bouillon granules and soy sauce can be increased and thickened slightly for a saucier product, then served over hot cooked brown rice. For a richer main dish, top with shredded cheese and allow it to melt before serving, or sprinkle with shredded cheese while serving. Vegetables can be substituted and/or increased according to taste and appetite. For example, try sliced yellow squash and/or zucchini.

Hot Chicken Salad

Serves 5

1 cup sliced fresh mushrooms

1/2 cup chopped onion

1 to 2 tablespoons minced garlic

1 tablespoon light olive oil

3 cups (bite-size) pieces roasted chicken

2 tablespoons chopped fresh tomato

1 tablespoon chopped jalapeño chiles

1/4 cup mayonnaise-type salad dressing

3 tablespoons sliced toasted almonds

1/2 cup (2 ounces) shredded sharp Cheddar cheese

1/2 cup (2 ounces) shredded Colby-Monterey Jack cheese

1/2 cup (2 ounces) shredded Cheddar cheese

1/3 cup crushed sour cream potato chips

Per serving
Calories 423
Protein 35 g
Carbohydrates 11 g
Total Fat 27 g
57% Calories from Fat
Cholesterol 112 mg
Fiber 1 g
Sodium 398 mg
Sugar 2 g

Preheat the oven to 375 degrees. Sauté the mushrooms, onion and garlic in the olive oil in a skillet until tender. Combine with the chicken, tomato and jalapeño chiles in a bowl and mix well. Add the salad dressing and mix well. Stir in the almonds, 1/2 cup Cheddar cheese and the Colby-Monterey Jack cheese. Spoon into a 9-inch pie plate. Sprinkle with 1/2 cup Cheddar cheese and the potato chips. Bake for 20 to 25 minutes or until bubbly and light brown. Do not overbake.

Chicken Spectacular

Serves 12

1 (6-ounce) package long grain and wild rice mix

3 cups chopped cooked chicken

1 (2-ounce) jar chopped pimento

1 onion, chopped

1 cup mayonnaise (do not substitute)

1 (15-ounce) can French-cut green beans

1 (8-ounce) can sliced water chestnuts

1 (10-ounce) can cream of celery soup

2 cups (8 ounces) shredded Cheddar cheese

Per serving
Calories 365
Protein 18 g
Carbohydrates 17 g
Total Fat 25 g
61% Calories from Fat
Cholesterol 63 mg
Fiber 3 g
Sodium 558 mg
Sugar 2 g

Preheat the oven to 350 degrees. Prepare the rice mix using the package directions. Combine with the chicken, pimento, onion, mayonnaise, green beans, water chestnuts and soup in a large bowl and mix well. Spoon into a 9×13-inch baking dish. Bake for 30 to 35 minutes or to 165 degrees on a meat thermometer, sprinkling with the Cheddar cheese during the last 15 minutes of baking.

Note: Instead of water chestnuts, cream of chicken soup can be used.

Spicy Pasta

Serves 2

Per serving
Calories 811
Protein 34 g
Carbohydrates 50 g
Total Fat 55 g
59% Calories from Fat
Cholesterol 68 mg
Fiber 7 g
Sodium 82 mg
Sugar 5 g

1	teaspoon butter	1/2	cup chopped fresh cilantro
1/4	cup olive oil		
2	jalapeño chiles, sliced	8	ounces chicken breast
1	bunch scallions, cut into 1-inch pieces	2	ounces chopped pecans
		2	cups cooked linguini
1/2	cup sliced mushrooms		

Melt the butter in a medium skillet. Add the olive oil. Add the jalapeño chiles, scallions and mushrooms and sauté for 5 minutes. Add the cilantro, chicken and pecans. Cook until the chicken registers 165 degrees on a meat thermometer. Spoon over the pasta.

Chicken Spaghetti

Serves 8

Per serving
Calories 495
Protein 31 g
Carbohydrates 41 g
Total Fat 23 g
42% Calories from Fat
Cholesterol 74 mg
Fiber 2 g
Sodium 1106 mg
Sugar 4 g

1/2	cup chopped green bell pepper	1	(2-ounce) jar pimento
1	onion, chopped	1	(4-ounce) can sliced mushrooms
1/4	cup (1/2 stick) butter or margarine	12	ounces spaghetti
1 1/2	cups chicken broth	8	ounces mozzarella cheese, shredded
2	(10-ounce) cans cream of mushroom soup	1/2	cup (2 ounces) shredded or grated Parmesan cheese
3	cups (bite-size) pieces cooked chicken		

Preheat the oven to 400 degrees. Sauté the bell pepper and onion in the butter in a skillet for 2 minutes. Add the broth. Cook over medium heat until the vegetables are tender. Remove from the heat. Stir in the soup, chicken, pimento and mushrooms.

Break the spaghetti into thirds. Cook the spaghetti using the package directions until tender; drain. Add to the chicken mixture with the mozzarella cheese and toss to coat. Spoon into a 9×13-inch baking dish sprayed with nonstick cooking spray. Cover with the Parmesan cheese. Bake for 30 minutes or to 165 degrees on a meat thermometer.

Chicken Tomato Spaghetti

Serves 10 to 12

3   (6-ounce) chicken
       breasts, cooked
       and chopped
1/2 cup chopped onion,
       sautéed
1/2 cup chopped bell
       pepper, sautéed
2   (10-ounce) cans cream of
       mushroom soup
1 1/2 cups milk
1   (15-ounce) can diced
       tomatoes
16 ounces spaghetti, cooked
8   ounces Cheddar
       cheese, shredded

Per serving
Calories 334
Protein 20 g
Carbohydrates 36 g
Total Fat 12 g
32% Calories from Fat
Cholesterol 46 mg
Fiber 2 g
Sodium 525 mg
Sugar 5 g

Preheat the oven to 350 degrees. Combine the chicken, onion, bell pepper, soup, milk, tomatoes, pasta and one-half of the cheese in a large bowl in the order listed and mix well. Spoon into a 9×13-inch baking dish. Cover with the remaining cheese. Bake for 30 minutes or to 165 degrees on a meat thermometer.

Note: You may use two large cans of white chicken instead of the chicken breasts.

Poblano Chicken Enchiladas

Serves 6

3   tablespoons
       chopped onion
3   tablespoons finely
       chopped poblano chiles
1/3 cup chopped
       fresh mushrooms
2   tablespoons light olive oil
1 1/2 cups chopped
       roasted chicken
1/2 teaspoon chili powder
1/4 teaspoon garlic powder
6   flour tortillas
       (8 ounces total)
2   cups (8 ounces) shredded
       Colby-Monterey
       Jack cheese
1   cup (4 ounces) shredded
       pizza-blend cheese
1   cup nonfat sour cream
1   (10-ounce) can cream of
       mushroom soup
1   (8-ounce) can green
       chile sauce

Per serving
Calories 501
Protein 28 g
Carbohydrates 34 g
Total Fat 29 g
51% Calories from Fat
Cholesterol 81 mg
Fiber 1 g
Sodium 1053 mg
Sugar 2 g

Preheat the oven to 375 degrees. Sauté the onion, poblano chiles and mushrooms in the olive oil in a skillet until tender. Stir in the chicken, chili powder and garlic powder. Cook until the chicken is heated through. Spread equally over the tortillas. Sprinkle with a small amount of the Colby-Monterey Jack cheese and pizza-blend cheese. Roll up and place seam side down in a single layer in an 8×8-inch baking dish. Combine the sour cream, soup and chile sauce in a bowl and mix well. Pour over the roll-ups. Sprinkle with the remaining Colby-Monterey Jack cheese and pizza-blend cheese. Bake for 30 to 40 minutes or until bubbly and the cheeses are melted.

Chicken Breasts and Wild Rice *Serves 8*

Per serving
Calories 370
Protein 31 g
Carbohydrates 32 g
Total Fat 13 g
31% Calories from Fat
Cholesterol 73 mg
Fiber 2 g
Sodium 368 mg
Sugar 2 g

1/3	cup wild rice	2 1/2	cups low-salt chicken broth
1/3	cup chopped onion	2	tablespoons chopped pimento
1/2	cup minced celery		
1/2	cup sliced mushrooms	1	(10-ounce) can cream of mushroom soup
1/2	cup slivered almonds		
2	tablespoons light margarine	1	cup light sour cream
1	cup uncooked white rice	2	pounds boneless skinless chicken breasts

Preheat the oven to 350 degrees. Rinse the wild rice. Cook the wild rice in water in a saucepan for 10 minutes. Rinse and drain. Sauté the onion, celery, mushrooms and almonds in the margarine in a skillet until tender. Combine the cooked wild rice, uncooked white rice, sautéed vegetables, broth, pimento, soup and sour cream in a large bowl and mix well. Cut the chicken into eight pieces. Place one-half of the rice mixture in a 2-quart baking dish. Add the chicken. Top with the remaining rice mixture. Bake, covered, for 1 1/4 hours or until the chicken registers 165 degrees on a meat thermometer.

Chicken and Wild Rice Casserole *Serves 10*

Per serving
Calories 277
Protein 21 g
Carbohydrates 20 g
Total Fat 12 g
40% Calories from Fat
Cholesterol 58 mg
Fiber 2 g
Sodium 602 mg
Sugar 3 g

1	(3-pound or larger) chicken	2	onions, chopped
2	ribs celery, chopped	1	tablespoon butter
1	bay leaf	8	ounces hot bulk sausage, crumbled
1/16	teaspoon salt		
1	(6-ounce) package wild rice	2	(10-ounce) cans cream of mushroom soup
		2	tablespoons bread crumbs

Preheat the oven to 350 degrees. Boil the chicken in water to cover with the celery, bay leaf and salt until cooked through; drain. Let the chicken stand until cool enough to handle and cut into pieces. Prepare the wild rice using the package directions. Sauté the onions in the butter in a skillet until translucent. Stir in the sausage and soup. Spoon into a 9×13-inch baking dish. Layer the chicken and wild rice over the sausage mixture. Sprinkle with the bread crumbs. Bake for 30 minutes or to 165 degrees on a meat thermometer.

Note: This recipe may be frozen.

Slow-Cooker Chicken and Salsa *Serves 6*

1   cup dried black beans
1¹/₂ pounds boneless chicken breasts,
         cut into serving-size pieces
1   (16-ounce) jar black bean salsa
1   (16-ounce) corn salsa
1   cup uncooked brown rice
2   cups water
1   cup sour cream
1   cup (4 ounces) shredded Cheddar cheese
         or Mexican cheese
1   avocado, sliced, for garnish
¹/₂ (5-ounce) package corn chips for garnish

Soak the beans in water to cover in a bowl for 8 to 10 hours; drain. Combine the beans, chicken, black bean salsa, corn salsa, brown rice and 2 cups water in a slow cooker. Cook on High for 4 hours or on Low for 8 to 10 hours, adding water if needed near the end of the cooking process.

To serve, place 1¹/₂ cups of the chicken mixture on individual serving plates or the entire amount on a serving platter. Top with the sour cream and cheese. Garnish with the avocado and corn chips.

Note: You may substitute two 15-ounce cans of black beans for the dried black beans to eliminate the soaking time. Use the liquid in the black beans for added moisture. Frozen unbreaded chicken tenders can also be used, but thaw them before placing in the slow cooker. Green salsa may also be used, or look for a combination of corn and black bean salsa. One cup of frozen corn kernels may also be added.

Per serving
Calories 734
Protein 43 g
Carbohydrates 76 g
Total Fat 29 g
35% Calories from Fat
Cholesterol 97 mg
Fiber 9 g
Sodium 1123 mg
Sugar 6 g

Egg Safety
What about pasteurized eggs and egg products? Pasteurized egg products are widely available. They are still raw, and still in their shells, but have undergone a very precise heat treatment, called pasteurizing, to eliminate any harmful bacteria and other pathogens which may cause illness. Pasteurized eggs and egg products are a safe alternative for recipes that call for raw or undercooked eggs such as eggnog, Caesar salad dressing, and homemade ice cream.

Smoked Turkey

Per serving
Calories 488
Protein 58 g
Carbohydrates 13 g
Total Fat 20 g
38% Calories from Fat
Cholesterol 169 mg
Fiber 1 g
Sodium 7824 mg
Sugar 12 g

1   pound apple, wild cherry or
      chicory wood
1/2   cup brine mix for Morton's
      Tender Quick Cure
16   cups water
2   cups apple juice
1   cup white grape juice
1   cup (or more) good-quality white wine
1/2   cup packed brown sugar
1   (20-pound) turkey
2   pounds apples

Preheat the oven to 300 degrees. Preheat a smoker with apple wood to 225 degrees. It usually takes two fires, so do this part late in the day and leave overnight. Smoke during the winter to early spring; do not attempt in warm weather. Combine the brine mix, water, apple juice, grape juice, wine and brown sugar in a large glass or plastic container. Soak the turkey in the mixture for 8 to 10 hours. The turkey should be totally submerged. Drain the turkey. Insert the apples into the turkey cavity. Tie the turkey with butcher cord. Place in a large roasting pan. Bake in the oven until a meat thermometer registers 150 degrees when inserted into the thickest portion of the turkey. Place in the smoker. Smoke until the turkey is a rich honey color and registers 165 degrees on the meat thermometer. Remove from the smoker and store in the refrigerator.

Note: As an alternative, you may inject or pump the turkey with the brine mix. Soak the turkey as directed with any remaining mix.

Nutritional information includes entire amount of brine.

Chile Cheese Appetizers

Serves 16

Per serving
Calories 143
Protein 9 g
Carbohydrates <1 g
Total Fat 11 g
71% Calories from Fat
Cholesterol 109 mg
Fiber <1 g
Sodium 285 mg
Sugar 1 g

1   (4-ounce) can chopped green chiles
16 ounces sharp Cheddar cheese, shredded
6   eggs
1/16 teaspoon paprika

Preheat the oven to 350 degrees. Drain the green chiles, reserving the liquid. Place one-half of the cheese in an 8×8-inch baking dish sprayed with nonstick cooking spray. Sprinkle with the green chiles. Layer with the remaining cheese. Beat the eggs and reserved chile liquid in a bowl. Pour over the layers. Sprinkle with the paprika. Bake for 35 to 45 minutes or to 145 degrees on a meat thermometer. Cut into 2-inch squares. Serve hot.

Note: These may be frozen and reheated. For a healthier version, use egg substitute.

Baked Egg Cups

Serves 6

Per serving
Calories 97
Protein 9 g
Carbohydrates 6 g
Total Fat 4 g
40% Calories from Fat
Cholesterol 118 mg
Fiber 2 g
Sodium 63 mg
Sugar 4 g

3/4 cup finely chopped onion
3/4 cup finely chopped red, yellow or
       green bell pepper
3/4 cup sliced mushrooms
2   cups chopped broccoli
1/2 cup chopped ham
3   eggs
1/2 cup low-fat milk
1   teaspoon dry mustard
1   tablespoon fresh dill weed, finely chopped

Preheat the oven to 350 degrees. Combine the onion, bell pepper, mushrooms, broccoli and ham in a large bowl and toss lightly to mix. Divide among twelve silicone muffin cups or foil-lined muffin cups. Whisk the eggs, milk, dry mustard and dill weed in a medium bowl with a spout. Pour over the vegetables. Bake for 30 minutes or until a knife inserted into the center comes out clean.

Note: Any combination of vegetables can be used, such as zucchini, summer squash, spinach, and/or potatoes.

Overnight Wine and Cheese Omelet

Serves 24

Per serving
Calories 331
Protein 18 g
Carbohydrates 15 g
Total Fat 22 g
59% Calories from Fat
Cholesterol 186 mg
Fiber 1 g
Sodium 823 mg
Sugar 3 g

1	loaf French bread, trimmed and cubed	1/2	cup dry white wine
6	tablespoons butter, melted	4	green onions, chopped
3/4	cup (3 ounces) shredded Swiss cheese	1	tablespoon dry mustard
		1/4	teaspoon black pepper
3/4	cup (3 ounces) shredded Monterey Jack cheese	1/8	teaspoon cayenne pepper
		1	cup sour cream
1	pound bacon, crisp-cooked and crumbled	1	cup (4 ounces) shredded Parmesan cheese
16	eggs	2	cups chopped tomatoes
3 1/2	cups milk	2	cups sliced black olives

Preheat the oven to 325 degrees. Butter two 9×13-inch baking pans. Spread the bread in the bottom of each. Drizzle with the butter. Sprinkle the Swiss cheese, Monterey Jack cheese and bacon over the bread. Beat the eggs, milk, wine, green onions, dry mustard, black pepper and cayenne pepper in a bowl until foamy. Pour over the bread. Chill, covered with foil, for 8 to 10 hours. Bake, covered, for 1 hour. Uncover and spread with the sour cream. Sprinkle with the Parmesan cheese. Bake, uncovered, for 10 minutes. Sprinkle with the tomatoes and olives. Cut into squares and serve.

Note: May substitute other varieties of cheese and meat.

Spinach Pie

Serves 8

Per serving
Calories 400
Protein 15 g
Carbohydrates 26 g
Total Fat 27 g
59% Calories from Fat
Cholesterol 106 mg
Fiber 4 g
Sodium 767 mg
Sugar 3 g

2	tablespoons olive oil	1	cup nonfat cottage cheese
1	cup chopped onion	1	(16-ounce) package frozen chopped spinach, thawed and drained
1	(2-crust) pie pastry		
3	eggs		
8	ounces feta cheese, crumbled	1/4	teaspoon pepper
		1/2	teaspoon salt (optional)

Preheat the oven to 425 degrees. Heat the olive oil in a skillet. Add the onion and sauté until tender. Roll out one-half of the pastry. Fit into a 9-inch pie plate. Separate one of the eggs. Brush the pie pastry with the egg white. Pour the excess egg white into a large bowl. Add the egg yolk and remaining eggs and beat well. Stir in the feta cheese, cottage cheese, spinach, pepper, salt and sautéed onion. Spoon into the prepared pie plate. Roll out the remaining pastry. Place over the top of the pie and crimp the edges. Bake for 30 minutes or until the crust is golden brown. Cool on a wire rack for 10 minutes.

Spinach Quiche

Serves 6

1/2 cup chopped
fresh spinach
1 (9-inch) deep-dish
pie shell
Chopped onion to taste
Garlic powder to taste
Nutmeg to taste

3 eggs, beaten
2 teaspoons all-purpose
flour
1/2 teaspoon salt
1 cup evaporated milk
1 cup (4 ounces) shredded
Cheddar cheese

Per serving
Calories 369
Protein 12 g
Carbohydrates 24 g
Total Fat 25 g
61% Calories from Fat
Cholesterol 139 mg
Fiber <1 g
Sodium 574 mg
Sugar 4 g

Preheat the oven to 350 degrees. Spread the spinach in the pie shell. Sprinkle with onion, garlic powder and nutmeg. Beat the eggs in a bowl. Add the flour, salt, evaporated milk and cheese and mix well. Pour over the spinach. Bake for 40 to 45 minutes or until set. Remove from the oven and cool for 10 minutes before serving.

Note: You may use frozen chopped spinach instead of fresh. Thaw and squeeze dry before using. You may spread 1/3 pound cooked sausage in the pie shell before the spinach and omit the nutmeg.

Chile Cheese Quiche

Serves 12

3/4 cup (3 ounces)
Mexican-blend cheese
1/2 cup (2 ounces)
Colby-Monterey
Jack cheese
12 frozen tart shells
3 eggs
1 teaspoon sugar

1/4 teaspoon pepper
1/2 teaspoon salt
11/2 cups half-and-half
1/4 cup chopped green chiles
2 tablespoons chopped
green onions
2 tablespoons sliced
black olives

Per serving
Calories 236
Protein 6 g
Carbohydrates 16 g
Total Fat 16 g
63% Calories from Fat
Cholesterol 74 mg
Fiber <1 g
Sodium 391 mg
Sugar 1 g

Preheat the oven to 325 degrees. Mix the Mexican-blend cheese and Colby-Monterey Jack cheese in a bowl. Fill each tart shell with 11/2 tablespoons of the cheese mixture. Mix the eggs, sugar, pepper, salt, half-and-half, green chiles, green onions and olives in a bowl. Pour 1/4 cup of the mixture into each tart shell. Bake for 20 to 25 minutes or until a knife inserted into the center comes out clean.

Meats

Shopping Tips

Shop for meat, poultry, and seafood last. Place these items in plastic bags and keep them separate from produce in your grocery cart to prevent them from dripping on other items.

Check the sell-by date on the package to ensure the date has not expired.

Limit your time from store to home to thirty minutes. If traveling more than thirty minutes, have an ice chest in your car to help limit the time that meats and refrigerated items are in the temperature danger zone.

Thawing Foods

There are three safe ways to defrost food:

In the refrigerator—this is the safest method for all foods.

In cold water—thaw meat and poultry in airtight packaging in cold water if they will be used immediately. Change the water every thirty minutes, so the food continues to thaw in cold water.

In the microwave—use the microwave only if you are going to cook the food immediately.

Safe Cooking Temperatures–as measured with a meat thermometer

PRODUCT	INTERNAL COOKED TEMPERATURE (F)
Fresh Beef, Veal, Lamb	
Ground meats (prepared as patties, meat loaf, etc.)	160°F
Whole cuts like roasts and steaks	
Medium-rare	145°F
Medium	160°F
Well-done	170°F
Fresh Pork	
All cuts, including ground meat	
Medium	160°F
Well-done	170°F
Lamb	
Ground meat	160°F
Roasts, steaks, and chops	145°F
Goat	
Ground meat	160°F
Roast, steaks, and chops	145°F

USDA Meat and Poultry Hotline—1-888-MPHotline (1-888-674-6854)

Chuck Roast Barbecue

Serves 6

Per serving
Calories 527
Protein 43 g
Carbohydrates 42 g
Total Fat 20 g
34% Calories from Fat
Cholesterol 134 mg
Fiber 2 g
Sodium 969 mg
Sugar 16 g

Moist Heat

Less tender cuts of meat are best when prepared by moist heat methods such as braising and cooking in liquid. Slowly cooking arm steaks, blade pot roasts, short ribs, stew meat, brisket, and round steak in moist heat will soften the connective tissue and produce a more tender product.

1	(2- to 2$^{1}/^{2}$-pound) boneless chuck roast, trimmed
2	large onions, chopped
$^{3}/^{4}$	cup cola
1	tablespoon apple cider vinegar
$^{3}/^{4}$	cup Worcestershire sauce
2	garlic cloves, minced
1	teaspoon beef bouillon granules
$^{1}/^{2}$	teaspoon dry mustard
$^{1}/^{2}$	teaspoon chili powder
$^{1}/^{4}$	teaspoon ground red pepper
$^{1}/^{2}$	cup ketchup
2	teaspoons butter or margarine
6	medium hamburger buns

Place the beef and onions in a 4-quart slow cooker. Combine the cola, vinegar, Worcestershire sauce, garlic, bouillon granules, dry mustard, chili powder and ground red pepper in a bowl and mix well. Reserve $^{1}/^{2}$ cup of the cola mixture and store in the refrigerator. Pour the remaining cola mixture over the beef. Cook, covered, on High for 6 hours; drain. Shred the beef. Place in a heatproof bowl and cover to keep warm. Combine the reserved cola mixture, ketchup and butter in a small saucepan. Cook over medium heat until heated through and of a sauce consistency. Pour over the shredded beef and stir gently to coat. Spoon equal amounts of the barbecue onto the buns and serve.

Burgundy Marinade Steak

Serves 4

1 cup burgundy wine
1 tablespoon Worcestershire sauce
1/2 teaspoon dried basil leaves
1/2 teaspoon dried thyme leaves
1/2 teaspoon garlic powder
1/4 teaspoon dry mustard
4 (4-ounce) rib-eye steaks
1/4 cup (1/2 stick) butter
1 cup fresh mushroom slices
1 (6-ounce) can French-fried onions

Per serving
Calories 560
Protein 23 g
Carbohydrates 20 g
Total Fat 37 g
61% Calories from Fat
Cholesterol 91 mg
Fiber <1 g
Sodium 442 mg
Sugar 1 g

Combine the wine, Worcestershire sauce, basil, thyme, garlic powder and dry mustard in a bowl and mix well. Reserve 1/2 cup of the marinade. Place the remaining marinade in a 1-gallon sealable freezer bag. Add the steaks and seal the bag. Marinate in the refrigerator for 8 to 10 hours, turning the bag occasionally. Drain the steaks, discarding the marinade. Melt the butter in a large skillet. Add the steaks. Cook until done to taste, turning several times. Place the steaks on a platter, reserving the drippings in the skillet. Add the mushrooms to the pan drippings. Cook just until tender, stirring constantly. Add the reserved marinade. Cook until heated through, stirring constantly. Place the steaks on serving plates and top with the mushroom sauce and French-fried onions.

SIGNATURE RECIPE

Diverse agriculture (panhandle plains yielding cattle feedlots, ranches, and large farms, to flat irrigated southwest growing cotton and wheat, to cross-timbered central sections emphasizing dairy, peanuts, and hay, to a wetter eastern third producing soybeans, pecans, and poultry) fosters rich culinary traditions. Chicken-fried steak, barbecue pork, fried okra and squash, corn, biscuits, sausage and gravy, grits, corn bread, black-eyed peas, strawberries, and pecan pie, combined via 1988 legislative resolution to create an "official meal" symbolizing Oklahoma foods!

Per serving
Calories 262
Protein 31 g
Carbohydrates 24 g
Total Fat 4 g
14% Calories from Fat
Cholesterol 64 mg
Fiber 2 g
Sodium 171 mg
Sugar 1 g

Chicken-Fried Steak— A Healthier Version

Serves 4

1	pound lean beef round steak, trimmed
1/4	teaspoon pepper
1/4	teaspoon garlic powder
2	egg whites, lightly beaten
3	tablespoons buttermilk
1/4	cup self-rising flour
3/4	cup mixture of half whole wheat flour and half all-purpose flour

Preheat the oven to 400 degrees. Pound the steak to tenderize or ask the butcher to pass the steak through a tenderizer machine. Sprinkle with pepper and garlic powder. Cut the steak into 4-ounce portions. Combine the egg whites and buttermilk in a container large enough to accommodate a steak portion and mix well. Sift the self-rising flour and the flour mixture into a container large enough to dredge a steak portion. Dip the steak into the buttermilk mixture and dredge in the flour mixture. Repeat again and set aside on a wire rack. Heat a 10-inch skillet sprayed with nonstick cooking spray. Add the steak and cook for a few minutes until brown on one side. Turn and brown on the other side. Place the steak in a baking pan lined with baking parchment. Bake for 20 minutes or until cooked through. Serve hot.

Grilled Orange Soy-Marinated Flank Steak

Serves 6

Per serving
Calories 344
Protein 27 g
Carbohydrates 23 g
Total Fat 16 g
42% Calories from Fat
Cholesterol 44 mg
Fiber <1 g
Sodium 1533 mg
Sugar 17 g

1	cup low-sodium soy sauce	2	teaspoons brown mustard
1/4	cup packed brown sugar	1/4	cup orange marmalade
3	tablespoons apple cider vinegar	1/4	teaspoon freshly ground pepper
1	tablespoon Worcestershire sauce	1	(2-pound) flank steak
		1/4	cup canola oil

Preheat a charcoal grill or gas grill to high. Mix the soy sauce, brown sugar, vinegar, Worcestershire sauce, brown mustard, marmalade and pepper in a 9×13-inch dish. Add the steak, turning to coat. Cover with plastic wrap. Marinate in the refrigerator for 1 to 2 hours, turning the steak occasionally. Remove the steak from the marinade, letting the excess drip off. Pour the marinade into a small saucepan. Simmer over medium heat until reduced by one-half. Brush the hot grill rack lightly with canola oil. Place the steak on the prepared rack. Grill to the desired degree of doneness, brushing with the reduced marinade. Remove to a serving platter. Let stand for 6 to 10 minutes before slicing. Cut diagonally into slices to serve.

Round Steak with Rich Gravy

Serves 9

Per serving
Calories 277
Protein 31 g
Carbohydrates 6 g
Total Fat 13 g
45% Calories from Fat
Cholesterol 91 mg
Fiber <1 g
Sodium 334 mg
Sugar 1 g

3	pounds beef round steak
1/3	cup all-purpose flour
3	tablespoons shortening
1	envelope dry onion soup mix
1/2	cup water
1	(10-ounce) can cream of mushroom soup

Cut the steak into serving pieces and coat with the flour. Melt the shortening in a large skillet over medium heat. Add the steak and cook until brown. Sprinkle with the onion soup mix. Mix the water and soup in a bowl. Pour over the steak. Simmer, tightly covered, for 1 1/2 to 2 hours or until tender.

Knife Safety

Keep your knives sharp. A dull blade can be dangerous, as it is more likely to slip and cause a cut. For maximum performance, knives should be sharpened after every couple of uses.

SIGNATURE RECIPE

In Nebraska, beef is more than an industry; it's a way of life. With more than twenty thousand beef producers and cattle outnumbering people, Nebraska is home to some of the best beef in the world. Nebraska produces one out of every five steaks and hamburgers in the United States, and through the efforts of the Beef Checkoff, organizations like the Nebraska Beef Council are able to promote, provide education, and fund research about this nutrient-rich food we all enjoy…beef.

Per serving
Calories 634
Protein 69 g
Carbohydrates 1 g
Total Fat 37 g
54% Calories from Fat
Cholesterol 239 mg
Fiber <1 g
Sodium 595 mg
Sugar <1 g

Cucumber Ranch Steaks

Serves 4

1/2 cup finely chopped seeded cucumber
1/4 cup prepared ranch salad dressing
1 tablespoon garlic pepper seasoning
4 pieces beef shoulder steaks or
   ranch steak, cut 3/4 inch thick
1 small tomato, seeded and chopped
   for garnish

Preheat a charcoal grill to medium, ash-covered coals. Combine the cucumber and salad dressing in a small bowl. Press the garlic pepper seasoning evenly onto the steaks. Place on a grill rack. Grill, covered, for 9 to 11 minutes for medium-rare to medium doneness, turning once. Garnish with the tomato. Serve with the cucumber sauce.

Flank Steak and Spinach Pinwheels

Serves 8

Per serving
Calories 123
Protein 17 g
Carbohydrates 3 g
Total Fat 5 g
35% Calories from Fat
Cholesterol 27 mg
Fiber 1 g
Sodium 114 mg
Sugar 1 g

1¹/2 pounds lean flank steak
¹/4 cup fat-free sour cream
1 teaspoon hot pepper sauce
1 (10-ounce) package frozen
   spinach, thawed and drained
¹/4 cup (1 ounce) grated
   Parmesan cheese

Preheat the broiler. Cut shallow diagonal cuts on one side of the steak and pound to ³/8-inch thickness. Combine the sour cream and hot sauce in a medium bowl. Stir in the spinach and cheese. Spread on the cut side of the steak. Roll up the steak beginning at the narrow end and secure at 1-inch intervals with wooden picks. Cut into 1-inch slices, leaving the wooden pick in the steak. Place on a rack in a broiler pan sprayed with nonstick cooking spray. Broil 6 inches from the heat source for 7 minutes on each side or to 145 degrees on a meat thermometer. Remove the wooden picks and serve.

Note: You may substitute 1 teaspoon red pepper for the hot sauce or omit the hot sauce. Serve with seasoned rice.

TEXAS

SIGNATURE RECIPE

Beef is What's for Dinner in Texas! Whether you grill it, broil it, or stir-fry it, nutrient-rich lean beef is a complete recipe for better health, supplying more than ten essential nutrients, including lean protein, B vitamins, phosphorus, zinc, selenium, and iron, as well as great taste. Check out the Texas Beef Council Web site, www.txbeef.org, for more absolutely mouthwatering recipes for beef, nutrition facts about beef, and information about the Texas beef industry.

Per serving
Calories 420
Protein 29 g
Carbohydrates 37 g
Total Fat 16 g
36% Calories from Fat
Cholesterol 54 mg
Fiber 3 g
Sodium 933 mg
Sugar 3 g

Texas Fajitas with Pico de Gallo

Serves 6 to 8

1/4	cup Hullabaloo Fajita Rub (page 159)	2	cups Pico de Gallo (page 159)
2	pounds beef skirt steak	12	lime wedges for garnish
12	all-purpose flour or whole wheat tortillas	12	sprigs of cilantro for garnish

Preheat a charcoal grill until the coals are medium-hot. Rub the fajita rub generously on all sides of the steak. Place in an airtight container or in a sealable plastic bag and seal the container or bag. Marinate in the refrigerator for at least 2 hours or up to 24 hours for ultimate flavor. Remove the steak, discarding the marinade. Place the steak on a grill rack. Grill 4 to 6 inches from the coals for 10 to 12 minutes or cover and grill for 8 minutes, turning once. Wrap the tortillas securely in heavy-duty foil. Place on the outer edge of the grill. Grill for 5 minutes, turning occasionally. Cut the steak crosswise into very thin slices. Serve in the tortillas with the pico de gallo. Garnish with the lime wedges and cilantro.

Hullabaloo Fajita Rub

Makes 1 1/4 cups

Per serving
Calories 76
Protein 4 g
Carbohydrates 16 g
Total Fat 2 g
18% Calories from Fat
Cholesterol 0 mg
Fiber 6 g
Sodium 2253 mg
Sugar 3 g

1/2 cup paprika
1/4 cup pepper
1/4 cup garlic powder
1   tablespoon salt
1   tablespoon seasoning salt
1   tablespoon ground cumin
1   tablespoon chopped
     dried cilantro
1   tablespoon onion powder
1/4 teaspoon hot pepper sauce

Mix the paprika, pepper, garlic powder, salt, seasoning salt, cumin, cilantro, onion powder and hot sauce in a bowl and mix well. Store in an airtight container.

Pico de Gallo

Makes 2 3/4 cups

Per serving
Calories 13
Protein 1 g
Carbohydrates 3 g
Total Fat <1 g
7% Calories from Fat
Cholesterol 0 mg
Fiber 1 g
Sodium 56 mg
Sugar 2 g

4   medium tomatoes,
     chopped
1   white onion or yellow
     onion, chopped
1   jalapeño chile, seeded and
     finely chopped
1/4 cup cilantro,
     finely chopped
2   tablespoons lime juice
1/2 teaspoon salt, or to taste
1/4 teaspoon pepper, or
     to taste

Combine the tomatoes, onion, chile, cilantro, lime juice, salt and pepper in an airtight container and mix well. Chill for 2 hours before serving.

Note: Heat will vary depending on the chile used and the number of seeds left.

Per serving
Calories 383
Protein 27 g
Carbohydrates 29 g
Total Fat 20 g
44% Calories from Fat
Cholesterol 68 mg
Fiber 4 g
Sodium 460 mg
Sugar 20 g

Tenderloin Salad with Cranberry and Pear

Serves 4

4	(4-ounce) tenderloin steaks, cut $3/4$ inch thick
$1/2$	teaspoon coarsely ground pepper
$1/2$	cup prepared honey mustard
2 to 3	tablespoons water
$1^1/2$	tablespoons olive oil
1	teaspoon white wine vinegar
$1/4$	teaspoon coarsely ground pepper
$1/8$	teaspoon salt
1	(5-ounce) package mixed baby salad greens
1	red pear or green pear, cut into 16 wedges
$1/4$	cup dried cranberries
$1/16$	teaspoon salt, or to taste
$1/4$	cup coarsely chopped pecans, toasted
$1/4$	cup crumbled goat cheese (optional)

Sprinkle the steaks with $1/2$ teaspoon pepper. Heat a large nonstick skillet over medium heat. Place the steaks in the skillet. Cook for 7 to 9 minutes for medium-rare to medium doneness, turning occasionally.

Whisk the honey mustard, water, olive oil, vinegar, $1/4$ teaspoon pepper and $1/8$ teaspoon salt in a bowl. Divide the salad greens among four serving plates. Top evenly with the pear wedges and dried cranberries. Cut the steak into thin slices. Sprinkle with $1/16$ teaspoon salt. Divide the steak slices evenly over the salads. Top each salad evenly with the dressing, pecans and goat cheese.

Chinese Beef and Broccoli

Serves 4

1	pound top round steak	1	garlic clove, chopped
1	bunch broccoli	1	teaspoon sugar
1/4	cup low-sodium soy sauce	1/4	teaspoon cayenne pepper
1/4	cup beef broth	1	tablespoon canola oil or
1	tablespoon cornstarch		sesame oil

Remove any visible fat from the steak. Cut the steak diagonally into very thin slices about 2 inches long. Cut the broccoli into florets; cut the stems into slices. Combine the soy sauce, broth, cornstarch, garlic, sugar and cayenne pepper in a 1-cup glass measure and mix well. Heat the canola oil in a wok or an electric skillet until hot. Add the steak and stir-fry for 3 minutes. Remove the steak with a slotted spoon to a clean plate. Add the broccoli to the drippings in the wok. Stir-fry for 5 minutes or until tender-crisp, covering the wok with a lid to steam the broccoli if desired. Return the steak to the wok. Add the soy sauce mixture and mix well. Bring to a boil and cook for 1 minute. Remove from the heat. Serve with steamed rice.

Per serving
Calories 237
Protein 31 g
Carbohydrates 12 g
Total Fat 8 g
28% Calories from Fat
Cholesterol 64 mg
Fiber 5 g
Sodium 655 mg
Sugar 4 g

Sukiyaki

Serves 6

1	pound thinly sliced beef sirloin tip	1	(8-ounce) can water chestnuts, sliced
2	cups sliced celery	1/3	cup light soy sauce
2	cups sliced green onions	1/3	cup beef consommé
2	cups torn spinach	1/3	cup water
2	cups sliced fresh mushrooms	1	tablespoon sugar
1	(15-ounce) can bean sprouts, drained	1/2	teaspoon salt
		2	tablespoons canola oil

Preheat a wok to 420 degrees. Arrange the beef and vegetables on a tray. Mix the soy sauce, consommé, water, sugar and salt in a bowl. Stir-fry the beef rapidly in the canola oil in the hot wok. Stir in the soy sauce mixture. Add the celery and green onions. Stir-fry for 2 minutes. Add the spinach, mushrooms, bean sprouts and water chestnuts. Cook until heated through. Serve with brown rice.

Per serving
Calories 188
Protein 16 g
Carbohydrates 14 g
Total Fat 8 g
38% Calories from Fat
Cholesterol 26 mg
Fiber 5 g
Sodium 1160 mg
Sugar 4 g

SIGNATURE RECIPE

"Red or green?" is the official New Mexico state question. This refers to being asked whether one prefers red or green chiles when ordering New Mexican cuisine. Green chile is a staple in the New Mexican diet, adding flavor and providing an excellent source of fiber, beta carotene, and vitamin C. In 2008 the New Mexico chile industry produced eighty-one thousand tons of chile valued at $32 million, one of our most important cash crops.

Per serving
Calories 199
Protein 17 g
Carbohydrates 22 g
Total Fat 5 g
23% Calories from Fat
Cholesterol 45 mg
Fiber 4 g
Sodium 1095 mg
Sugar 9 g

Green Chile Stew

Serves 6

1	pound lean cubed beef
2	garlic cloves, minced
1	large onion, chopped
4	(4-ounce) cans chopped green chiles
2	(14-ounce) cans diced tomatoes
2	cups cubed potatoes
	Salt and pepper to taste

Brown the beef, garlic and onion in a skillet, stirring constantly. Place in a slow cooker with the green chiles, tomatoes, potatoes, salt and pepper. Cook on High for 3 to 4 hours.

Note: The stew may be simmered in a Dutch oven over low heat for 1 hour or until the flavors are blended and the potatoes are tender. It can be made ahead and frozen. Instead of lean cubed beef, it can be made with cubed pork, chicken or ground beef. Frozen green chiles can be substituted where available.

Ground Beef Zucchini Casserole

Serves 9

Per serving
Calories 296
Protein 22 g
Carbohydrates 22 g
Total Fat 14 g
41% Calories from Fat
Cholesterol 60 mg
Fiber 1 g
Sodium 592 mg
Sugar 4 g

2	tablespoons butter	2	cups cooked rice
1/2	cup fine dry bread crumbs	1 1/2	pounds zucchini, sliced
1 1/2	pounds lean ground beef	16	ounces small curd low-fat cottage cheese
1/2	cup chopped onion	1	(10-ounce) can cream of mushroom soup
1	teaspoon garlic salt		
1	teaspoon dried oregano leaves		

Preheat the oven to 350 degrees. Melt the butter in a skillet over low heat. Remove from the heat and stir in the bread crumbs. Brown the ground beef with the onion in a skillet, stirring until the ground beef is crumbly; drain. Add the garlic salt, oregano and rice and mix well. Layer one-half of the unpeeled zucchini, the ground beef mixture, cottage cheese and remaining zucchini in a 9×9-inch baking pan. Spread the soup over the top and sprinkle with the bread crumbs. Bake for 45 minutes.

New Mexico Ground Beef Chili Bake

Serves 12

Per serving
Calories 398
Protein 24 g
Carbohydrates 24 g
Total Fat 21 g
49% Calories from Fat
Cholesterol 81 mg
Fiber 3 g
Sodium 773 mg
Sugar 4 g

2	pounds lean ground beef	6	tablespoons picante sauce
1	onion, chopped	6	(10-inch) flour tortillas, cut into quarters
2	(10-ounce) cans cream of chicken soup	2	cups (8 ounces) shredded longhorn cheese or Cheddar cheese
1	(12-ounce) can evaporated milk		

Preheat the oven to 350 degrees. Brown the ground beef with the onion in a skillet, stirring until the ground beef is crumbly; drain. Combine the soup, evaporated milk and picante sauce in a bowl and mix well. Add to the ground beef mixture and mix well. Cover the bottom of a greased 9×13-inch baking dish with one-half of the tortilla quarters. Layer one-half of the ground beef mixture, the remaining tortilla quarters and the remaining ground beef mixture over the tortilla quarters. Sprinkle with the cheese. Bake, uncovered, for 30 minutes.

Note: This recipe is also great made with ground wild meat, such as elk or venison. You can use low-sodium, low-fat cream of chicken soup to be more health-conscious. The amount of picante sauce used can be increased or decreased, depending on how spicy your family likes their food.

Oriental Ground Beef Skillet Supper

Serves 4

Per serving
Calories 425
Protein 25 g
Carbohydrates 35 g
Total Fat 20 g
42% Calories from Fat
Cholesterol 70 mg
Fiber 1 g
Sodium 635 mg
Sugar 0 g

1	pound ground beef	2	cups water
2	(3-ounce) packages oriental-flavor ramen noodles	2	cups frozen broccoli florets, thawed

Brown the ground beef in a skillet, stirring until crumbly; drain. Add the ramen noodles, contents of one of the seasoning packets and the water. Bring to a boil. Cook for 3 minutes or until the ramen noodles are tender. Add the broccoli. Cook for 3 minutes or until tender.

Note: Vary the recipe by using different flavors of ramen noodles and different frozen vegetable mixes.

Company Lasagna

Serves 8

Per serving
Calories 449
Protein 28 g
Carbohydrates 30 g
Total Fat 25 g
49% Calories from Fat
Cholesterol 75 mg
Fiber 6 g
Sodium 1036 mg
Sugar 1 g

8	ounces whole wheat lasagna noodles	1	cup shredded carrots
1	pound lean ground beef	10	ounces fresh spinach
1	(10-ounce) can low-fat low-salt cream of mushroom soup	8	ounces mushrooms, sliced
		1	(16-ounce) can black olives, sliced
6	ounces low-fat cream cheese	8	ounces mozzarella cheese, shredded
2/3	cup water	1/2	cup (2 ounces) freshly grated Parmesan cheese

Preheat the oven to 350 degrees. Cook the noodles in boiling water in a saucepan until al dente. Brown the ground beef in a skillet, stirring until crumbly; drain. Mix the soup, cream cheese and water in a saucepan. Heat until the cream cheese melts, stirring constantly. Spread one-third of the soup mixture in a 9×13-inch baking dish. Layer the noodles, ground beef, carrots, spinach, mushrooms, olives, mozzarella cheese and remaining soup mixture one-half at a time over the soup mixture. Sprinkle with the Parmesan cheese. Bake for 45 to 50 minutes or until hot and bubbly.

Meat Loaf with Tomato Sauce

Serves 12

Per serving
Calories 153
Protein 12 g
Carbohydrates 10 g
Total Fat 7 g
42% Calories from Fat
Cholesterol 56 mg
Fiber 1 g
Sodium 490 mg
Sugar 6 g

1	small onion, chopped
1/2	green bell pepper, chopped
2	tablespoons water
1 1/2	pounds lean ground beef
2	slices bread, crumbled
1	(15-ounce) can tomato sauce
1/2	cup evaporated milk
1	egg
1 1/2	teaspoons sugar
1	teaspoon salt
1/2	teaspoon pepper
1/2	cup water
2	teaspoons Worcestershire sauce
3	tablespoons vinegar
2	tablespoons mustard
2	tablespoons brown sugar

Preheat the oven to 350 degrees. Place the onion, bell pepper and 2 tablespoons water in a 2-cup glass measure. Microwave on High for 2 minutes; drain. Combine with the ground beef, bread, one-half of the tomato sauce, the evaporated milk, egg, sugar, salt and pepper in a large bowl and mix well. Shape into a loaf and place in a 9×13-inch glass baking dish. Mix the remaining one-half of the tomato sauce, 1/2 cup water, the Worcestershire sauce, vinegar, mustard and brown sugar in a bowl. Spread over the meat loaf. Bake for 1 to 1 1/4 hours or until cooked through. Cool for 5 minutes before serving.

Note: Reheats well in the microwave by the slice with sauce over the top. To chill leftovers, remove the meat loaf from the sauce and chill separately. Fat will form on the top of the sauce and can be removed before reheating.

Mom's Meat Loaf

Serves 8

Per serving
Calories 241
Protein 21 g
Carbohydrates 11 g
Total Fat 12 g
46% Calories from Fat
Cholesterol 72 mg
Fiber <1 g
Sodium 662 mg
Sugar 6 g

2	pounds ground beef	1/2	teaspoon pepper
1	tablespoon minced onion	2/3	cup cracker crumbs
1	tablespoon minced green bell pepper	1/2	cup milk
1	teaspoon salt	3/4	cup ketchup

Preheat the oven to 325 degrees. Combine the ground beef, onion, bell pepper, salt, pepper, cracker crumbs, milk and 1/2 cup of the ketchup in a bowl and mix well. Shape into a loaf. Place in a 9×13-inch baking pan. Spread the remaining 1/4 cup ketchup over the meat loaf. Bake for 1 to 1 1/2 hours or until cooked through.

Note: You may substitute ground turkey or ground pork for the ground beef. Ground whole grain crackers or rolled oats may be substituted for the cracker crumbs.

Pork Tenderloin

Serves 8

Per serving
Calories 265
Protein 11 g
Carbohydrates 15 g
Total Fat 18 g
62% Calories from Fat
Cholesterol 41 mg
Fiber <1 g
Sodium 1621 mg
Sugar 14 g

10	slices bacon	1	garlic clove, minced
2	medium pork tenderloins	1	teaspoon grated onion
1/2	cup soy sauce	1/4	teaspoon pepper
1/2	cup sugar	1/4	teaspoon seasoned salt
1	tablespoon cider vinegar		

Preheat the oven to 300 degrees. Wrap the bacon around the pork and secure with wooden picks. Place in a baking dish. Combine the soy sauce, sugar, vinegar, garlic, onion, pepper and seasoned salt in a bowl and mix well. Pour over the pork. Bake for 1 1/2 to 2 hours or to 160 degrees on a meat thermometer, basting occasionally with the pan drippings. Let stand for 5 minutes before serving to seal in the juices. Remove the wooden picks before serving.

Carving Meat

Carving meat is easy when you have the right tools and understand the technique. Make sure you have a sharp knife, a carving fork, and a cutting board. To carve a roast, remove from the oven and let stand for 10 to 15 minutes. Look at the direction the muscle fibers run in the meat. This is called the grain. Hold the roast firmly in place with the carving fork and slice the roast across (at a right angle to) the grain.

Simply Delicious Smoked Pork Chops

Serves 4

Per serving
Calories 313
Protein 43 g
Carbohydrates 7 g
Total Fat 12 g
34% Calories from Fat
Cholesterol 133 mg
Fiber 1 g
Sodium 89 mg
Sugar 6 g

| 4 | (8-ounce) center-cut lean smoked pork chops |
| 4 | (1/2-inch) slices fresh pineapple |

Preheat the oven to 300 degrees. Place the pork chops on a rack in a 9×13-inch baking dish. Top each with a pineapple slice. Bake for 1 hour.

Note: Canned pineapple slices can be used instead of the fresh pineapple. Makes a great meal with cooked rice, cooked carrots, mixed green salad and whole wheat rolls.

Honey Mustard Pork Chops

Serves 4

Per serving
Calories 210
Protein 20 g
Carbohydrates 19 g
Total Fat 6 g
26% Calories from Fat
Cholesterol 62 mg
Fiber <1 g
Sodium 239 mg
Sugar 18 g

1/4	cup honey
2	tablespoons Dijon mustard
1	tablespoon orange juice
1	teaspoon balsamic vinegar
1/2	teaspoon Worcestershire sauce
1/4	teaspoon onion powder
4	(1-inch) pork loin chops

Preheat a grill for direct heat method. Mix the honey, Dijon mustard, orange juice, vinegar, Worcestershire sauce and onion powder in a bowl. Place the pork chops on a grill rack brushed with vegetable oil. Grill, covered, 4 to 5 inches from medium heat for 14 to 16 minutes or to 160 degrees on a meat thermometer, brushing occasionally with the honey mixture and turning once. Discard any remaining honey mixture.

Accidental Thawing

Leaving the freezer door open is probably the most common cause of accidental thawing. Little damage is done if the foods are only partially thawed (crystals visible). They can be refrozen but the food should be used as soon as possible because even though the food is safe to eat, the quality may be impaired. If the food has completely thawed, it should not be refrozen.

Peachy Pork Picante

Serves 4

Per serving
Calories 401
Protein 23 g
Carbohydrates 43 g
Total Fat 15 g
34% Calories from Fat
Cholesterol 67 mg
Fiber 2 g
Sodium 586 mg
Sugar 17 g

1   pound boneless pork,
          cut into 3/4-inch cubes
1   tablespoon taco seasoning mix
1   tablespoon olive oil
1   (8-ounce) jar chunky picante sauce
1/3   cup peach preserves
2   cups hot cooked brown rice

Sprinkle the pork with the taco seasoning mix. Heat the olive oil in a medium nonstick skillet over medium-high heat. Add the pork. Cook until brown, stirring occasionally. Add the picante sauce and preserves. Reduce the heat. Simmer, covered, for 15 to 20 minutes or until the pork is cooked through. Serve over the rice.

Vegetable Stir-Fry

Serves 5

Per serving
Calories 163
Protein 17 g
Carbohydrates 5 g
Total Fat 8 g
45% Calories from Fat
Cholesterol 48 mg
Fiber 2 g
Sodium 418 mg
Sugar 3 g

1   pound lean pork
1   garlic clove, crushed
1   (2-inch) piece of ginger, crushed
1   tablespoon soy sauce
1   teaspoon cornstarch
1/2   teaspoon sugar
1   head wong bok cabbage
          (about 1 1/2 pounds)

Cut the pork into thin strips. Mix the garlic, ginger, soy sauce, cornstarch and sugar in a bowl. Add the pork and stir to coat. Marinate for 15 to 20 minutes. Cut the cabbage into 1- to 2-inch lengths. Stir-fry the pork mixture in a wok or large skillet sprayed with nonstick cooking spray until cooked through. Add the cabbage. Stir-fry for a few minutes.

Note: Other fresh or frozen vegetable or a combination of vegetables could be used.

Colorado Green Chile Stew

Serves 8

3 tablespoons canola oil
1¹/2 pounds pork butt, cut into
     1-inch cubes
1¹/2 cups chopped onions
1 tablespoon minced garlic
6 cups low-sodium chicken broth or
     beef broth
1 pound potatoes, cut into ³/4-inch cubes
2 teaspoons salt
3 cups chopped peeled roasted fresh
     green chiles
1 (15-ounce) can diced tomatoes

Heat the canola oil in a 6-quart saucepan over high heat. Add the pork and cook until brown, stirring frequently. Remove the pork and set aside. Add the onions to the pan drippings and sauté until golden brown. Add the garlic and sauté for 1 minute. Return the undrained pork to the saucepan. Add the broth, potatoes and salt. Bring to a boil; reduce the heat. Simmer for 1 hour or until the potatoes are tender. Add the green chiles and tomatoes. Cook for 15 to 20 minutes or until heated through.

Note: You may use canned or frozen commercial green chiles.

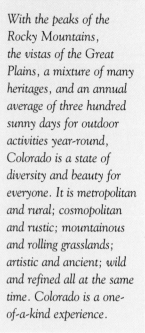

SIGNATURE RECIPE

With the peaks of the Rocky Mountains, the vistas of the Great Plains, a mixture of many heritages, and an annual average of three hundred sunny days for outdoor activities year-round, Colorado is a state of diversity and beauty for everyone. It is metropolitan and rural; cosmopolitan and rustic; mountainous and rolling grasslands; artistic and ancient; wild and refined all at the same time. Colorado is a one-of-a-kind experience.

Per serving
Calories 262
Protein 21 g
Carbohydrates 24 g
Total Fat 10 g
34% Calories from Fat
Cholesterol 45 mg
Fiber 3 g
Sodium 739 mg
Sugar 6 g

Adobo Meat

Per serving
Calories 189
Protein 23 g
Carbohydrates 6 g
Total Fat 7 g
36% Calories from Fat
Cholesterol 58 mg
Fiber 2 g
Sodium 214 mg
Sugar 3 g

3	tablespoons vinegar
1/2	cup water
1	tablespoon light soy sauce
1	garlic clove, crushed
1	pound boneless pork, cut into bite-size pieces
1	bay leaf
	Salt to taste
1/2	teaspoon peppercorns
1	cup frozen peas

Mix the vinegar, water and soy sauce in a medium saucepan. Add the garlic, pork, bay leaf, salt and peppercorns. Bring to a boil, stirring constantly. Reduce the heat. Simmer, covered, for 45 minutes. Uncover and simmer until the liquid evaporates and the pork is light brown. Discard the bay leaf. Add the peas. Cook until heated through, stirring constantly. Discard the peppercorns.

Note: Chicken may be used instead of the pork.

BLT Wrap

Serves 4

3   ounces vegetable-flavor low-fat
      cream cheese, softened
4   flour tortillas
2   tomatoes, seeded and chopped
1   avocado, chopped
2   cups mixed salad greens
10   slices bacon, crisp-cooked and crumbled
1/3   cup reduced-calorie ranch salad dressing

Spread a thin layer of the cream cheese on each tortilla. Combine the tomatoes, avocado, salad greens, bacon and salad dressing in a large bowl and mix well. Place over the cream cheese layer and roll up. Serve immediately.

Per serving
Calories 366
Protein 14 g
Carbohydrates 27 g
Total Fat 23 g
55% Calories from Fat
Cholesterol 35 mg
Fiber 3 g
Sodium 983 mg
Sugar 5 g

Appetizer Pinwheels

Serves 20

8   ounces fat-free cream
      cheese, softened
1   tablespoon minced onion
1   tablespoon horseradish
10   thin slices ham
10   slices American cheese

Whip the cream cheese in a bowl until smooth. Stir in the onion and horseradish. Spread each ham slice with some of the cream cheese mixture. Top each with a cheese slice and spread with the remaining cream cheese mixture. Roll up and place on a platter. Chill, covered, in the refrigerator. Uncover and cut each roll-up into four pieces.

Note: For variation, roll around a dill pickle spear.

Per serving
Calories 155
Protein 21 g
Carbohydrates 1 g
Total Fat 7 g
42% Calories from Fat
Cholesterol 60 mg
Fiber <1 g
Sodium 985 mg
Sugar <1 g

Ham and Cheese Quiche

Serves 6 to 7

Per serving
Calories 399
Protein 23 g
Carbohydrates 17 g
Total Fat 26 g
60% Calories from Fat
Cholesterol 191 mg
Fiber 1 g
Sodium 473 mg
Sugar 1 g

4	medium eggs	1	cup (4 ounces) shredded
1	cup half-and-half		Swiss cheese
1	tablespoon mustard	1	tablespoon chopped
1/4	teaspoon salt		green onions
1/4	teaspoon pepper	1	unbaked (9-inch)
1 1/2	cups chopped ham		pie shell
2	slices bacon, crisp-cooked and crumbled		

Preheat the oven to 350 degrees. Beat the eggs, half-and-half, mustard, salt and pepper in a bowl. Sprinkle the ham, bacon, Swiss cheese and green onions in the pie shell. Pour the egg mixture over the top. Bake for 45 to 50 minutes or until set.

Breakfast Casserole

Serves 8

Per serving
Calories 793
Protein 55 g
Carbohydrates 45 g
Total Fat 46 g
51% Calories from Fat
Cholesterol 346 mg
Fiber 5 g
Sodium 2266 mg
Sugar 19 g

The Importance of Breakfast

All of us need to eat breakfast for energy to start the day and to improve our mood and memory. Children who eat breakfast are better prepared to learn at school. Adults who eat breakfast feel better all morning and aren't tempted to snack on high-calorie foods.

1/2	cup (1 stick) butter, softened	3	cups skim milk
		1/2	teaspoon dry mustard
16	slices whole wheat bread, crusts trimmed	8	ounces fresh mushrooms, sliced
8	slices sharp Cheddar cheese	1	tablespoon butter
		1	cup crushed cornflakes
8	slices cooked ham	1/2	cup (1 stick) butter, melted
6	eggs		

Preheat the oven to 350 degrees. Spread 1/2 tablespoon butter on one side of each bread slice. Place one-half of the buttered bread slices in a well-greased 9×13-inch baking pan. Top each with a slice of the cheese and ham. Place the remaining bread slices buttered side up on top of the ham. Beat the eggs, milk and dry mustard in a bowl. Pour over the bread. Chill for 8 to 10 hours. Sauté the mushrooms in 1 tablespoon butter in a nonstick skillet until tender. Spread over the bread. Mix the cornflakes and 1/2 cup melted butter in a bowl. Sprinkle over the top. Bake for 45 minutes.

Kentucky Ham Slices

Serves 8

6   slices country ham,
       3/8 to 1/2 thick (about 2 pounds)
1 1/2 cups packed light brown sugar

Preheat the oven to 325 degrees. Trim the rind, fat and bone residue from the ham. Cut the slices into serving-size pieces. Line a 9×13-inch baking dish with foil, leaving enough overhang to fold and seal. Sprinkle a generous amount of the brown sugar on the bottom. Alternate layers of the ham and remaining brown sugar in the prepared pan until all of the ingredients are used, ending with the brown sugar. Bring the overhanging foil over the top and fold and seal. Bake for 1 1/2 to 2 hours or until the ham is cooked through and tender.

Note: The uncooked ham can be either smoked, salt-cured, or sugar-cured.

SIGNATURE RECIPE

Kentucky foods represent the unique culture of the state—dried apple stack cakes from the mountain region, bourbon balls from the Bluegrass region, and barbecue from the western region. While Bibb lettuce (see Almond Bibb Salad, page 97) was developed in Kentucky by Major John Bibb, most Kentuckians agree that country ham is one of our most notable traditions. Families often pass down secret recipes for curing and cooking the meat that becomes the featured dish at special gatherings.

Per serving
Calories 241
Protein 12 g
Carbohydrates 41 g
Total Fat 4 g
13% Calories from Fat
Cholesterol 30 mg
Fiber 0 g
Sodium 1173 mg
Sugar 40 g

Asparagus and Ham Confetti Fettuccini

Serves 6

Per serving
Calories 703
Protein 30 g
Carbohydrates 52 g
Total Fat 43 g
54% Calories from Fat
Cholesterol 174 mg
Fiber 5 g
Sodium 513 mg
Sugar 6 g

12 ounces fettuccini
   White portion of 1 small bunch
     green onions, thinly sliced
1 (8-ounce) can sliced button or
   baby bella mushrooms
1 pound fresh asparagus, trimmed and
   cut into 2-inch pieces
2 tablespoons butter
2 cups chopped cooked ham
2 cups heavy cream
2 tablespoons ketchup
2 teaspoons Italian seasoning
1 cup (4 ounces) grated Parmesan cheese

Cook the pasta using the package directions. Sauté the green onions, mushrooms and asparagus in the butter in a large skillet until tender. Add the ham, cream, ketchup, Italian seasoning and cheese. Cook over medium heat until hot and slightly thickened, stirring constantly. Drain the pasta and place in a large serving bowl. Spoon the sauce over the pasta.

Horseshoe Sandwich

Serves 2

1 (8-ounce) package frozen
    French fries
1/2 cup (1 stick) butter
1/4 cup all-purpose flour
2 cups milk or light cream
2 cups (8 ounces) shredded
    Cheddar cheese
1/4 teaspoon pepper
1 teaspoon hot pepper sauce, or
    to taste
1 slice cooked spiral ham
2 slices thick-sliced bread, toasted

Prepare the French fries in the oven using the package directions. Melt the butter in a saucepan. Whisk in the flour. Cook until thick and bubbly, stirring constantly. Whisk in the milk gradually until smooth. Bring to a simmer and remove from the heat. Add the cheese and stir until melted. Stir in the pepper and hot sauce.

Cut the ham into two serving pieces. Heat the ham in a skillet until heated through. Place a slice of toast on each serving plate. Top with a ham slice and French fries. Pour the cheese sauce over each sandwich and serve immediately.

Note: This can be made with ground beef, chicken breast, pork tenderloin, bacon, or any meat you desire. Some restaurants add sliced tomato to the sandwich between the meat and French fries.

SIGNATURE RECIPE

The Horseshoe Sandwich was developed in Springfield, Illinois, and is still a popular menu item today. The Horseshoe actually uses two slices of bread and two servings of meat per person. The smaller version is called the Ponyshoe. There are many variations of the cheese sauce used to top the sandwich, and each restaurant has its own "secret" ingredient.

Per serving
Calories 1438
Protein 60 g
Carbohydrates 74 g
Total Fat 101 g
63% Calories from Fat
Cholesterol 311 mg
Fiber 4 g
Sodium 2140 mg
Sugar 14 g

SIGNATURE RECIPE

The majestic buffalo is the central focus of our Wyoming flag and is also our state mammal. This recipe was served when Lady Bird Johnson, wife of President Lyndon Johnson, visited Green River, Wyoming, in connection with the dedication of the Flaming Gorge Recreation Area on August 17, 1964. This recipe appeared in the Cooking in Wyoming Woman's Suffrage Centennial Edition Cookbook *and was submitted by Mrs. Gale McGee, wife of Wyoming's United States Senator.*

Per serving
Calories 965
Protein 53 g
Carbohydrates 18 g
Total Fat 71 g
64% Calories from Fat
Cholesterol 134 mg
Fiber 3 g
Sodium 856 mg
Sugar 10 g

Buffalo Tips à la Bourgogne   *Serves 10*

2	cups olive oil
2	cups dry red wine
1	tablespoon oregano
1	tablespoon pepper
1	tablespoon sweet basil
3	garlic cloves, chopped
1/4	teaspoon salt
1/4	teaspoon pepper
1	(16-ounce) can tomato sauce
1	(5-pound) buffalo roast
2	large onions
1	cup olive oil
2	cups burgundy wine
2	cups tomato purée
3	cups chicken broth
3	bay leaves
1/4	teaspoon salt
1/4	teaspoon pepper

Preheat the oven to 275 degrees. Process 2 cups olive oil, the red wine, oregano, 1 tablespoon black pepper, the basil, garlic, 1/4 teaspoon salt, 1/4 teaspoon pepper and the tomato sauce in a blender until smooth. Place the buffalo in a greased roaster. Bake to 160 degrees on a meat thermometer, basting on all sides with the sauce while roasting. Do not overcook (buffalo is lean and juicy with very little fat). Cut the buffalo into 1-inch cubes. Sauté with the onions in 1 cup olive oil in a large skillet until the onions are golden brown. Add the burgundy. Cook until the wine is reduced by two-thirds. Add the tomato purée, broth and bay leaves. Simmer for 1 hour. Sprinkle with 1/4 teaspoon salt and 1/4 teaspoon pepper. Discard the bay leaves before serving.

Note: This is best served over buttered pasta. The buffalo can be barbecued over a slow open fire and smoked.

Buffalo Stew

Serves 6

Per serving
Calories 279
Protein 31 g
Carbohydrates 27 g
Total Fat 5 g
16% Calories from Fat
Cholesterol 95 mg
Fiber 4 g
Sodium 587 mg
Sugar 7 g

2	pounds bison for stew, cut into 1-inch cubes	1	(28-ounce) can tomatoes
5	large carrots, cut into 1-inch pieces	1/2	cup quick-cooking tapioca
		1/2	teaspoon ground cloves
1	large onion, cut into chunks	2	bay leaves
		3/4	teaspoon salt
3	ribs celery, sliced	1/2	teaspoon pepper

Trim the fat from the bison. Combine the bison, carrots, onion, celery, tomatoes, tapioca, cloves, bay leaves, salt and pepper in a 3-quart slow cooker and mix well. Cook on Low for 12 hours or on High for 5 to 6 hours. Discard the bay leaves before serving.

Note: Green bell peppers, potatoes or mushrooms may be added. For extra seasoning, use canned Mexican-style tomatoes.

All-American Goat Burgers

Serves 8

Per serving
Calories 124
Protein 23 g
Carbohydrates 1 g
Total Fat 3 g
20% Calories from Fat
Cholesterol 64 mg
Fiber <1 g
Sodium 149 mg
Sugar <1 g

2 pounds ground goat
1 envelope dry onion soup mix
1 teaspoon garlic powder

Preheat a gas or charcoal grill. Combine the ground goat, onion soup mix and garlic powder in a bowl and mix well. Shape into eight patties and place on a grill rack. Grill to 160 degrees on a meat thermometer.

Note: The goat burgers may also be cooked in a skillet on the stovetop.

Goat Meat

Goat meat is generally quite lean, although its high moisture content makes it tender when handled properly. Meat of adult goats is best prepared by stewing because of its relative toughness; however, in stews it is flavorful and tender. Kid meat (goats under a year of age) lends itself to all recipes for lamb: chops, leg or shoulder, crown roasts, rack or saddle, and kabobs.

Per serving
Calories 759
Protein 33 g
Carbohydrates 35 g
Total Fat 50 g
59% Calories from Fat
Cholesterol 109 mg
Fiber 4 g
Sodium 592 mg
Sugar 5 g

Lamb Chops with Mushroom Gnocchi

Serves 4

Lamb

Lamb is meat from a sheep less than one year old. If the phrase "spring lamb" is on the meat label, it means the lamb was slaughtered between March and October. Mutton is meat from a sheep more than a year old. It is usually less tender than lamb and has a stronger flavor.

1	(16-ounce) package gnocchi
3	tablespoons fresh rosemary, finely crushed
1¹/₂	tablespoons fresh thyme, finely crushed
3	garlic cloves, minced
¹/₂	teaspoon sea salt
¹/₂	teaspoon pepper
¹/₂	cup olive oil
4	(5-ounce) lamb chops
8	ounces shiitake mushrooms
10	plum tomatoes, cut into halves
1	tablespoon unsalted butter
1	tablespoon olive oil
9	ounces fresh baby spinach
1	cup white wine
¹/₈	teaspoon salt, or to taste
¹/₈	teaspoon pepper, or to taste

Preheat the oven to 375 degrees. Cook the gnocchi using the package directions. Mix the rosemary, thyme, garlic, ¹/₂ teaspoon salt and ¹/₂ teaspoon pepper with ¹/₂ cup olive oil in a bowl to form a paste. Brush onto each side of the lamb chops and place on end or edge in an ovenproof skillet. Bake for 15 minutes or until medium-rare. Remove the lamb chops to a platter and keep warm, reserving the pan drippings.

Sauté the mushrooms and tomatoes in the butter and 1 tablespoon olive oil in a skillet until almost tender. Add the spinach. Cook, covered, until the spinach wilts. Pour the wine into the reserved drippings in the ovenproof skillet. Cook for 1 minute, stirring to scrape up the brown bits. Add ¹/₈ teaspoon salt and ¹/₈ teaspoon pepper. Cook until the mixture is reduced to about ¹/₄ cup. Combine the vegetables, gnocchi and sauce in a bowl and mix well. Serve with the lamb chops.

Big Sky Elk Roast

Serves 8

1   (2¹/2- to 3-pound) elk roast
2   onions, cut into wedges
¹/2 teaspoon cinnamon
1   teaspoon salt
¹/4 teaspoon pepper
3 or 4 potatoes
1   cup water or beef bouillon

Place the elk and onions in a slow cooker. Sprinkle with the cinnamon, salt and pepper. Add the potatoes and water. Cook on Low for 8 to 10 hours.

Note: Venison may be used instead of the elk. Sweet potatoes or squash may be used instead of the potatoes.

SIGNATURE RECIPE

Montana, an outdoor enthusiast's haven, is known for its big skies, rich natural resources, recreation, hunting, and fishing. Deemed "the treasure state" by seekers of fortune during the gold rush days, Montanans now treasure clean air, wide open spaces, and pristine lakes and rivers. A heritage rich in hunting, fishing, and outdoor recreation is valued by Montana families. Our featured recipe is an elk roast with cinnamon, which brings out the flavor of the meat.

Per serving
Calories 252
Protein 40 g
Carbohydrates 16 g
Total Fat 2 g
9% Calories from Fat
Cholesterol 93 mg
Fiber 1 g
Sodium 370 mg
Sugar 2 g

Pheasant Wild Rice Soup

Serves 10

SIGNATURE RECIPE

South Dakota's state bird is the Chinese ring-necked pheasant, one of the world's most hunted birds. Pheasant can be found throughout most of South Dakota, except for the Black Hills, and is known for its delicious meat. Although high in cholesterol, pheasant is low in sodium and saturated fat. Since it is primarily a Midwestern bird, pheasant is considered a delicacy in many other states.

1	(6-ounce) package long grain and wild rice mix
1	(4-ounce) can mushrooms, drained
1	small onion, chopped
1/2	cup (1 stick) butter
1/2	cup all-purpose flour
1	cup milk
8	cups chicken broth
1	envelope dry onion soup mix
1	pheasant, cooked and chopped

Prepare the rice mix using the package directions. Sauté the mushrooms and onion in the butter in a skillet until tender. Stir in the flour but do not let brown. Whisk in the milk and broth gradually. Add the cooked rice, sautéed vegetables, onion soup mix and pheasant. Cook until heated through. Ladle into soup bowls.

Per serving
Calories 419
Protein 34 g
Carbohydrates 21 g
Total Fat 22 g
47% Calories from Fat
Cholesterol 112 mg
Fiber 1 g
Sodium 1236 mg
Sugar 3 g

Dove with Lemon Sauce

Serves 6

Per serving
Calories 566
Protein 54 g
Carbohydrates 1 g
Total Fat 37 g
60% Calories from Fat
Cholesterol 263 mg
Fiber <1 g
Sodium 218 mg
Sugar <1 g

12 medium dove, cleaned
1/2 teaspoon herb seasoning
1/4 teaspoon freshly ground pepper
1/4 cup water
1/4 cup (1/2 stick) margarine
3/4 cup water
2 tablespoons lemon juice

Rinse the dove briefly under cool running water and pat dry with paper towels. Place the dove in a large skillet. Sprinkle with the herb seasoning and pepper. Add 1/4 cup water to the skillet. Do not pour over the dove. Cook, covered, over medium heat for 20 minutes to steam the dove. Uncover and continue to cook until the liquid evaporates. Remove the dove to a platter. Melt the margarine in the skillet. Return the dove to the skillet and cook until brown. Remove again to the platter. Stir 3/4 cup water into the pan drippings. Cook over medium-high heat for 2 minutes, stirring to scrape up any brown bits. Stir in the lemon juice. Pour over the dove and serve immediately.

Fish & Seafood

How Do I Know My Fish Is Fresh?

Clear eyes that bulge a little

Firm, shiny flesh that springs back when pressed

Gills that are bright red and not slimy

No darkening or discoloration around the edges

Fresh, mild smell that is not "fishy" or ammonia-like

How Do I Know My Seafood Is Safe?

Buy seafood from a reputable source.

Seafood must be refrigerated or on ice when purchased.

Don't buy frozen seafood if the packages are open, torn, or crushed on the edges. Visible frost or ice crystals in the package indicates the seafood has been stored for a long time, or was thawed and then refrozen.

Clams, mussels, and oysters should be purchased live. Open, cracked, or broken shells mean they are dead and should not be eaten.

If seafood will be used within two days of purchase, then store it in the refrigerator. If it will not be used within two days, then it needs to be stored in the freezer.

I Know Fish Is Good For Me, but What About Mercury?

Almost all fish contain trace amounts of methyl mercury. Unborn babies and young infants are sensitive to methyl mercury's effects. FDA recommends that women who are pregnant, or may become pregnant, and nursing mothers avoid fish that may contain unsafe levels of methyl mercury. These include shark, swordfish, king mackerel, and tilefish.

However, fish and seafood are good sources of omega-3 fatty acids, important nutrients for brain development. Therefore, pregnant and nursing women, as well as young children, may eat up to twelve ounces per week of cooked fish that contain low amounts of methyl mercury. Some of the most popular varieties are shrimp, canned light tuna, salmon, pollock, and catfish.

SAFE COOKING

Fin Fish
145°F or until opaque and flakes easily with fork

Shrimp, Lobster, and Crabs
Flesh pearly and opaque

Clams, Oysters, and Mussels
Shells open during cooking

Scallops
Milky white or opaque and firm

Smoked Salmon Spread

Serves 4

Per serving
Calories 143
Protein 9 g
Carbohydrates 2 g
Total Fat 12 g
72% Calories from Fat
Cholesterol 31 mg
Fiber <1 g
Sodium 84 mg
Sugar <1 g

1   (4-ounce) can smoked salmon
4   ounces soft cheese spread
2   tablespoons chopped red onion
2   teaspoons fresh dill weed, chopped

Combine the smoked salmon, cheese spread, red onion and dill weed in a small bowl and mix well. Chill, covered, until serving time.

Baked Salmon Croquettes

Serves 7

Per serving
Calories 146
Protein 14 g
Carbohydrates 9 g
Total Fat 6 g
38% Calories from Fat
Cholesterol 70 mg
Fiber 1 g
Sodium 355 mg
Sugar 1 g

1   (15-ounce) can salmon, drained
1/4   green bell pepper, chopped
1   small onion, chopped
1   tablespoon lemon juice
1   egg
2/3   cup dried bread crumbs
1   teaspoon dried parsley
1/2   teaspoon dill weed
1/2   teaspoon pepper

Preheat the oven to 350 degrees. Remove any bones from the salmon. Break the salmon into small pieces into a bowl. Add the bell pepper, onion, lemon juice, egg, bread crumbs, parsley, dill weed and pepper and mix well. Drop by small scoopfuls 1 inch apart onto a baking sheet. Bake for 20 minutes or until light brown. Serve warm.

Note: Instead of discarding the salmon bones, crush some of them and stir into the mixture to add more calcium. Whole grain soft bread crumbs or dried bread crumbs can be used to make it healthier. If the mixture is dry, add a small amount of the liquid from the can of salmon. Frozen chopped onion or frozen chopped green bell pepper can be substituted for fresh. Egg substitute can be used instead of a fresh egg.

Baked Salmon

Serves 6

1   (1¹/₂-pound) salmon fillet
1¹/₂ teaspoons dried dill weed
1   large lemon, sliced

Preheat the oven to 350 degrees. Rinse the salmon and pat dry. Place skin side down on a large sheet of heavy-duty foil. Sprinkle with the dill weed. Place the lemon slices over the salmon. Bring the foil over the salmon and fold the edges together. Fold the foil ends together to create a sealed packet. Place on a baking sheet. Bake for 20 minutes or to 145 degrees on a meat thermometer. Serve with additional lemon wedges.

Note: Using the foil makes cleanup easy. The foil packet may be placed on a grill rack and grilled. Alternatively, the salmon can be placed in a baking dish. Cover and bake as directed. Leftover salmon is great as salmon patties, in a casserole, or made into a dip for vegetables or crackers.

SIGNATURE RECIPE

Salmon is a staple of many people's diets in Alaska. It may be prepared in many ways. Baking in the oven or on the grill is a simple way to prepare salmon. When the runs are plentiful, extra fish is frozen or canned for future use.

Per serving
Calories 206
Protein 26 g
Carbohydrates 1 g
Total Fat 10 g
46% Calories from Fat
Cholesterol 82 mg
Fiber <1 g
Sodium 62 mg
Sugar <1 g

Salmon Surprise

Serves 6

Per serving
Calories 338
Protein 25 g
Carbohydrates 26 g
Total Fat 15 g
40% Calories from Fat
Cholesterol 161 mg
Fiber 2 g
Sodium 1078 mg
Sugar 4 g

Fat Recommendations

USDA recommends using fewer solid fats from butter, margarine, shortening, and lard. Have most of your fat sources in the diet from fish, nuts, and vegetable oils. Making fat-free and low-fat choices when possible will also reduce fat in the diet.

1	(15-ounce) can salmon, drained
2	medium eggs, beaten
3/4	cup rolled oats
1/2	cup fat-free ranch salad dressing
1	teaspoon minced garlic
1/2	cup chopped marinated artichokes
1	teaspoon wasabi horseradish
1/4	cup (1 ounce) grated Parmesan, Romano and asiago cheese blend
1/3	cup milk
2	tablespoons olive oil
1	medium egg
2	tablespoons water
1	cup Italian bread crumbs

Break the salmon into small pieces into a bowl. Stir in 2 eggs. Add the oats, salad dressing, garlic, artichokes, horseradish, cheese and milk and mix well. Shape into 1/2-cup patties. Heat the olive oil in a 10-inch skillet over medium heat. Beat 1 egg and the water in a small bowl to create an egg wash. Dip each patty in the egg wash and roll in the bread crumbs to coat. Fry in the hot olive oil for 5 minutes per side or until cooked through.

Note: This is great as a main dish served with vegetables. To serve as an appetizer, shape into one-tablespoon patties. To lower cholesterol, use egg substitute equal to two eggs.

Pecan-Encrusted Salmon

Serves 4

Per serving
Calories 381
Protein 29 g
Carbohydrates 9 g
Total Fat 25 g
60% Calories from Fat
Cholesterol 84 mg
Fiber 1 g
Sodium 501 mg
Sugar 1 g

1/3	cup pecans	
1/3	cup bread crumbs	
2	tablespoons grated Parmesan cheese	
1/4	teaspoon salt	
1/4	teaspoon freshly ground pepper	

1 to 2 tablespoons olive oil
1 pound sockeye or coho salmon fillets
2 tablespoons Dijon mustard

Preheat the oven to 425 degrees. Pulse the pecans, bread crumbs, cheese, salt and pepper in a small food processor until finely ground. Spread in a shallow bowl. Drizzle with the olive oil and toss with a fork until moistened. Loosely fold the tapered ends of the fillets under to create an even thickness, if needed. Spread the top of each fillet evenly with Dijon mustard. Press the mustard-coated side of each fillet into the crumb mixture to coat generously. Place coated side up on a baking sheet sprayed with nonstick cooking spray. Sprinkle the remaining crumb mixture over the fillets to form a thick encrustment. Bake for 10 to 12 minutes or until the topping is crisp and brown and the fillet is cooked through.

Orange Snapper

Serves 6

Per serving
Calories 132
Protein 23 g
Carbohydrates 2 g
Total Fat 3 g
21% Calories from Fat
Cholesterol 40 mg
Fiber <1 g
Sodium 49 mg
Sugar 2 g

6 (4-ounce) red snapper fillets
3 tablespoons water
2 tablespoons thawed frozen orange juice concentrate
2 teaspoons olive oil

1/2 teaspoon grated orange zest
1/4 teaspoon freshly ground pepper
1/8 teaspoon ground nutmeg
Orange wedges for garnish
Parsley for garnish

Preheat the oven to 350 degrees. Place the fillets in an 8×12-inch baking dish coated with nonstick cooking spray. Combine the water, orange juice concentrate, olive oil and orange zest in a small bowl and mix well. Pour over the fillets. Sprinkle with the pepper and nutmeg. Bake, uncovered, for 20 to 25 minutes or until the fillets flake easily when tested with a fork or to 145 degrees on a meat thermometer. Garnish with orange wedges and parsley.

Tuna Tofu Salad

Serves 8

Per serving
Calories 127
Protein 14 g
Carbohydrates 10 g
Total Fat 5 g
30% Calories from Fat
Cholesterol 9 mg
Fiber 2 g
Sodium 901 mg
Sugar 6 g

Sesame Dressing

1/3 cup soy sauce
1 teaspoon sesame oil
1 tablespoon sugar
 Toasted sesame seeds to taste

Salad

1 head lettuce, chopped
1 bunch Chinese parsley, chopped
1 onion, chopped
1/2 bunch green onions, chopped
2 tomatoes, chopped
20 ounces firm tofu, drained and cut into bite-size pieces
1 (6-ounce) can water-packed tuna, drained

To prepare the dressing, mix the soy sauce, sesame oil, sugar and toasted sesame seeds in a jar with a tight-fitting lid. Seal the jar and shake well. Chill until serving time.

To prepare the salad, toss the lettuce, parsley, onion, green onions, tomatoes, tofu and tuna together in a large bowl. Chill until serving time. To serve, pour the dressing over the salad and toss to coat.

Baked Fish Fillets with Dill Sauce

Serves 4

Per serving
Calories 223
Protein 20 g
Carbohydrates 8 g
Total Fat 12 g
47% Calories from Fat
Cholesterol 58 mg
Fiber <1 g
Sodium 410 mg
Sugar 3 g

1	pound catfish, crappie or salmon fillets
2	tablespoons white cooking wine
1/4	teaspoon salt
1/2	teaspoon pepper
2	tablespoons dried onion flakes
1/4	cup mayonnaise-type salad dressing
1/4	cup fat-free milk
1	tablespoon dried dill weed
1	tablespoon lemon juice
2	teaspoons Dijon mustard

Preheat the oven to 425 degrees. Place the fish in a single layer in a 9×13-inch baking dish coated with nonstick cooking spray. Sprinkle with the wine, salt, pepper and onion flakes. Bake, covered with foil, for 20 to 25 minutes or to 145 degrees on a meat thermometer.

Place the mayonnaise-type salad dressing in a saucepan. Whisk in the milk gradually. Whisk over medium-low heat for 2 minutes or until smooth and heated through but not bubbly. Remove from the heat. Stir in the dill weed, lemon juice and Dijon mustard.

Remove the fish to a serving platter. Pour the drippings from the baking pan into the dill mixture and mix well. Spoon over the fish.

Note: This is a quick and healthier way to cook catfish or crappie. Also, it cooks quickly.

Tips for Staying Safe When You Catch Your Own

Before: *Always check local advisories and sign postings for information about the safety of fish and shellfish in your area.*

During: *Be sure to keep fish and shellfish well iced while fishing and while transporting the seafood home.*

After: *Fish caught in some lakes and streams may have harmful levels of polychlorinated biphenyls, or PCBs, which can cause a variety of health problems. Harmful levels of PCBs have not been found in fish that are sold in the commercial marketplace, including farm-raised species.*

Since PCBs accumulate in fat, trim the fat and skin from fish before cooking. This can lessen the risk of exposure to these contaminants.

Parmesan Fish Bake

Per serving
Calories 279
Protein 28 g
Carbohydrates 11 g
Total Fat 13 g
43% Calories from Fat
Cholesterol 80 mg
Fiber 1 g
Sodium 392 mg
Sugar 5 g

1/4	cup chopped onion
1	tablespoon vegetable oil
2	tablespoons all-purpose flour
1/4	teaspoon salt
3/4	cup skim milk
3/4	cup shredded carrots
1/2	cup (2 ounces) shredded Parmesan cheese
6 to 8 tablespoons lemon juice	
1	pound fish fillets

Preheat the oven to 350 degrees. Sauté the onion in the oil in a skillet until translucent. Stir in the flour and salt. Add the milk. Cook until thickened, stirring constantly. Add the carrots, cheese and lemon juice. Place the fish in a 7×11-inch baking dish. Pour the sauce over the fish. Bake for 25 minutes or to 145 degrees on a meat thermometer. Serve with hot cooked rice or pasta.

Note: You may substitute chicken broth for the skim milk. Try adding other vegetables, such as green bell pepper or peas.

Mexican Crab Salad

Per serving
Calories 154
Protein 6 g
Carbohydrates 25 g
Total Fat 4 g
23% Calories from Fat
Cholesterol 9 mg
Fiber 2 g
Sodium 418 mg
Sugar 4 g

1	pound imitation crab meat, chopped
1/2	bunch cilantro, chopped
1	large cucumber, peeled and cut into small cubes
1	small red onion, chopped
1	large tomato, cut into small cubes
1	large avocado, cut into small cubes
	Salt to taste
3	small limes
10	(6-inch) tortillas, toasted
	Tapatío hot sauce to taste

Combine the crab meat, cilantro, cucumber, onion, tomato, avocado and salt in a large bowl and mix well. Cut the limes into halves. Squeeze the juice over the crab meat mixture and mix well. Spoon onto the tortillas and sprinkle with hot sauce.

Maryland Crab Cakes

Serves 6

1	pound crab meat
1/2	cup cracker meal
4	egg whites
1/2	cup mayonnaise
1 1/2	teaspoons seafood seasoning
1	teaspoon Worcestershire sauce
1/8	teaspoon ground red pepper
1/2	teaspoon dry mustard
1/4	cup fresh parsley, chopped

Preheat the oven to 350 degrees. Place the crab meat in a medium bowl. Gently work the crab meat between your fingers to find and remove any shells. Be careful not to mash the crab meat and break it up too much. Toss the cracker meal gently with the crab meat.

Beat the egg whites in a bowl. Add the mayonnaise and mix until smooth. Add the seafood seasoning, Worcestershire sauce, ground red pepper, dry mustard and parsley and mix well. Add to the crab meat mixture and toss gently to mix. Do not overmix. Divide the mixture into six 1/2-cup portions using an ice cream scoop or #8 scoop. Shape each portion into a patty. Place on a baking sheet sprayed with nonstick cooking spray. Coat the patties with nonstick cooking spray. Bake for 12 minutes or to 160 degrees on a meat thermometer.

Note: Always keep crab meat chilled at 38 degrees or below. You may use jumbo lump, special or claw meat, blue crab meat, or any kind of cooked crab meat. Substitute 1 cup of bread crumbs or crushed saltine crackers for the cracker meal. For color and flavor, add sautéed green or red bell peppers and onions to the crab cakes.

SIGNATURE RECIPE

Maryland blue crab is the state crustacean. Its scientific name means "beautiful swimmer that is savory." The Chesapeake Bay supplies about one-third of the nation's catch, and blue crabs are Maryland's top commercial fishing industry. The blue crab meat is sweet like lobster. Cracking and eating steamed hard crabs is a favorite summertime festivity. Blue crab is also enjoyed in a soft-shell stage, and in soups, dips, omelets, casseroles, salads, and crab imperial.

Per serving
Calories 256
Protein 18 g
Carbohydrates 8 g
Total Fat 16 g
57% Calories from Fat
Cholesterol 75 mg
Fiber <1 g
Sodium 537 mg
Sugar <1 g

SIGNATURE RECIPE

Crawfish Étouffée— A Healthier Way

Serves 8

Laissez les bon temps rouler (pronounced lay-zay lay bon ton rule-ay)... "Let the good times roll!" And nothing says good times quite like a Cajun crawfish boil. If you are lucky enough to have leftover crawfish, it's expected that you'll make an étouffée (pronounced ay-to-fay), a traditional seafood stew eaten over rice. The Bayou State produces about 90 percent of the nation's crawfish, making it just one of the many unique agricultural commodities produced in Louisiana.

2	pounds peeled crawfish tails
2	teaspoons light salt
1/2	teaspoon black pepper
1/2	teaspoon red pepper
1/4	cup polyunsaturated oil
1	cup chopped white onion
1/2	cup chopped celery
1/4	cup chopped bell pepper
2	garlic cloves, minced
2	cups water
2	tablespoons cornstarch
2	tablespoons chopped green onions and tops
2	tablespoons minced parsley
1	teaspoon low-sodium Worcestershire sauce

Sprinkle the crawfish tails with salt, black pepper and red pepper. Heat the oil in a heavy stockpot. Add the onion, celery, bell pepper and garlic. Sauté until soft, stirring frequently. Add the crawfish tails. Cook over medium heat for 5 to 10 minutes, stirring frequently. Add 1 1/2 cups of the water. Bring just to a boil and simmer for 15 minutes, stirring occasionally. Dissolve the cornstarch in the remaining 1/2 cup water. Add to the crawfish mixture. Cook until thickened and smooth, stirring constantly. Add the green onions, parsley and Worcestershire sauce. Simmer for 10 minutes, adding additional water if needed. Cover and let stand for 10 minutes for the flavors to blend. Serve over hot fluffy rice.

Note: The flavor is often better if the étouffée is made one day in advance and chilled in shallow containers. This recipe freezes well. If freezing boiled crawfish to make the étouffée later, the fat must be rinsed off the tail meat before freezing. Adding two tablespoons tomato paste will give the red color that you normally get from the crawfish fat.

Nutritional analysis does not include rice.

Per serving
Calories 159
Protein 16 g
Carbohydrates 5 g
Total Fat 8 g
47% Calories from Fat
Cholesterol 124 mg
Fiber 1 g
Sodium 384 mg
Sugar 1 g

Blend of the Bayou

Serves 8

8	ounces cream cheese	1	tablespoon garlic salt
1/2	cup (1 stick) butter	1	teaspoon Tabasco sauce
1	pound shrimp, peeled	1/2	teaspoon red pepper
1	large onion, chopped	1	pint crab meat
1	large bell pepper, chopped	3/4	cup rice, cooked
2	ribs celery, chopped	12	ounces sharp Cheddar cheese, shredded
2	tablespoons butter	3	cups cracker crumbs
1	(10-ounce) can cream of mushroom soup		
1	(8-ounce) can mushrooms, drained		

Preheat the oven to 350 degrees. Place the cream cheese and 1/2 cup butter in a microwave-safe bowl. Microwave for 1 minute. Sauté the shrimp, onion, bell pepper and celery in 2 tablespoons butter in a skillet until the vegetables are tender. Stir into the cream cheese mixture. Add the soup, mushrooms, garlic salt, Tabasco sauce, red pepper, crab meat and rice and mix well. Spoon into a 9×13-inch or 2-quart baking dish. Sprinkle with the Cheddar cheese and cracker crumbs. Bake for 20 to 30 minutes or until bubbly.

Note: You may substitute two cans of shrimp and one can of crab meat for the fresh.

Per serving
Calories 697
Protein 33 g
Carbohydrates 40 g
Total Fat 45 g
58% Calories from Fat
Cholesterol 228 mg
Fiber 2 g
Sodium 1653 mg
Sugar 3 g

Easy Shrimp Casserole

Serves 6

1	cup rice	1/2	teaspoon pepper
1	green bell pepper, chopped	1	(10-ounce) can cream of shrimp soup
1/2	small onion, finely chopped	1	pound freshwater shrimp or frozen shrimp, peeled and deveined
8	ounces sliced mushrooms, drained	4	slices processed cheese or Cheddar cheese
2	tablespoons butter, melted		
1	teaspoon seasoning salt or garlic		

Preheat the oven to 375 degrees. Cook the rice using the package directions. Sauté the bell pepper, onion and mushrooms in the butter in a large skillet. Add the seasoning salt, pepper, soup and shrimp. Spoon into a greased 8×8-inch baking dish. Bake for 15 minutes or until hot and bubbly. Top with the cheese. Bake for 5 minutes or until the cheese begins to melt.

Per serving
Calories 326
Protein 21 g
Carbohydrates 31 g
Total Fat 13 g
36% Calories from Fat
Cholesterol 146 mg
Fiber 1 g
Sodium 1066 mg
Sugar 1 g

Per serving
Calories 342
Protein 19 g
Carbohydrates 18 g
Total Fat 21 g
57% Calories from Fat
Cholesterol 166 mg
Fiber 1 g
Sodium 812 mg
Sugar 1 g

Shrimp and Grits Southeast North Carolina Style

Serves 6

1/2	cup (1 stick) butter	3	cups cooked stone-ground grits
1	large sweet onion, chopped		
1	pound uncooked deveined peeled shrimp	8	ounces bacon, crisp-cooked and crumbled
1/2	teaspoon lemon pepper		Sliced green onions for garnish
1/2	teaspoon seafood seasoning		
1/2	teaspoon salt		

Melt the butter in a large saucepan. Add the onion and shrimp. Sauté until the shrimp turn pink and the onion is soft and translucent. Add the lemon pepper, seafood seasoning and salt. Pour over the grits and sprinkle with the bacon. Garnish with green onions.

Per serving
Calories 345
Protein 24 g
Carbohydrates 32 g
Total Fat 14 g
35% Calories from Fat
Cholesterol 173 mg
Fiber 2 g
Sodium 754 mg
Sugar 3 g

Shrimp Fajitas

Serves 4

1	pound uncooked peeled shrimp	2	tablespoons vegetable oil
1/2	teaspoon salt	6	green onions, sliced
1/2	teaspoon ground cumin	2	large green bell peppers, cut into strips
1/2	teaspoon chili powder	4	(8-inch) tortillas
1/2	teaspoon dried oregano	1/4	cup sour cream
1/4	teaspoon garlic powder	1	bunch fresh cilantro, chopped
2	tablespoons lime juice		

Preheat the oven to 350 degrees. Combine the shrimp, salt, cumin, chili powder, oregano, garlic powder and lime juice in a bowl and toss to coat. Marinate for 10 minutes. Heat the oil in a large skillet over high heat. Add the green onions and bell peppers. Stir-fry for 2 minutes. Add the undrained shrimp. Stir-fry for 3 minutes or until the shrimp turn pink. Wrap the tortillas in foil. Bake for 10 minutes. Spoon 1/2 cup of the shrimp mixture onto each warm tortilla and roll up. Top each with 1 tablespoon sour cream and cilantro. Serve with chopped onions and salsa as desired.

Cooking Freshwater Shrimp

Freshwater shrimp (prawns) should be kept refrigerated—preferably on crushed ice. Use them immediately. Rinse the shrimp in cold water just before cooking to remove any sediment. Shrimp are transparent and gelatinous when uncooked. When properly cooked (about two to three minutes depending on the size), they become firm and opaque, appearing white, dappled with pink. Overcooking causes shrimp to become tough.

Low-Country Boil

Serves 6

1¹/2 gallons water
    Salt to taste
2 to 4 tablespoons seafood seasoning or
    crab boil
3   pounds small red potatoes
1¹/2 pounds smoked sausage, cut into
    2-inch pieces
6   ears of corn on the cob, cut into halves
3   pounds unpeeled shrimp

Bring the water and salt to a boil in a stockpot or Dutch oven. Add the seafood seasoning and potatoes. Cook for 5 minutes. Reduce the heat to medium-high. Add the sausage and cook for 5 minutes. Add the corn and cook for 5 minutes. Add the shrimp and cook for 3 minutes. Do not overcook the shrimp. Remove to a serving platter or serving container with a slotted spoon.

Note: For additional flavor, add two to four crushed garlic cloves to the water before boiling. Add two onions, cut into wedges, and one or two sliced lemons when you add the shrimp.

SIGNATURE RECIPE

South Carolina is known as the Palmetto State. During the Colonial period, coastal South Carolina was the largest producer of rice in America. Grits were named the official state food in 1976. Shrimp and grits are served on menus across the state. Today, South Carolina promotes the use of fresh, locally grown foods, protects fish for the future, and provides links to agricultural markets. Their efforts include such programs as the Sustainable Seafood initiative, Certified SC, and SC MarketMaker®.

Per serving
Calories 620
Protein 55 g
Carbohydrates 57 g
Total Fat 20 g
29% Calories from Fat
Cholesterol 372 mg
Fiber 6 g
Sodium 2594 mg
Sugar 5 g

Shrimp Seashell Pasta

Serves 8

Per serving
Calories 457
Protein 21 g
Carbohydrates 53 g
Total Fat 18 g
36% Calories from Fat
Cholesterol 106 mg
Fiber 7 g
Sodium 309 mg
Sugar 6 g

1	pound seashell pasta	1	(14-ounce) can diced tomatoes
1/4	cup olive oil	1/4	cup fresh chives, chopped
1/4	cup (1/2 stick) butter	6	fresh basil leaves, chopped
1	cup chopped sweet onion	4	ounces fresh pea pods (optional)
2	garlic cloves, finely chopped	1/2	cup toasted pine nuts
1	pound uncooked deveined peeled shrimp	1/2	cup (2 ounces) grated Romano cheese
2	green onions, sliced		

Cook the pasta using the package directions. Heat the olive oil and butter in a saucepan over medium heat. Add the onion and garlic. Cook until the onion is translucent. Add the shrimp, green onions, undrained tomatoes, chives, basil and pea pods. Cook, covered, until the shrimp turn pink and the pea pods are tender, stirring constantly. Drain the pasta and place in a large serving dish. Pour the shrimp mixture over the pasta. Sprinkle with the pine nuts and half the cheese. Serve with the remaining cheese.

Seafood Linguini

Serves 8

Per serving
Calories 355
Protein 27 g
Carbohydrates 38 g
Total Fat 9 g
23% Calories from Fat
Cholesterol 128 mg
Fiber 2 g
Sodium 350 mg
Sugar 3 g

12	ounces linguini	1	cup chicken broth
2	tablespoons butter	1/2	cup dry white wine
4	green onions, sliced	2	tablespoons lemon juice
1	teaspoon minced garlic	2	tablespoons chopped fresh parsley
1	cup sliced baby bella mushrooms	1	teaspoon dried basil leaves
1	pound frozen uncooked large shrimp, thawed and drained	1	teaspoon dried oregano leaves
8	ounces frozen bay scallops, thawed and drained	1/4	teaspoon white pepper
		2	tablespoons cornstarch
1	(6-ounce) can minced clams	2	tablespoons cold water
		2	tablespoons butter
		1/3	cup light sour cream

Cook the pasta using the package directions. Melt 2 tablespoons butter in a skillet over medium heat. Add the green onions, garlic and mushrooms. Cook until the green onions are tender. Stir in the shrimp, scallops, undrained clams and next 7 ingredients. Bring to a boil; reduce the heat. Simmer for 5 minutes. Dissolve the cornstarch in the water. Stir into the seafood mixture gradually. Cook until the mixture boils and thickens, stirring constantly. Drain the pasta; rinse with hot water. Toss with 2 tablespoons butter in a bowl until melted. Stir in the sour cream. Pour the seafood sauce over the pasta.

Summer Rolls

Serves 4

16 shrimp, peeled and deveined
3 ounces rice vermicelli noodles
4 sheets rice paper
16 mint leaves
1/4 cup cilantro, chopped
1/2 cup julienned carrots
16 Thai basil leaves
1/2 cup bean sprouts
2 Manoa lettuce leaves, cut into halves
1 green onion, cut into 4-inch strips
1 cup Nuoc Mam (below)

Per serving
Calories 167
Protein 9 g
Carbohydrates 32 g
Total Fat 1 g
4% Calories from Fat
Cholesterol 32 mg
Fiber 2 g
Sodium 627 mg
Sugar 8 g

Cook the shrimp in boiling water in a saucepan for 2 minutes or until the shrimp turn pink. Drain and set aside. Soak the noodles in warm water in a bowl for 15 minutes. Drain and set aside.

Dip the rice paper in warm water one sheet at a time and lay on a flat wet surface. Stack the mint, cilantro, carrots, basil, bean sprouts and lettuce leaves 1 inch from one end of each rice paper. Place four shrimp in the middle of each rice paper next to the vegetable stack. Place the noodles on top of the shrimp. Lay the green onion strips next to the shrimp. Fold up each rice paper, beginning at the end nearest you, and then fold in the sides. Roll the rice paper upwards into a tight roll. Cut each roll into four pieces. Serve with nuoc mam.

Nuoc Mam (Vietnamese Dipping Sauce)

Makes 1 1/2 cups

1 cup water
1/4 cup Vietnamese fish sauce
1 garlic clove, crushed
1/4 cup sugar
1 tablespoon rice wine vinegar
1 tablespoon lime juice
1 teaspoon chili paste

Per serving
Calories 50
Protein 1 g
Carbohydrates 12 g
Total Fat <1 g
2% Calories from Fat
Cholesterol 0 mg
Fiber <1 g
Sodium 1131 mg
Sugar 11 g

Bring the water, fish sauce, garlic and sugar to a rolling boil in a saucepan. Remove from the heat. Mix the vinegar, lime juice and chili paste in a small bowl. Add the fish sauce mixture and mix well. Chill for 15 minutes before serving.

Clam Chowder

Serves 20

SIGNATURE RECIPE

Clams are native to the Connecticut shoreline and have been a longtime favorite in recipes. Most are purchased fresh in the marketplace. You can buy them in their shells and clean them at home. Most people opt for shucked clams (opened with outer shell removed) or buy them in containers. Clams should be plump, with clear to opalescent liquid and a pleasant, sea breeze odor. They're delicious baked, fried in batter, or added to chowders.

3/4 cup (1 1/2 sticks) butter
12   ounces salt pork, chopped
3/4 cup chopped onion
3/4 cup chopped celery
3   pints chopped clams
4   cups clam broth
8   cups water
1/2 cup chopped parsley
1/2 teaspoon pepper
5   pounds potatoes, chopped

Melt the butter in a large stockpot over low heat. Increase the heat to medium. Add the pork and sauté until cooked through. Add the onion and celery and sauté until tender. Reduce the heat to a simmer. Add the clams, broth, water, parsley and pepper. Simmer for 1 1/2 hours. Do not boil or the clams will become tough. Add the potatoes. Simmer for 2 to 2 1/2 hours. Ladle into soup bowls.

Per serving
Calories 270
Protein 16 g
Carbohydrates 24 g
Total Fat 12 g
41% Calories from Fat
Cholesterol 55 mg
Fiber 2 g
Sodium 334 mg
Sugar 2 g

Rhode Island Stuffies

Serves 12

3	tablespoons extra-virgin olive oil
10	slices lean bacon, minced
8	garlic cloves, minced
1	cup finely chopped celery
1	cup finely chopped onion
2	quarts quahogs, chopped with juice
1/2	cup parsley, chopped
1/4	cup lemon juice
2	tablespoons hot pepper sauce
2	tablespoons Worcestershire sauce
1/2	cup (1 stick) unsalted butter
6	cups bread crumbs
24	clean quahog shells
1/4	teaspoon paprika

Preheat the oven to 425 degrees. Heat the olive oil in a large skillet or sauté pan. Add the bacon, garlic, celery and onion. Cook over medium heat for 10 to 15 minutes or until the bacon renders its fat and the vegetables soften, stirring frequently. Spoon off the excess fat. Add the clams, parsley, lemon juice, hot sauce and Worcestershire sauce. Increase the heat to high. Cook just until the mixture begins to simmer. Reduce the heat to low. Add the butter and bread crumbs. Cook gently, stirring constantly and adding additional bread crumbs if needed to absorb most of the liquid. The mixture should hold its shape but not be dry. Remove from the heat. Pack the clam mixture into the shells, filling generously. Chill, covered, until 30 minutes before serving time. Place the stuffed clams on a baking sheet. Bake for 25 to 30 minutes or until the filling is heated through and light brown. Finish under a broiler if the clam mixture is not brown enough. Sprinkle with paprika. Serve with lemon.

Note: The stuffed clams may be frozen before baking and baked for forty-five minutes.

Rhode Island's state shellfish is the quahog, more commonly known as the hard clam. Quahogs, whose shells can be four inches or larger, may be found on the menu in almost every Rhode Island restaurant, whether in the form of clam chowder or clam cakes. A "stuffie," in particular, is Rhode Island's staple way to prepare quahogs. Since Rhode Island also provides 25 percent of the country's commercial quahog catch, it's no wonder that Rhode Island is known as "Quahog Country."

Per serving
Calories 541
Protein 41 g
Carbohydrates 49 g
Total Fat 19 g
33% Calories from Fat
Cholesterol 109 mg
Fiber 3 g
Sodium 785 mg
Sugar 8 g

Fruits

Steps for Washing Fresh Fruits and Vegetables

Fresh fruits and vegetables should be washed immediately before they are eaten or prepared. The following steps should be taken:

Wash hands for twenty seconds with hot soapy water. Rinse.

Dry with a paper towel.

Throw away outer leaves from heads of lettuce and cabbage before washing them.

Wash whole fruits and vegetables thoroughly under cool, clean, running water. Do not soak fruits and vegetables in water. Do not use beach, soaps, or detergents.

Rub soft fruits and vegetables, such as tomatoes and pears, with your hands.

Wash berries in a clean colander and spray with a kitchen sink sprayer. If you do not have a kitchen sink sprayer, rinse and agitate berries under cool, slow, running water. Turn and gently shake the colander as the berries are washed.

Scrub the skins and rinds of firm fruits and vegetables, such as melons and potatoes, under cool, clean running water with a clean and sanitized fruit/vegetable brush.

Wash ALL fruits and vegetables even if the rind or skin is not eaten.

Safe Storage of Fruits and Vegetables

Fresh fruits and vegetables must be separated from raw meat, poultry, fish, and seafood.

Store fruits and vegetables in the refrigerator crisper.

Store cut fruits and vegetables in clean, airtight packages (containers, plastic bags, or plastic wrap).

Fruits and vegetables should be refrigerated after cutting or peeling until ready to serve.

FRUITS FOOD EQUIVALENTS

Bananas
1 medium = $1/3$ cup mashed

Lemons
1 medium = 3 tablespoons juice, 2 teaspoons grated peel

Limes
1 medium = 2 tablespoons juice, $1^1/2$ teaspoons grated peel

Oranges
1 medium = $1/4$ to $1/3$ cup juice, 4 teaspoons grated peel

Soda Pop Salad

Serves 9

Per serving
Calories 127
Protein 10 g
Carbohydrates 8 g
Total Fat <1 g
1% Calories from Fat
Cholesterol 0 mg
Fiber 1 g
Sodium 524 mg
Sugar 7 g

2	cups unsweetened applesauce
2	(3-ounce) packages lemon sugar-free gelatin
3/4	cup orange juice
1 1/4	cups diet lemon-lime soda

Place the applesauce in a 2-quart microwave-safe bowl. Microwave on High until hot. Dissolve the gelatin in the hot applesauce. Stir in the orange juice. Add the soda gradually, stirring gently to minimize foaming. Pour into a 9×9-inch glass dish. Chill until firm. Cut into nine squares to serve.

Note: Delicious with ham, poultry, and barbecue.

Apple Crisp

Serves 9

Per serving
Calories 275
Protein 2 g
Carbohydrates 43 g
Total Fat 11 g
36% Calories from Fat
Cholesterol 27 mg
Fiber 3 g
Sodium 143 mg
Sugar 29 g

6	apples, peeled and sliced
1 1/2	cups rolled oats
3/4	cup packed brown sugar
1/4	cup all-purpose flour
1/4	teaspoon nutmeg
1	teaspoon cinnamon
1/4	teaspoon salt
1/2	cup (1 stick) butter or margarine

Preheat the oven to 375 degrees. Arrange the apples in a lightly greased 9×9-inch baking pan. Place the oats, brown sugar, flour, nutmeg, cinnamon and salt in a sealable plastic bag. Seal the bag and shake to mix well. Cut the butter into 1-inch pieces. Add to the oat mixture and seal the bag. Squeeze until the mixture holds together. Open the bag and crumble the mixture evenly over the apples. Bake for 40 to 45 minutes or until the topping is golden brown and the juices begin to bubble around the edges. Cool slightly before serving. Serve with whipped cream or ice cream.

Love Apple Pie

Serves 8

SIGNATURE RECIPE

1/3   cup Heinz ketchup
2   teaspoons lemon juice
6   cups sliced peeled cooking apples
1   unbaked (9-inch) pie shell
2/3   cup all-purpose flour
1/3   cup sugar
1   teaspoon cinnamon
1/3   cup butter, softened

Preheat the oven to 425 degrees. Mix the ketchup and lemon juice in a large bowl. Add the apples and toss to coat. Place in the pie shell. Mix the flour, sugar and cinnamon in a bowl. Cut in the butter until crumbly. Sprinkle over the apples. Bake for 40 to 45 minutes or until the apples are cooked through. Serve warm with ice cream, if desired.

Created some twenty-five years ago in the H. J. Heinz test kitchen, the Love Apple Pie recipe is unique. Ketchup gives the apple pie a spicy flavor and a delicate pink tint. In the mid-1800s, people called tomatoes "love apples," hence the recipe's name. H. J. Heinz Company, located in Pittsburgh, Pennsylvania, is one of the leading producers and marketers of ketchup, condiments, and sauces. Pennsylvania ranks fourth in the nation in apple production.

Per serving
Calories 188
Protein 2 g
Carbohydrates 30 g
Total Fat 8 g
36% Calories from Fat
Cholesterol 20 mg
Fiber 1 g
Sodium 166 mg
Sugar 19 g

Banana Punch

Serves 35

Per serving
Calories 71
Protein 1 g
Carbohydrates 18 g
Total Fat <1 g
1% Calories from Fat
Cholesterol 0 mg
Fiber <1 g
Sodium 7 mg
Sugar 15 g

1/4	cup lemon juice	3	cups water
1/4	cup sugar	1	(46-ounce) can
3	large bananas		unsweetened
1	(12-ounce) can		pineapple juice
	frozen orange	2	(1-liter) bottles ginger ale
	juice concentrate		or lemon-lime soda

Blend the lemon juice, sugar, bananas and frozen orange juice concentrate in a blender. Combine the water, pineapple juice and banana mixture in a large bowl and mix well. Pour 7 cups of the mixture into each of two freezer containers. Freeze until firm.

Remove from the freezer and place in the refrigerator. Chill for 1 day before serving. To serve, combine one container of the slushy mixture with 1 liter of ginger ale in a punch bowl. Ladle into punch cups. Repeat with the remaining slushy mixture and ginger ale.

Festive Cake

Serves 16

Per serving
Calories 453
Protein 5 g
Carbohydrates 57 g
Total Fat 24 g
47% Calories from Fat
Cholesterol 40 mg
Fiber 4 g
Sodium 177 mg
Sugar 36 g

3	cups whole wheat	3/4	cup honey
	pastry flour	1	teaspoon almond extract
1	teaspoon baking soda	2	cups chopped firm
1	teaspoon baking powder		ripe bananas
1	teaspoon cinnamon	1	(8-ounce) can
1	cup chopped almonds		crushed pineapple
3	eggs	1	(16-ounce) can cream
1	cup extra-virgin olive oil		cheese frosting

Preheat the oven to 300 degrees. Mix the whole wheat flour, baking soda, baking powder and cinnamon in a bowl. Stir in the almonds. Beat the eggs lightly in a mixing bowl. Add the olive oil, honey and almond extract. Add the bananas and undrained pineapple and mix well. Add the flour mixture and mix well but do not beat. Spoon into a well-oiled 10-inch tube pan. Bake for 1 hour and 15 minutes to 1 hour and 20 minutes or until the cake tests done. Remove from the oven. Let stand for 10 to 15 minutes. Invert onto a wire rack to cool completely. Spread with the frosting. Chill in the refrigerator.

Storing Honey

Store honey at room temperature, not in the refrigerator. If honey crystallizes, a naturally occurring process, place the container of honey in warm water and stir until the crystals dissolve.

Blackberry Cobbler

Serves 9 to 12

2 cups sugar
2 tablespoons all-purpose flour
2 cups fresh blackberries or
    thawed frozen blackberries
2 cups all-purpose flour
2 teaspoons sugar
1 teaspoon salt
$^3/_4$ cup plus 2 tablespoons shortening
$^3/_4$ cup water
1 medium egg
$1^1/_2$ teaspoons vinegar
$^1/_4$ cup ($^1/_2$ stick) butter,
    cut into pieces

Preheat the oven to 350 degrees. Mix 2 cups sugar and 2 tablespoons flour in a bowl. Spoon over the blackberries in a bowl and mix well. Let stand while preparing the pastry. Mix 2 cups flour, 2 teaspoons sugar and the salt in a bowl. Cut in the shortening until crumbly. Beat the water, egg and vinegar in a bowl. Add to the flour mixture and stir just until moistened. Divide the dough into two portions, one portion slightly larger than the other. Roll each portion into a rectangle on a lightly floured surface. Fit the larger rectangle into a 9×13-inch baking dish. Fill with the blackberry mixture. Top with the remaining pastry. Place dots of the butter around the outer edge of the top pastry to prevent the juices from boiling over the edges. Cut vents in the center of the top pastry to allow steam to escape. Bake for 1 hour or until the filling thickens and bubbles out the steam vents, covering with foil if needed to prevent overbrowning.

SIGNATURE RECIPE

Blackberries, one of Missouri's favorite native wild berries, ripen around July Fourth, and part of the fun of picking is eating fresh berries. While picking berries has its hardships, briers and chiggers, the victory is well worth the pain of endurance! Cobblers are so named due to their "cobbled" appearance. Cobblers created in pioneer days were prepared in a cast-iron Dutch oven with a lid holding hot coals set on top of the pan.

Per serving
Calories 395
Protein 3 g
Carbohydrates 54 g
Total Fat 19 g
44% Calories from Fat
Cholesterol 26 mg
Fiber 2 g
Sodium 227 mg
Sugar 36 g

Bubbling Blackberry Crisp

Serves 6

Per serving
Calories 191
Protein 2 g
Carbohydrates 28 g
Total Fat 8 g
39% Calories from Fat
Cholesterol 20 mg
Fiber 3 g
Sodium 58 mg
Sugar 15 g

2 cups fresh or frozen blackberries
2 tablespoons granulated sugar
1 teaspoon cornstarch
1¹/2 teaspoons water
1/2 teaspoon lemon juice
1/2 cup quick-cooking oats
1/4 cup all-purpose flour
1/4 cup packed brown sugar
1/2 teaspoon cinnamon
1/4 cup (1/2 stick) butter

Preheat the oven to 375 degrees. Place the blackberries in a greased 1-quart baking dish. Mix the granulated sugar, cornstarch, water and lemon juice in a small bowl until smooth. Pour over the blackberries. Mix the oats, flour, brown sugar and cinnamon in a bowl. Cut in the butter until crumbly. Sprinkle over the blackberries. Bake, uncovered, for 20 to 25 minutes or until the filling is bubbly.

Wild Blueberry Gingerbread

Serves 12

2 cups all-purpose flour
1/2 teaspoon ginger
1 teaspoon cinnamon
1/2 teaspoon salt
1 teaspoon baking soda
1 cup sour milk or buttermilk
1/2 cup (1 stick) margarine, softened
1 cup sugar
1 egg
3 tablespoons molasses
1 cup wild or cultivated blueberries
3 tablespoons sugar

Preheat the oven to 350 degrees. Sift the flour, ginger, cinnamon and salt together. Dissolve the baking soda in the milk. Cream the margarine and 1 cup sugar in a mixing bowl. Add the egg and mix well. Add the flour mixture and milk mixture alternately, beating well after each addition. Stir in the molasses. Fold in the blueberries gently. Do not overmix. Pour into a greased and floured 7×9-inch baking pan or an 8×8-inch baking pan. Sprinkle 3 tablespoons sugar over the top. Bake for 50 minutes or until the gingerbread tests done.

SIGNATURE RECIPE

The low-bush blueberry grown in Maine is valued for its small size and sweet taste. Maine produces more wild blueberries than any other state. Wild blueberries are harvested commercially in Maine with over seventy million pounds produced each year. Wild blueberries have a higher antioxidant capacity per serving compared to most fruits. This recipe was in one of Mildred "Brownie" Schrumpf's cookbooks. Brownie was a 1925 Home Economics graduate of the University of Maine.

Per serving
Calories 260
Protein 3 g
Carbohydrates 42 g
Total Fat 9 g
30% Calories from Fat
Cholesterol 20 mg
Fiber 1 g
Sodium 308 mg
Sugar 25 g

Per serving
Calories 410
Protein 18 g
Carbohydrates 73 g
Total Fat 5 g
10% Calories from Fat
Cholesterol 8 mg
Fiber 3 g
Sodium 636 mg
Sugar 32 g

Cherry Bread Pudding

Serves 6

Bread Pudding

1   loaf French bread, cut into
       1-inch pieces
2   cups fat-free milk
1/2   (12-ounce) can fat-free
       evaporated milk
3/4   cup no-calorie sweetener
3/4   cup egg substitute
1/4   cup sugar
1   tablespoon butter, melted
1   teaspoon vanilla extract
1/2   teaspoon cinnamon
1/4   teaspoon nutmeg

Cherry Sauce

1   (15-ounce) can water-packed pitted
       tart cherries
3   tablespoons light brown sugar
2   tablespoons cherry-flavored liqueur
       Toasted slivered almonds for garnish

Preheat the oven to 350 degrees. To prepare the bread pudding, place the bread in six 8-inch ramekins coated with nonstick cooking spray. Place the ramekins on a baking sheet. Whisk the milk, evaporated milk, sweetener, egg substitute, sugar, butter, vanilla, cinnamon and nutmeg in a bowl until blended. Pour over the bread. Let stand for 30 minutes, pressing the bread to absorb the mixture after 15 minutes. Bake for 30 to 35 minutes or just until a knife inserted in the center comes out clean. Let stand for 10 minutes.

To prepare the sauce, combine the cherries, brown sugar and liqueur in a small saucepan and mix well. Cook over medium-high heat for 16 to 18 minutes or until most of the liquid is reduced, stirring constantly. Spoon over the bread pudding. Garnish with toasted slivered almonds.

Note: Instead of ramekins, place the bread in a 7×11-inch baking dish coated with nonstick cooking spray and proceed with the recipe as directed.

Cranberry Apple Punch

Serves 25

Per serving
Calories 73
Protein <1 g
Carbohydrates 18 g
Total Fat <1 g
2% Calories from Fat
Cholesterol 0 mg
Fiber <1 g
Sodium 8 mg
Sugar 16 g

1 (46-ounce) bottle
  cranberry juice cocktail
8 cups apple juice
1¼ cups bottle tonic water
1¼ cups club soda
1 orange, sliced
1 lemon, sliced

Mix ½ cup of the cranberry juice cocktail, ½ cup of the apple juice, ¼ cup of the tonic water, ¼ cup of the club soda and some of the orange slices and lemon slices in a pitcher. Pour into a ring mold. Freeze until firm. Mix the remaining cranberry juice cocktail, apple juice, tonic water and club soda in a punch bowl. Unmold the ice ring and float in the punch. Add the remaining orange and lemon slices. Ladle into punch cups.

Note: This punch may also be served hot. Heat the juice mixture, orange slices, lemon slices and a cinnamon stick in a large stockpot on the stovetop or in a slow cooker. Serve around Thanksgiving and Christmas.

Holiday Punch

Serves 20

Per serving
Calories 77
Protein <1 g
Carbohydrates 14 g
Total Fat <1 g
1% Calories from Fat
Cholesterol 0 mg
Fiber <1 g
Sodium 1 mg
Sugar 13 g

4 cups cranberry juice cocktail
1 (6-ounce) can frozen lemonade
  concentrate
1¾ cups water
⅓ cup sugar
1 cup vodka

Combine the cranberry juice cocktail, lemonade concentrate, water, sugar and vodka in a freezer container and mix well. Freeze for 8 hours. Serve slushy.

Mulled Cider

Per serving
Calories 86
Protein 0 g
Carbohydrates 21 g
Total Fat <1 g
0% Calories from Fat
Cholesterol 0 mg
Fiber 0 g
Sodium 13 mg
Sugar 19 g

1/2 teaspoon whole allspice
1/2 teaspoon whole cloves
1   cinnamon stick
1/2 cup water
1 1/2 cups cranberry juice cocktail
4   cups apple cider

Mix the allspice, cloves, cinnamon stick, water, cranberry juice cocktail and apple cider in a 2-quart microwave-safe container. Cover with waxed paper. Microwave on High for 6 to 8 minutes or until hot. Strain to remove the spices.

Note: You may also heat the mixture in a slow cooker or in a saucepan on the stovetop.

Cranberry Salsa

Per serving
Calories 91
Protein <1 g
Carbohydrates 23 g
Total Fat <1 g
1% Calories from Fat
Cholesterol 0 mg
Fiber 3 g
Sodium 1 mg
Sugar 19 g

12   ounces fresh cranberries
1   large Granny Smith apple,
        cut into quarters
2 or 3 navel oranges, ends trimmed
1 or 2 fresh jalapeño chiles, or
        to taste, trimmed
1 to 3 sprigs of cilantro, or to taste
1/4 to 1/2 cup sugar, or to taste

Chop the cranberries, apple, oranges, jalapeño chiles and cilantro separately in a food processor. Mix the chopped ingredients in a large bowl. Stir in the sugar. Chill for 3 to 10 hours for the flavors to blend.

Keep on Hand

Stock your pantry with dried fruit such as apples, apricots, cherries, cranberries, and raisins. Add these to salads for color and flavor. Canned fruits like mandarin oranges and pineapple are great added to chicken salad. Blueberries and other fruits are welcome additions to pancakes and breads.

Cran-Apple Crisp

Serves 6

4   large apples, thinly sliced
1   (16-ounce) can whole
        cranberry sauce
2   teaspoons tub margarine, melted
1   cup rolled oats
1/3 cup packed brown sugar
1   teaspoon cinnamon

Preheat the oven to 400 degrees. Mix the apples and cranberry sauce in a bowl. Spoon into an 8×8-inch baking dish. Mix the oats, brown sugar and cinnamon in a bowl. Add the margarine and mix well. Sprinkle over the fruit. Bake, covered, for 15 minutes. Bake, uncovered, for 10 minutes longer or until the topping is crisp and brown. Serve warm or cold.

Note: Two individual packets of flavored instant oatmeal can be substituted for the oat mixture. This is a great recipe to serve for breakfast.

SIGNATURE RECIPE

Cranberries are one of three commercially grown fruits that are native to North America. The first commercial bog was planted on Cape Cod in 1816. American Indians used cranberries gathered from the wild for food, medicine, and fabric dye. Cranberries are harvested in the fall. This recipe of apples and cranberries makes a great combination of sweet and tart flavors, especially on Thanksgiving. They are both great sources of vitamin C, anti-oxidants, and fiber.

Per serving
Calories 293
Protein 2 g
Carbohydrates 70 g
Total Fat 3 g
7% Calories from Fat
Cholesterol 0 mg
Fiber 6 g
Sodium 36 mg
Sugar 46 g

Florida Key Lime Pie

Serves 6

SIGNATURE RECIPE

Florida Key limes are also called West Indian or Mexican limes. They are small, thin-skinned, and yellow-green in color. Famous as an ingredient in Key lime pie, the official Florida dessert, they also can be used the same as limes or lemons. Select limes that are fresh, not leathery or shriveled at the stem end. A brownish circle at the pointed end can indicate rot or dryness. Bottled Key lime juice is available commercially.

Per serving
Calories 741
Protein 14 g
Carbohydrates 104 g
Total Fat 30 g
36% Calories from Fat
Cholesterol 45 mg
Fiber 1 g
Sodium 401 mg
Sugar 94 g

1/4 cup (1/2 stick) margarine
1 1/4 cups graham cracker crumbs
1/3 cup sugar
1/2 cup egg substitute
      (equivalent to 4 eggs)
2 (14-ounce) cans sweetened
      condensed milk
1/2 cup Key lime juice
8 ounces whipped topping

Preheat the oven to 350 degrees. Place the margarine in a 1-quart microwave-safe bowl. Microwave on High for 1 minute. Stir in the graham cracker crumbs and sugar. Pat the crumb mixture into a 9-inch microwave-safe pie plate. Microwave on High for 1 1/2 minutes. Let stand until cool. Beat the egg substitute in a mixing bowl until frothy. Add the condensed milk and beat until blended. Stir in the lime juice. Pour into the crumb crust. Bake for 10 minutes. Cool for 10 minutes. Chill in the refrigerator. Spread the whipped topping over the pie just before serving.

Note: Low-fat sweetened condensed milk is not recommended for this recipe.

Rocky Top Orange Cake

Serves 12

Per serving
Calories 436
Protein 4 g
Carbohydrates 66 g
Total Fat 20 g
39% Calories from Fat
Cholesterol 54 mg
Fiber 1 g
Sodium 481 mg
Sugar 38 g

Cake

1 (2-layer) package yellow cake mix or
     orange cake mix
1 (11-ounce) can mandarin oranges
1/2 cup vegetable oil
3 eggs

Orange Pineapple Frosting

1 (6-ounce) package vanilla instant
     pudding mix
8 ounces whipped topping
1 (28-ounce) can crushed pineapple
2 teaspoons orange zest

Preheat the oven to 350 degrees. To prepare the cake, combine the cake mix, undrained mandarin oranges, oil and eggs in a mixing bowl and mix well. Spoon into two greased 9-inch cake pans. Bake for 35 minutes or until the layers test done. Cool in the pans for 10 minutes. Invert onto wire racks to cool completely.

To prepare the frosting, combine the pudding mix, whipped topping, undrained pineapple and orange zest in a bowl and mix well.

To assemble, cut the cooled cake layers horizontally into halves. Spread between the layers and over the top and side of the cake. Chill until serving time.

Note: Orange food coloring may be added for a Big Orange look.

Orange Cranberry Delight

Serves 32

Per serving
Calories 54
Protein 1 g
Carbohydrates 5 g
Total Fat 4 g
61% Calories from Fat
Cholesterol 8 mg
Fiber <1 g
Sodium 22 mg
Sugar 4 g

1   cup cream cheese, softened
1/4   cup orange juice concentrate
1/2   cup pecans, chopped
1/2   cup dried cranberries, chopped
1/3   cup sugar or Splenda

Beat the cream cheese in a mixing bowl until fluffy. Add the orange juice concentrate. Stir in the pecans, cranberries and sugar. Chill, covered, for 8 to 10 hours. Serve with crackers or Cranberry Nut Bread (page 61).

Fresh Peach Crumble

Serves 4

Per serving
Calories 67
Protein 1 g
Carbohydrates 14 g
Total Fat 1 g
18% Calories from Fat
Cholesterol 0 mg
Fiber 2 g
Sodium 43 mg
Sugar 9 g

2 1/2 cups sliced fresh or frozen peaches
1/4   cup graham cracker crumbs
1/3   teaspoon cinnamon
1/4   teaspoon nutmeg
2   teaspoons reduced-calorie
       margarine, melted

Preheat the oven to 350 degrees. Layer the peaches in an 8-inch baking pan sprayed with nonstick cooking spray. Mix the graham cracker crumbs, cinnamon, nutmeg and margarine in a bowl. Sprinkle over the peaches. Bake for 45 minutes.

Peach Crumble

Serves 3

3 large sheets graham crackers
2 teaspoons sugar
1 tablespoon margarine, melted
1 (15-ounce) can sliced peaches or
    peach chunks, drained
1 1/2 cups plain nonfat yogurt

Place the graham crackers in a sealable plastic bag or between two pieces of foil. Crumble the graham crackers using the unopened can of peaches or a rolling pin. Combine the graham cracker crumbs, sugar and margarine in a bowl and mix well. Heat the peaches in a saucepan for 1 to 2 minutes or until warm. Spoon 1/2 cup yogurt into each of three 1-cup dessert bowls. Spoon the warm peaches over the yogurt. Top with the graham cracker mixture and serve.

SIGNATURE RECIPE

Nothing is more refreshing than a Georgia peach on a hot sunny day! Georgia became known as the Peach State when this delicious treat became the official state fruit in 1995. Over forty different varieties are grown statewide, and each year Georgia produces over one hundred thirty million pounds. An excellent source of fiber, peaches are packed with nutrition including vitamins A and C and potassium. A medium-size peach contains thirty-eight calories, which makes them a perfect snack.

Per serving
Calories 264
Protein 7 g
Carbohydrates 47 g
Total Fat 5 g
18% Calories from Fat
Cholesterol 3 mg
Fiber 2 g
Sodium 232 mg
Sugar 39 g

Spiced Pear Salad

Serves 4

Per serving
Calories 197
Protein 2 g
Carbohydrates 37 g
Total Fat 5 g
23% Calories from Fat
Cholesterol 8 mg
Fiber 2 g
Sodium 55 mg
Sugar 27 g

1	(15-ounce) can pear halves	1/16	teaspoon nutmeg
1/4	cup packed brown sugar	1/16	teaspoon ground cloves
2	tablespoons sherry	2	ounces reduced-fat cream cheese
1 1/2	teaspoons apple cider vinegar	2	tablespoons chopped pecans
1/16	teaspoon cinnamon	4	small lettuce leaves

Drain the pear halves, reserving 1 tablespoon of the juice. Mix the brown sugar, sherry, reserved juice, vinegar, cinnamon, nutmeg and cloves in a 1-quart microwave-safe dish. Microwave on High for 1 to 2 minutes or until boiling, stirring after half the time. Add the pear halves, stirring to coat. Microwave on High for 1 to 2 minutes or until heated through. Chill in the refrigerator.

To serve, cut the cream cheese into four pieces. Shape the cream cheese into four balls and roll in the pecans. Place each pear half on a lettuce leaf on a serving plate. Spoon the sauce over the pear half. Place the cheese ball in the hollow of each pear half.

Note: The pears and sauce may be made one to two days in advance. Assemble the salad just before serving.

Pear Walnut Salad

Serves 8 to 12

Per serving
Calories 218
Protein 2 g
Carbohydrates 28 g
Total Fat 12 g
47% Calories from Fat
Cholesterol 2 mg
Fiber 4 g
Sodium 281 mg
Sugar 21 g

1	(5-ounce) package lettuce greens	2	red apples, sliced
1	(5-ounce) package mixed salad greens	1	small red onion, sliced
		1/4	cup crumbled blue cheese
3	pears, peeled and sliced	1/2	cup toasted walnuts
2	Granny Smith apples, sliced	1	(16-ounce) bottle raspberry vinaigrette salad dressing

Rinse the lettuce greens and salad greens and pat dry. Tear into bite-size pieces. Combine with the pears, Granny Smith apples, red apples, onion, cheese and walnuts in a bowl and toss to mix. Chill, covered, until serving time. Pour the salad dressing over the salad and toss lightly. Serve immediately.

Note: You may add fresh raspberries or blueberries if in season. Cooked chicken may be added also.

Piña Colada Slush

Serves 12

1   (18-ounce) can unsweetened
        pineapple juice
2   cups water
1   (10-ounce) can frozen nonalcoholic
        piña colada mix
1   tablespoon lime juice
1   envelope Crystal light
6   cups lemon-lime soda, chilled

Combine the pineapple juice, water, piña colada mix, lime juice
and Crystal light in a pitcher and stir until dissolved. Pour into a 2-quart
freezer container. Freeze for 6 to 10 hours. Remove from the freezer
45 minutes before serving. To serve, mix 1/2 cup slush and 1/2 cup soda
for each serving.

Per serving
Calories 106
Protein <1 g
Carbohydrates 26 g
Total Fat <1 g
1% Calories from Fat
Cholesterol 0 mg
Fiber <1 g
Sodium 36 mg
Sugar 23 g

Pineapple Cookies

Makes 5 to 6 dozen

2/3   cup butter, softened
1 2/3   cups sugar
2   eggs
1/2   cup crushed pineapple
2 2/3   cups self-rising flour
2   teaspoons lemon extract

Preheat the oven to 350 degrees. Beat the butter and sugar in a
mixing bowl until light and fluffy. Add the eggs one at a time, beating
well after each addition. Add the undrained crushed pineapple,
flour and lemon extract and mix well. Drop by teaspoonfuls onto a
greased cookie sheet. Bake for 12 to 15 minutes or until light brown.
Remove from the oven and let stand for 5 seconds. Remove to
a wire rack to cool completely.

Per serving
Calories 53
Protein 1 g
Carbohydrates 8 g
Total Fat 2 g
32% Calories from Fat
Cholesterol 10 mg
Fiber <1 g
Sodium 73 mg
Sugar 5 g

Per serving
Calories 512
Protein 5 g
Carbohydrates 72 g
Total Fat 24 g
41% Calories from Fat
Cholesterol 74 mg
Fiber 3 g
Sodium 407 mg
Sugar 47 g

Raspberry Cake with Butter Sauce

Serves 9

Cake

2 cups all-purpose flour
1 tablespoon baking powder
1/2 teaspoon salt
2 tablespoons butter, softened
1 teaspoon vanilla extract
1 cup sugar
1 1/4 cups milk
2 cups raspberries

Butter Sauce

1/2 cup (1 stick) butter
1 cup heavy whipping cream or
     evaporated milk
1 teaspoon vanilla extract
1 cup sugar

Preheat the oven to 350 degrees. To prepare the cake, mix the flour, baking powder and salt in a bowl. Cream the butter, vanilla and sugar in a mixing bowl until light and fluffy. Add the milk alternately with the flour mixture, beating after each addition. Pour one-half of the batter into a greased 9×9-inch cake pan. Place the raspberries on top of the batter. Pour the remaining batter over the raspberries. Bake for 35 minutes or until a wooden pick inserted near the center comes out clean.

To prepare the sauce, combine the butter, whipping cream, vanilla and sugar in a saucepan. Simmer for 5 minutes. Serve warm over the cake.

Note: Blackberries, black raspberries, marionberries, boysenberries, loganberries, blueberries, or cranberries may be substituted for the raspberries.

Raspberry-Rhubarb Slump

Serves 8

★

WASHINGTON

SIGNATURE RECIPE

4 cups whole fresh raspberries
4 cups sliced rhubarb
1/2 to 3/4 cup sugar
1/4 cup water
2 tablespoons apple juice
1 tablespoon cornstarch
1 cup all-purpose flour
1/4 cup sugar
1 teaspoon baking powder
1/4 teaspoon baking soda
1/4 teaspoon salt
1/4 cup (1/2 stick) cold butter
1/2 cup buttermilk
1/2 teaspoon almond extract
    Coarse sugar for sprinkling
      (optional)

In 2008, Washington grew over fifty-three million pounds of raspberries, which thrive in the relatively cool, marine climate west of the Cascades. The Crimson Red variety of rhubarb is grown commercially. The arid and semi-arid land east of the Cascade Mountains is home to vineyards and vast orchards producing pears, peaches, cherries, apricots, and apples, the state's largest crop. More than half of all apples grown in the United States for fresh eating come from Washington.

Preheat the oven to 400 degrees. Combine the raspberries, rhubarb, 1/2 cup sugar and the water in a large skillet. Bring to a boil; reduce the heat. Simmer, covered, for 10 minutes. Add a mixture of the apple juice and cornstarch to the fruit mixture. Cook until thickened and bubbly, stirring constantly. Spoon into a 2 1/2-quart square baking dish and keep warm.

Mix the flour, 1/4 cup sugar, the baking powder, baking soda and salt in a bowl. Cut in the butter until the mixture resembles coarse crumbs. Blend the buttermilk and almond extract together. Add to the flour mixture, stirring until moistened. Drop by spoonfuls onto the hot fruit, forming eight mounds. Sprinkle with coarse sugar. Bake for 20 minutes or until golden brown.

Per serving
Calories 255
Protein 3 g
Carbohydrates 51 g
Total Fat 6 g
21% Calories from Fat
Cholesterol 16 mg
Fiber 6 g
Sodium 233 mg
Sugar 27 g

Per serving
Calories 290
Protein 2 g
Carbohydrates 66 g
Total Fat 2 g
5% Calories from Fat
Cholesterol 8 mg
Fiber 1 g
Sodium 56 mg
Sugar 57 g

Raspberry Sizzle

Serves 2

1¹/₂ cups raspberry juice or
      cran-raspberry juice
1¹/₂ cups raspberry sherbet
¹/₂ cup sparkling water
¹/₂ cup frozen raspberries

Process the raspberry juice, sherbet, sparkling water and raspberries in a blender until smooth. Serve chilled.

Per serving
Calories 21
Protein <1 g
Carbohydrates 3 g
Total Fat 1 g
40% Calories from Fat
Cholesterol 0 mg
Fiber 1 g
Sodium 1 mg
Sugar 2 g

Strawberry Salsa

Serves 15

1 pint fresh strawberries,
      coarsely chopped
¹/₂ cup chopped onion
1 tablespoon finely chopped
      jalapeño chiles
4 Roma tomatoes, seeded
      and chopped
    Juice of 1 lime
1 tablespoon olive oil
1 tablespoon chopped fresh mint
      or cilantro

Combine the strawberries, onion, jalapeño chiles, tomatoes, lime juice, olive oil and mint in a bowl and mix well. Chill, covered, for 2 hours. Serve over grilled fish or chicken.

Roasted Strawberry and Tomato Soup

Serves 4

Per serving
Calories 216
Protein 2 g
Carbohydrates 23 g
Total Fat 14 g
56% Calories from Fat
Cholesterol 0 mg
Fiber 4 g
Sodium 54 mg
Sugar 18 g

2	pints fresh strawberries, stems removed	1/4	cup olive oil
1	pint cherry tomatoes	1	cup bottled strawberry daiquiri mix
1/4	cup chopped fresh fennel		Salt and pepper to taste

Preheat the oven to 350 degrees. Toss the strawberries, tomatoes, fennel and olive oil in a bowl until coated. Spread in a single layer on a baking sheet. Roast for 15 minutes. Process the roasted strawberry mixture in a blender or food processor until puréed. Add the daiquiri mix and process until blended. Strain the soup through a fine mesh strainer into a bowl. Sprinkle with salt and pepper. Chill until serving time. Ladle into individual soup bowls.

Frozen Strawberry Salad

Serves 15

Per serving
Calories 136
Protein 2 g
Carbohydrates 17 g
Total Fat 6 g
40% Calories from Fat
Cholesterol 8 mg
Fiber 2 g
Sodium 57 mg
Sugar 13 g

3/4	cup confectioners' sugar	4	bananas, chopped
8	ounces low-fat cream cheese, softened	1/2	cup chopped pecans
1	(16-ounce) package frozen sliced strawberries, thawed	8	ounces fat-free whipped topping
1	(8-ounce) can crushed pineapple, drained		Sliced fresh strawberries for garnish

Cream the confectioners' sugar and cream cheese in a bowl until fluffy. Add the undrained strawberries, pineapple, bananas and pecans and mix well. Fold in the whipped topping. Pour into a 9×13-inch pan and freeze until firm. Thaw for 10 minutes before serving. Garnish with fresh strawberry slices.

Strawberry Pie

Per serving
Calories 417
Protein 3 g
Carbohydrates 68 g
Total Fat 16 g
33% Calories from Fat
Cholesterol 0 mg
Fiber 3 g
Sodium 193 mg
Sugar 46 g

1   cup all-purpose flour
1/2 cup (1 stick) margarine, softened
3 1/2 tablespoons confectioners' sugar
3   tablespoons cornstarch
1   cup granulated sugar
1   cup water
1 or 2 drops of red food coloring
1   tablespoon lemon juice
3   tablespoons strawberry gelatin
1   quart strawberries

Preheat the oven to 450 degrees. Combine the flour, margarine and confectioners' sugar in a bowl and mix well. Pat over the bottom and up the side of a 9-inch pie plate. Bake until brown. Cool on a wire rack. Cook the cornstarch, granulated sugar and water in a saucepan over low heat until thick, stirring constantly. Remove from the heat. Stir in the food coloring, lemon juice and gelatin. Stir in the strawberries. Pour into the pie shell. Chill until set.

Note: You may top the pie with whipped topping, if desired.

Strawberry Shortcake

Serves 9

Per serving
Calories 377
Protein 5 g
Carbohydrates 45 g
Total Fat 20 g
48% Calories from Fat
Cholesterol 37 mg
Fiber 2 g
Sodium 429 mg
Sugar 21 g

1/2 cup (1 stick) margarine
2 cups all-purpose flour
2/3 cup sugar
1 tablespoon baking powder
1/2 teaspoon salt
2/3 cup skim milk
1 tablespoon sugar

3 to 4 cups lightly sugared sliced fresh strawberries
1 cup whipped cream or whipped topping
Sprigs of fresh mint for garnish

Preheat the oven to 450 degrees. Melt the margarine in a 9×9-inch cake pan in the preheated oven. Mix the flour, 2/3 cup sugar, the baking powder and salt in a bowl. Add the melted margarine and stir to form coarse crumbs. Add the milk all at once and stir just until moistened. Do not overmix. The batter will be thick and will not be smooth. Spoon into the cake pan, spreading the batter evenly to the edges of the pan. Sprinkle 1 tablespoon sugar evenly over the top of the batter. Bake for 15 to 18 minutes or until golden brown. Let cool for 15 minutes. Remove from the pan to a wire rack to cool completely.

Cut the cake into 3-inch squares. Cut the squares horizontally into halves and place on a serving plate. Spoon one-half of the strawberries over the bottom halves. Replace the top halves and spoon the remaining strawberries over the top. Top each with a dollop of whipped cream. Garnish with a sprig of mint.

Recipe Collections

Write in your cookbooks! Don't hesitate to make notes about the recipe when you prepare it or if it is someone's favorite. It makes the book priceless to other family members.

Hot Citrus Drink

Serves 16

Per serving
Calories 170
Protein 1 g
Carbohydrates 43 g
Total Fat <1 g
0% Calories from Fat
Cholesterol 0 mg
Fiber <1 g
Sodium 1 mg
Sugar 43 g

1 (12-ounce) can frozen lemonade concentrate, thawed
1 (12-ounce) can frozen orange juice concentrate, thawed

2 teaspoons vanilla extract
2 teaspoons almond extract
2 cups sugar
10 concentrate cans water

Blend the lemonade concentrate, orange juice concentrate, vanilla, almond extract, sugar and water in a large stockpot. Cook until heated through. Ladle into serving cups.

Jersey Tomato Peach Salsa

Serves 12

SIGNATURE RECIPE

New Jersey, The Garden State, is known for its tomatoes, peaches, and other Jersey Fresh™ produce. New Jersey has been breeding and growing tomatoes since the 1920s and is famous for the Rutgers and Ramapo tomato varieties. New Jersey's excellent growing conditions for peaches result in beautiful color and great taste. This recipe combines these fresh flavors for a yummy salsa—perfect for grilled fish or chicken, or enjoyed with crudités or chips.

2	cups chopped tomatoes
1	cup chopped peeled peaches
1/2	cup chopped yellow, red or green bell pepper
3	tablespoons minced seeded fresh jalapeño chiles
1/2	cup minced red onion
1/4	cup chopped cilantro
1/4	teaspoon salt
3	tablespoons balsamic vinegar

Combine the tomatoes, peaches, bell pepper, jalapeño chiles, onion, cilantro, salt and vinegar in a nonmetallic bowl and mix well. Chill, covered, for 1 hour or longer for the flavors to blend. Serve with fresh vegetables or baked chips, or use as an accompaniment to grilled fish or chicken.

Per serving
Calories 19
Protein 1 g
Carbohydrates 4 g
Total Fat <1 g
6% Calories from Fat
Cholesterol 0 mg
Fiber 1 g
Sodium 51 mg
Sugar 3 g

Fruit Salsa

Serves 4

1 cup chopped cantaloupe
1 cup chopped watermelon
3 tomatoes, seeded and chopped
1/2 cup chopped red onion
1 jalapeño chile, minced
2 small limes
1 teaspoon salt
1/4 teaspoon pepper

Per serving
Calories 61
Protein 2 g
Carbohydrates 14 g
Total Fat <1 g
6% Calories from Fat
Cholesterol 0 mg
Fiber 3 g
Sodium 596 mg
Sugar 10 g

Combine the cantaloupe, watermelon, tomatoes, onion and jalapeño chile in a medium bowl. Squeeze the juice from the limes over the top of the mixture. Add the salt and pepper. Toss lightly to mix together. Serve with tortilla chips.

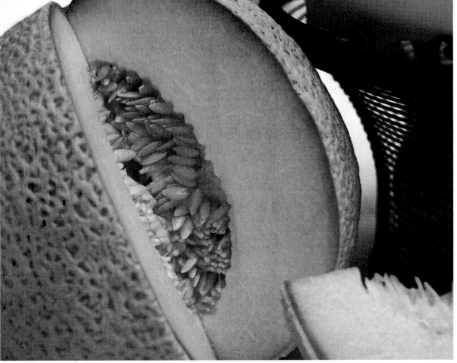

Fruit Soup

Per serving
Calories 106
Protein 1 g
Carbohydrates 27 g
Total Fat <1 g
3% Calories from Fat
Cholesterol 0 mg
Fiber 3 g
Sodium 3 mg
Sugar 19 g

3   tablespoons tapioca
1/2   cup sugar (optional)
1/16 teaspoon salt
1   cup cold water
1   (6-ounce) can frozen orange
          juice concentrate
1 1/2 cups water
1   (11-ounce) can mandarin
          oranges, drained
1   (8-ounce) package sliced strawberries
2   bananas, sliced
2   cups chopped drained peaches
2   apples, chopped

Mix the tapioca, sugar, salt and 1 cup cold water in a saucepan. Let stand for 5 minutes. Cook for 6 to 8 minutes or until clear, stirring frequently. Stir in the orange juice concentrate, 1 1/2 cups water, the mandarin oranges, strawberries, bananas, peaches and apples. Chill until serving time. Serve cold.

Note: You may serve topped with sherbet.

Heavenly Healthful Ambrosia

Serves 4

Per serving
Calories 240
Protein 7 g
Carbohydrates 39 g
Total Fat 9 g
30% Calories from Fat
Cholesterol 3 mg
Fiber 4 g
Sodium 94 mg
Sugar 23 g

1   cup vanilla low-fat or nonfat yogurt
1/2   cup reduced-calorie whipped topping
1/4   cup shredded coconut
1   cup pineapple chunks
1   cup orange sections
1   cup red seedless grapes or
          green seedless grapes
1/2   cup wheat germ
      Additional fruit for garnish

Combine the yogurt, whipped topping, coconut, pineapple chunks, orange sections and grapes in a bowl and mix well. Fold in 1/4 cup of the wheat germ. Sprinkle with the remaining wheat germ. Garnish with additional fruit. Serve immediately.

Note: To serve as a parfait, layer the fruit, yogurt, whipped topping and coconut in parfait glasses. Sprinkle with the wheat germ. Garnish with additional fruit.

Summer Fruit Salad

Serves 12

Per serving
Calories 93
Protein 1 g
Carbohydrates 20 g
Total Fat 1 g
13% Calories from Fat
Cholesterol 4 mg
Fiber 2 g
Sodium 89 mg
Sugar 14 g

1/2	cup blueberries
1	pear, chopped
1	peach, peeled and chopped
1	apple, chopped
1	cup sliced fresh strawberries
1 1/2	cups seedless grapes
1	teaspoon lemon juice
4	ounces low-fat strawberry cream cheese spread
1/4	cup packed light brown sugar
1	teaspoon vanilla extract
1/4	teaspoon cinnamon
1	cup broken pretzels

Combine the blueberries, pear, peach, apple, strawberries and grapes in a large bowl. Add the lemon juice and toss to mix. Beat the cream cheese spread, brown sugar, vanilla and cinnamon in a bowl until smooth. Fold into the fruit. Stir in the pretzels gently. Serve immediately or chill until serving time.

Chilling Injury

Sometimes refrigeration may actually cause injury to the flesh or rinds of some fruits and vegetables. This is known as a chilling injury. The chilling injury can cause surface lesions, internal discoloration, water-soaking of the tissue, and failure of a fruit or vegetable to ripen normally.

Curried Fruit

Serves 8

Per serving
Calories 311
Protein 1 g
Carbohydrates 64 g
Total Fat 8 g
22% Calories from Fat
Cholesterol 20 mg
Fiber 4 g
Sodium 72 mg
Sugar 58 g

1	(29-ounce) can pear halves, drained
1	(29-ounce) can peach halves, drained
1	(20-ounce) can pineapple chunks, drained
8	maraschino cherries
1/3	cup butter
3/4	cup packed brown sugar
4	teaspoons curry powder

Preheat the oven to 325 degrees. Place the fruit in a 9×13-inch baking dish. Melt the butter in a small saucepan. Add the brown sugar and curry powder and mix well. Pour over the fruit. Bake, uncovered, for 1 hour.

Note: This is a great side dish for ham or turkey.

Fruit Salad

Per serving
Calories 132
Protein 2 g
Carbohydrates 32 g
Total Fat 1 g
5% Calories from Fat
Cholesterol 21 mg
Fiber 2 g
Sodium 13 mg
Sugar 25 g

1   (20-ounce) can juice-packed
       pineapple chunks
2   large apples, chopped
1   cup marshmallows
2   bananas, sliced
1   cup seedless grapes
1/4 cup sugar
2   tablespoons all-purpose flour
1   egg

Drain the pineapple, reserving the liquid. Add enough water to the reserved liquid to measure 1 cup. Combine the apples, marshmallows, bananas, pineapple chunks and grapes in a large bowl. Mix the sugar, flour, reserved pineapple liquid and egg in a small saucepan. Cook over medium heat until thickened, stirring constantly. Pour over the fruit mixture and toss to coat. Chill for 2 hours or longer before serving.

Fruit Pizza

Serves 10

Per serving
Calories 396
Protein 4 g
Carbohydrates 54 g
Total Fat 19 g
43% Calories from Fat
Cholesterol 71 mg
Fiber 1 g
Sodium 213 mg
Sugar 39 g

1 1/4	cups sifted all-purpose flour
1/4	teaspoon baking powder
1/4	teaspoon salt
1/2	cup (1 stick) butter, softened
3/4	cup sugar
1	tablespoon milk
1	egg
1	teaspoon vanilla extract
8	ounces cream cheese, softened
2/3	cup sugar
1	banana, sliced
1	apple, chopped
1/2	cup seedless green grapes, cut into halves
1	(11-ounce) can mandarin oranges, drained
1	cup whipped topping

Preheat the oven to 425 degrees. Sift the flour with the baking powder and salt into a bowl. Beat the butter in a mixing bowl until creamy. Add 3/4 cup sugar gradually, beating constantly. Add the milk, egg and vanilla and beat well. Stir in the flour mixture to form a soft dough. Reserve enough dough to make seven cookies later so the pizza crust will not be too thick. Pat the remaining dough into a circle on a lightly oiled baking sheet. Bake for 5 to 7 minutes or until light brown. Do not overbake. Cool on a wire rack.

Beat the cream cheese and 2/3 cup sugar in a mixing bowl until light and fluffy. Spread over the cooled crust. Chill for 24 hours, if desired, to enhance the flavor.

Combine the banana, apple, grapes and mandarin oranges in a bowl and mix well. Fold in the whipped topping. Spread over the cream cheese mixture. Chill before serving.

Note: You may add 1/2 cup maraschino cherries to the fruit mixture.

Hot Gingered Fruit

Serves 12

Per serving
Calories 205
Protein 1 g
Carbohydrates 36 g
Total Fat 8 g
32% Calories from Fat
Cholesterol 20 mg
Fiber 2 g
Sodium 63 mg
Sugar 34 g

1   (14-ounce) can large pineapple slices
1   (14-ounce) can large
       peach halves, drained
1   (14-ounce) can large
       apricot halves, drained
1   (14-ounce) can large
       pear halves, drained
10   large maraschino cherries
1/2   cup (1 stick) butter
1/2   teaspoon ginger
3/4   cup packed light brown sugar

Preheat the oven to 325 degrees. Drain the pineapple, reserving
2 tablespoons of the syrup. Pat the pineapple, peaches, apricots, pears
and maraschino cherries dry with paper towels. Arrange the fruit in a
2-quart baking dish, placing the maraschino cherries on top. Melt the
butter with the ginger in a small saucepan. Stir in the reserved pineapple
syrup and the brown sugar. Cook for a few minutes or until the brown
sugar melts, stirring frequently. Pour over the fruit. Bake for 40 minutes
or until the fruit is hot and light brown.

Frozen Fruit Mix

Serves 24

Per serving
Calories 166
Protein 1 g
Carbohydrates 42 g
Total Fat <1 g
1% Calories from Fat
Cholesterol 0 mg
Fiber 2 g
Sodium 1 mg
Sugar 35 g

2³/4   cups sugar or sugar substitute
        such as Splenda
3   cups water
1   (12-ounce) can frozen orange juice
        concentrate, thawed
10   bananas, sliced
1   quart fresh strawberries, sliced
1   (20-ounce) can crushed pineapple

Bring the sugar and water to a boil in a saucepan. Remove from the heat and let stand until cool. Add the orange juice concentrate and mix well. Stir in the bananas, strawberries and pineapple. Spoon into a large freezer container. Freeze until firm. Remove from the freezer to partially thaw before serving.

Note: The fruit mixture may be frozen in smaller amounts, if desired. You may use frozen strawberries instead of the fresh strawberries.

Poppy Seed Dressing

Serves 16

Per serving
Calories 160
Protein <1 g
Carbohydrates 10 g
Total Fat 14 g
76% Calories from Fat
Cholesterol 0 mg
Fiber <1 g
Sodium 73 mg
Sugar 10 g

³/4   cup sugar
1   teaspoon dry mustard
¹/2   teaspoon salt
1   teaspoon garlic powder
¹/3   cup half red wine vinegar and
        half white vinegar
1   cup vegetable oil
1   teaspoon poppy seeds

Mix the sugar, dry mustard, salt, garlic powder and vinegar in a mixing bowl. Add the oil gradually, beating constantly with an electric mixer. Continue to beat until thick. Stir in the poppy seeds. Store in the refrigerator.

Note: Delicious with a salad of mandarin oranges or fresh strawberries, spinach, water chestnuts, almonds, and red onions.

Sweets

Tempering Chocolate

To make chocolate suitable for dipping without the use of paraffin, it should be tempered so it will stay glossy and firm at room temperature. Begin by melting 2/3 of your chocolate to 118 degrees so it melts but does not separate. Transfer the chocolate to a second bowl. Gradually add the remaining chocolate, some of it in large lumps, to the melted chocolate. By adding this new "tempered chocolate," the warm chocolate will cool and form the desired crystals needed for decorating and coating. Continue stirring in the pieces until it reaches a temperature of 88 degrees. Remove any remaining chocolate lumps and reuse to temper another batch of chocolate. At this point, the chocolate is ready to use. Do not allow the chocolate to cool to 77 degrees or the tempering process will need to be repeated.

Perfect Piecrust

4 cups all-purpose flour
1 tablespoon sugar
2 teaspoons salt
1 3/4 cups shortening
1 egg
1/2 cup water
1 tablespoon vinegar

Mix the flour, sugar and salt in a bowl. Cut the shortening into the flour mixture until it is the size of peas (use a pastry blender or fork). Beat the egg, water and vinegar in a bowl. Pour over the flour mixture and gently blend together just until moistened. Cover and place in the refrigerator for 30 minutes. Makes 5 balls of dough.

Wrap each in plastic wrap and place in a sealable container.

Because of the vinegar in this recipe, this dough will keep in the refrigerator for 2 weeks. Take out as needed.

COOKING WITH SWEETENERS

1. Sugar substitutes cannot contribute to the volume, tenderness, moistness, or browning factor in baked desserts.

2. Replacing a small amount of the required sugar with artificial sweeteners will improve the nutritional quality of your baked products without sacrificing the overall quality.

3. When adapting recipes for diabetics, the number of teaspoons of sugar should not exceed the number of servings. Make up the difference in the recipe requirement for sugar with sweetener.

4. Recipes that rely on sugar only for sweetness are better suited for artificial sweeteners, such as beverages, frozen desserts, gelatins, and puddings.

Kuchen

Serves 48

Per serving
Calories 192
Protein 4 g
Carbohydrates 35 g
Total Fat 5 g
22% Calories from Fat
Cholesterol 23 mg
Fiber 2 g
Sodium 65 mg
Sugar 16 g

1	envelope dry yeast
1	tablespoon sugar
1/4	cup lukewarm water
2	cups warm milk
2	eggs
1/2	cup shortening
6 to 8	cups all-purpose flour
1/2	cup sugar
1	teaspoon salt
32	apples, peeled and sliced
2	cups sweet cream or sour cream
2	eggs, beaten
1/2	cup sugar
2	tablespoons all-purpose flour
1/2	teaspoon vanilla extract
	Cinnamon to taste

Preheat the oven to 350 degrees. Dissolve the yeast and 1 tablespoon sugar in the lukewarm water in a bowl. Beat the milk and 2 eggs in a bowl. Add the shortening and beat well. Stir in the yeast mixture. Mix 6 cups of the flour, 1/2 cup sugar and the salt in a large bowl. Add the yeast mixture and mix well. Knead on a lightly floured surface until smooth and elastic, sprinkling with the remaining 2 cups flour a small amount at a time. Place in a greased bowl, turning to coat the surface. Let rise in a warm place until doubled in bulk. Divide the dough into eight equal portions. Roll each portion into a circle. Fit each into an 8-inch pie plate. Let rise for 20 minutes. Spoon the apples over the dough. Combine the cream, 2 eggs, 1/2 cup sugar, 2 tablespoons flour and the vanilla in a bowl and mix well. Spoon over the apples. Sprinkle with cinnamon. Bake for 20 to 25 minutes or until brown.

Note: Peaches, raisins or prunes may be used with or as a replacement for the apples in this recipe.

Sugar on Snow

Serves 16

1   quart grade A 100% pure
       maple syrup
4   pounds crushed or chipped ice

Heat the maple syrup in a 4-quart heavy saucepan to 233 degrees on a candy thermometer, thread stage. Do not stir. Immediately pour or drizzle the syrup over the crushed ice in a bowl to form a thin coating. A soft taffy will form. The easiest way to eat it is to wind it up with a fork and enjoy.

Note: Sugar on Snow is traditionally served with raised doughnuts, sour dill pickles, and coffee. The pickles and coffee serve to counter the intense sweetness of the candy.

SIGNATURE RECIPE

Introduced to early settlers by Native Americans, Maple Sugaring and Sugar on Snow parties have been a spring tradition in Vermont for centuries. Vermont is the largest producer of maple syrup in the United States. The climate is ideal for growing sugar maple trees and for good sap flow. Forty years are required to grow a maple tree large enough to tap, and it takes forty gallons of sap to make one gallon of syrup.

Per serving
Calories 209
Protein 0 g
Carbohydrates 54 g
Total Fat <1 g
1% Calories from Fat
Cholesterol 0 mg
Fiber 0 g
Sodium 7 mg
Sugar 48 g

Summer Dessert

Per serving
Calories 204
Protein 8 g
Carbohydrates 20 g
Total Fat 10 g
44% Calories from Fat
Cholesterol 32 mg
Fiber 1 g
Sodium 195 mg
Sugar 14 g

2	egg whites
1/4	cup (scant) superfine sugar
1	teaspoon cornstarch
1	teaspoon vanilla extract
1	teaspoon vinegar
1 1/3	cups low-fat cream cheese, softened
2/3	cup plain low-fat yogurt
1/2 to 1	teaspoon vanilla extract, or to taste
10 1/2	ounces fresh or frozen mixed fresh berries, thawed

Preheat the oven to 250 degrees. Whisk the egg whites in a grease-free mixing bowl until soft peaks form. Whisk in the sugar a spoonful at a time until stiff peaks form. Stir in the cornstarch, 1 teaspoon vanilla and the vinegar. Spoon onto a baking sheet lined with baking parchment. Shape into a 6-inch circle, forming a well in the center. Bake for 1 1/2 to 2 hours or until crisp. Turn off the oven and let cool in the oven. Remove from the oven. Let stand until cold before removing from the baking sheet to avoid breakage. Store in an airtight container until serving time.

Beat the cream cheese and yogurt in a mixing bowl until smooth. Stir in 1/2 to 1 teaspoon vanilla. Cut the berries into bite-size pieces if needed. Mound the cream cheese mixture into the meringue shell and top with the berries. Cut into six slices or serve whole and let your guests serve themselves.

Sopaipilla Cheesecake

Serves 12

Per serving
Calories 591
Protein 8 g
Carbohydrates 64 g
Total Fat 34 g
52% Calories from Fat
Cholesterol 41 mg
Fiber 1 g
Sodium 790 mg
Sugar 32 g

2	(8-count) cans refrigerator crescent roll dough	1	cup sugar
8	ounces cream cheese, softened	1/2	cup (1 stick) butter, softened
1	teaspoon vanilla extract	1/2	cup sugar
		2	teaspoons cinnamon

Preheat the oven to 350 degrees. Unroll one can of the crescent roll dough, pressing the perforations to seal. Place in a 9×13-inch baking pan. Beat the cream cheese, vanilla and 1 cup sugar in a mixing bowl until smooth. Spread over the crescent roll dough. Unroll the remaining can of crescent roll dough, pressing the perforations to seal. Place on top of the cream cheese mixture. Mix the butter and 1/2 cup sugar in a bowl. Spread over the top. Sprinkle with the cinnamon. Bake for 30 minutes.

Chocolate Chip Pie with Raspberry Lime Cream

Serves 6

Per serving
Calories 835
Protein 8 g
Carbohydrates 84 g
Total Fat 54 g
57% Calories from Fat
Cholesterol 152 mg
Fiber 3 g
Sodium 392 mg
Sugar 54 g

1	cup Splenda no-calorie sweetener	1/2	cup (3 ounces) chocolate chips
1	cup packed brown sugar	1	unbaked (8-inch) pie shell
1	cup all-purpose flour		
2	eggs, lightly beaten	1/4	cup raspberry preserves
1	teaspoon vanilla extract	1	teaspoon lime juice
1	cup (2 sticks) butter, melted	1	cup whipped topping
1/2	cup pecans, coarsely chopped		

Preheat the oven to 325 degrees. Mix the sweetener, brown sugar and flour in a large bowl. Stir in the eggs, vanilla and butter. Fold in the pecans and chocolate chips. Spoon into the pie shell. Bake for 60 to 70 minutes or until a knife inserted in the center comes out clean. Place the raspberry preserves in a microwave-safe bowl. Microwave on High for 15 seconds. Stir in the lime juice. Fold in the whipped topping. Cut the pie into slices. Top with the raspberry mixture.

Note: Mint chocolate chips or white chocolate chips can be used in this recipe.

Sugar Cream Pie

Serves 8

SIGNATURE RECIPE

On January 23, 2009, Indiana passed a resolution proclaiming Sugar Cream Pie as the official Hoosier pie. The recipe is believed to have originated in Indiana around 1800 as a great substitute for fruit pie when there was no fruit left after a long winter. Using only the staples on the shelf, an industrious homemaker created a tasty treat that is now the featured pie of the Hoosier pie company Wick's. There are many variations of the recipe using the following staples: milk, sugar, all-purpose flour, shortening, vanilla extract, and nutmeg.

Per serving
Calories 550
Protein 3 g
Carbohydrates 54 g
Total Fat 37 g
59% Calories from Fat
Cholesterol 107 mg
Fiber 1 g
Sodium 156 mg
Sugar 38 g

1¹/₂ cups sugar
¹/₃   cup all-purpose flour
2¹/₂ cups whipping cream
2   teaspoons vanilla extract
1   tablespoon butter, melted
1   unbaked (9-inch) pie shell
¹/₄   teaspoon nutmeg

Preheat the oven to 450 degrees. Mix the sugar and flour in a bowl. Add the cream, vanilla and butter and beat well. Pour into the pie shell. Sprinkle with the nutmeg. Bake for 10 minutes. Reduce the oven temperature to 350 degrees. Bake for 30 minutes longer. Cool the pie on a wire rack. Chill in the refrigerator. Serve cold.

Old-Fashioned Jam Cake

Serves 8

Cake

1 1/2 cups sifted all-purpose
    flour
1/2 teaspoon ground allspice
1/2 teaspoon cinnamon
1/2 teaspoon ground cloves
1/2 teaspoon baking soda
1/4 teaspoon salt
1/2 cup (1 stick)
    butter, softened
1 cup sugar
3 eggs
1/2 teaspoon vanilla extract
1/2 cup buttermilk

1 cup blackberry jam
1/2 cup strawberry preserves
1/2 cup raisins
1/2 cup chopped
    black walnuts

Caramel Glaze

1/4 cup (1/2 stick) butter
1/2 cup packed dark
    brown sugar
1/4 cup milk
2 cups sifted
    confectioners' sugar
1 teaspoon vanilla extract

Per serving
Calories 740
Protein 8 g
Carbohydrates 128 g
Total Fat 24 g
29% Calories from Fat
Cholesterol 126 mg
Fiber 1 g
Sodium 325 mg
Sugar 105 g

Preheat the oven to 325 degrees. To prepare the cake, grease the bottoms of two 8-inch square or 8-inch round cake pans and line with waxed paper. Grease and flour the waxed paper and sides of the pans. Sift the flour, allspice, cinnamon, cloves, baking soda and salt together. Cream the butter and sugar in a mixing bowl until light and fluffy. Add the eggs one at a time, beating well after each addition. Blend in the vanilla. Add the flour mixture, buttermilk, jam and preserves. Beat at medium speed for 2 minutes, scraping the bowl occasionally. Stir in the raisins and walnuts. Pour into the prepared pans. Bake for 45 to 50 minutes or until a wooden pick inserted in the centers comes out clean. Cool in the pans for 10 minutes. Invert onto wire racks and remove the waxed pepper. Let stand to cool completely.

To prepare the glaze, melt the butter in a saucepan over medium-low heat. Stir in the brown sugar. Cook for 2 minutes, stirring constantly. Add the milk. Bring to a boil, stirring constantly. Remove from the heat. Stir in the confectioners' sugar gradually. Blend in the vanilla. Add a little more additional milk if the glaze becomes too thick.

To assemble, place one of the cake layers on a serving plate. Cover with about one-third of the warm glaze. Top with the remaining cake layer. Drizzle with the remaining glaze.

Note: This cake is best made two days in advance. Store, tightly covered, at room temperature. The cake may be frozen for up to three months.

Festive Fudge-Filled Bars

Serves 24

Per serving
Calories 314
Protein 4 g
Carbohydrates 38 g
Total Fat 17 g
47% Calories from Fat
Cholesterol 28 mg
Fiber 2 g
Sodium 211 mg
Sugar 27 g

2 cups rolled oats
1 1/2 cups all-purpose flour
1 cup pecans or walnuts, chopped
1 cup packed brown sugar
1 teaspoon baking soda
3/4 teaspoon salt
1 cup (2 sticks) butter or margarine
2 tablespoons shortening
1 1/2 cups candy-coated chocolate pieces
1 (14-ounce) can sweetened condensed milk

Preheat the oven to 375 degrees. Mix the oats, flour, pecans, brown sugar, baking soda and salt in a mixing bowl. Cut in the butter until crumbly. Reserve 1 1/2 cups of the crumb mixture. Press the remaining crumb mixture into a greased 9×13-inch or 10×15-inch baking pan. Bake for 10 minutes. Melt the shortening in a heavy saucepan. Add 1 cup of the chocolate pieces. Cook over very low heat until almost melted but pieces of the colored coating remain, stirring constantly with a metal spoon and pressing with the back of the spoon to break up. Remove from the heat. Stir in the condensed milk. Spread over the partially baked crust to within 1/2 inch of the edge. Combine the reserved crumb mixture with the remaining 1/2 cup candies. Sprinkle evenly over the chocolate mixture and press lightly. Bake for 20 minutes or until golden brown. Cool on a wire rack before cutting into bars.

Whole Wheat Peanut Butter Bars

Serves 36

Per serving
Calories 134
Protein 3 g
Carbohydrates 15 g
Total Fat 8 g
50% Calories from Fat
Cholesterol 6 mg
Fiber 1 g
Sodium 118 mg
Sugar 9 g

1/2 cup (1 stick) margarine, softened
1 cup packed brown sugar
1 egg
1 cup creamy or chunky peanut butter
1 teaspoon vanilla extract
1 1/2 cups whole wheat flour
1 teaspoon baking soda
1/4 teaspoon salt
1/2 cup quick-cooking oats
1 cup (6 ounces) chocolate chips

Preheat the oven to 350 degrees. Cream the margarine and brown sugar in a mixing bowl. Add the egg, peanut butter and vanilla and mix well. Mix in the flour, baking soda and salt. Stir in the oats and chocolate chips. Pat into a greased 9×13-inch baking pan. Bake for 15 minutes or until slightly puffed and light brown. Cool on a wire rack before cutting into bars.

Note: Sprinkle the top of the unbaked dough with 1 tablespoon coarse or granulated sugar for a sparkly top. Bake for 20 minutes if using an insulated baking pan.

Biscochitos

Serves 36 to 48

3 cups all-purpose flour
1 1/2 teaspoons baking powder
1/2 teaspoon salt
1/2 cup (1 stick) butter, softened
1/2 cup shortening

1/2 cup sugar
1 1/2 teaspoons anise seeds
1 egg
2 to 4 tablespoons cold water
1/4 cup sugar
1 teaspoon cinnamon

Preheat the oven to 350 degrees. Mix the flour, baking powder and salt together. Cream the butter, shortening, 1/2 cup sugar and the anise seeds in a mixing bowl. Add the egg and beat until fluffy. Add the flour mixture alternately with the water, beating constantly just until blended and using only enough of the water to produce a dough that is soft and stiff, but not sticky. Roll 1/4 inch thick on a lightly floured surface. Cut with a round-, diamond- or fleur de lis–shaped cookie cutter. Dip each into a mixture of 1/4 cup sugar and the cinnamon and place on an ungreased cookie sheet. Bake for 10 to 12 minutes or until light brown. Cool on a wire rack. Store in an airtight container.

Per serving
Calories 78
Protein 1 g
Carbohydrates 9 g
Total Fat 4 g
48% Calories from Fat
Cholesterol 9 mg
Fiber <1 g
Sodium 55 mg
Sugar 3 g

Praline Biscotti

Serves 36

1/4 cup canola oil
1/2 cup granulated sugar
1/2 cup packed dark brown sugar
2 eggs
1 teaspoon maple extract

2 cups all-purpose flour
1 teaspoon baking powder
1/4 teaspoon salt
3/4 cup finely chopped toasted pecans

Preheat the oven to 350 degrees. Mix the canola oil, granulated sugar, brown sugar, eggs and maple extract in a medium bowl by hand. Add the flour, baking powder and salt and stir until moistened. Stir in the pecans. Divide the dough into two equal portions. Shape each portion into a 1 1/2×12-inch log on a lightly floured surface. Place the logs on a lightly greased cookie sheet about 3 inches apart. The logs will spread. Bake for 25 to 30 minutes or until the logs begin to crack. Remove to a wire rack to cool for 15 to 20 minutes. Reduce the oven temperature to 300 degrees. Cut each log diagonally into 1/2-inch slices with a serrated knife. Place cut side down on a cookie sheet. Bake for 10 to 15 minutes or until golden brown on each side, turning once. Cool completely on a wire rack. Store in a glass jar or tin.

Per serving
Calories 83
Protein 1 g
Carbohydrates 12 g
Total Fat 4 g
39% Calories from Fat
Cholesterol 12 mg
Fiber <1 g
Sodium 35 mg
Sugar 6 g

Chocolate Chip Cookies

Per serving
Calories 335
Protein 4 g
Carbohydrates 41 g
Total Fat 19 g
49% Calories from Fat
Cholesterol 31 mg
Fiber 2 g
Sodium 99 mg
Sugar 25 g

Get Ready to Cook
Wash your hands before starting to cook. Clear a work area, and make sure it is clean. Set out all ingredients and equipment.

2/3	cup butter, chilled and cut into cubes
2/3	cup butter-flavor shortening
1	cup packed brown sugar
1	cup granulated sugar
2	eggs
2	teaspoons vanilla extract

3 1/2	cups all-purpose flour
1	teaspoon baking soda
1	cup chopped pecans
2	cups (12 ounces) semisweet chocolate chips or milk chocolate chips

Preheat the oven to 375 degrees. Beat the butter and shortening in a mixing bowl until smooth. Add the brown sugar, granulated sugar, eggs and vanilla and mix well. Add the flour and baking soda and mix just until blended. Stir in the pecans and chocolate chips. Drop by large ice cream scoopfuls 1 1/2 inches apart onto an ungreased cookie sheet. Bake for 13 minutes or until the edges are golden brown. Cool on the cookie sheet for 5 to 10 minutes. Remove to a wire rack to cool completely. Store in an airtight container or sealable plastic bag.

Note: The dough may be shaped into balls and flash frozen on a cookie sheet. Place in a freezer bag. Bake in small batches or all at once when you are craving the truly best chocolate chip cookie ever.

Peanut Butter Cookies

Per serving
Calories 212
Protein 4 g
Carbohydrates 25 g
Total Fat 11 g
47% Calories from Fat
Cholesterol 22 mg
Fiber 1 g
Sodium 153 mg
Sugar 15 g

1 1/2	cups sifted all-purpose flour
1	teaspoon baking soda
1/4	cup (1/2 stick) butter, softened

1/4	cup shortening
1/2	cup granulated sugar
1/2	cup packed brown sugar
1	egg
1/2	cup peanut butter

Preheat the oven to 350 degrees. Sift the flour and baking soda together. Beat the butter and shortening in a mixing bowl until creamy. Beat in the granulated sugar and brown sugar until fluffy. Add the egg and beat well. Beat in the peanut butter. Stir in the flour mixture. Roll into 1-inch balls and place on an ungreased cookie sheet. Flatten with a fork. Bake for 10 to 12 minutes or until firm. Cool on a wire rack. Store any leftover cookies with one slice of bread to keep the cookies soft.

Pyramid Cookies

Serves 24

1	cup rolled oats or quick-cooking oats
3/4	cup milled flaxseed
1	cup all-purpose flour
1/2	teaspoon baking soda
1/2	teaspoon salt
1/2	cup packed brown sugar
1/2	cup granulated sugar
1	cup mixed dried fruit
2/3	cup pecans
2/3	cup shredded uncooked carrots
1	egg
1	teaspoon vanilla extract
1/4	cup 2% milk or skim milk
1/2	cup (1 stick) butter, softened

Preheat the oven to 350 degrees. Mix the oats, flaxseed, flour, baking soda, salt, brown sugar, granulated sugar, dried fruit and pecans in a large bowl. Combine the carrots, egg, vanilla, milk and butter in a bowl and mix well. Add to the oat mixture and mix well with a wooden spoon or your hands. Drop by tablespoonfuls 2 inches apart onto a greased cookie sheet. Bake for 10 to 14 minutes or until the edges are light brown. Cool on a wire rack.

Per serving
Calories 165
Protein 3 g
Carbohydrates 22 g
Total Fat 8 g
43% Calories from Fat
Cholesterol 19 mg
Fiber 2 g
Sodium 110 mg
Sugar 13 g

Sour Cream Sugar Cookies

Serves 48

1 1/2	cups sugar
3	eggs
1	cup fat-free sour cream
1	cup (2 sticks) butter or margarine, softened
1	teaspoon vanilla extract
2	teaspoons baking soda
2	pounds all-purpose flour

Preheat the oven to 375 degrees. Combine the sugar, eggs, sour cream, butter and vanilla in a mixing bowl and mix well. Stir in the baking soda and flour to form a stiff dough. Knead on a lightly floured surface. Roll into a circle 1/2 inch thick. Cut with desired cookie cutters. Place on a cookie sheet. Bake for 10 minutes or until brown. Cool on a wire rack.

Note: These cookies may be decorated as desired.

Per serving
Calories 137
Protein 3 g
Carbohydrates 22 g
Total Fat 4 g
29% Calories from Fat
Cholesterol 23 mg
Fiber 1 g
Sodium 88 mg
Sugar 7 g

Buckeye Candy

Serves 200

SIGNATURE RECIPE

The buckeye tree is the state tree of Ohio. The tree is called the buckeye because its nuts resemble the shape and color of a deer's eye. These candies look like the nuts from buckeye trees that are common in Ohio. This is also the recipe that Ohio members made for hospitality for NEAFCS annual session in St. Paul, Minnesota, in 2007.

Per serving
Calories 85
Protein 1 g
Carbohydrates 9 g
Total Fat 5 g
54% Calories from Fat
Cholesterol 0 mg
Fiber <1 g
Sodium 38 mg
Sugar 8 g

2   cups (4 sticks) margarine, softened
1   (18-ounce) jar creamy peanut butter
2   teaspoons vanilla extract
1   (2-pound) package (more or less)
      confectioners' sugar
3   pounds dipping chocolate

Cream the margarine in a mixing bowl. Add the peanut butter and vanilla and beat until smooth. Add the confectioners' sugar one-third at a time, beating well after each addition and adding additional confectioners' sugar if the dough is too soft. You may need to use a spoon to finish mixing. Chill, covered, for 8 to 10 hours.

Shape into 1-inch balls and place close together but not touching in a single layer on a baking sheet. Freeze for 8 to 10 hours.

Place the dipping chocolate in a medium microwave-safe bowl. Microwave on Defrost for 2 minutes and then stir. Microwave for 2 minutes longer and stir again. Microwave for 1 to 2 minutes longer or until melted. Remove a few peanut butter balls from the freezer at a time and insert a wooden pick into each one. Dip each ball into the chocolate to cover three-fourths of the surface; the "eye of the buckeye" (about the size of a dime) remains uncovered. Place on waxed paper and let stand until set. Store in a tin or plastic container with waxed paper between each layer. Freeze or chill until serving time.

Note: Three pounds of dipping chocolate does a little more than one batch of buckeyes. If dipping chocolate is not available, use 12 ounces chocolate chips and 1/2 block paraffin.

Nutritional information includes the entire amount of dipping chocolate.

Caramels by the Sea

Serves 100

Per serving
Calories 62
Protein <1 g
Carbohydrates 11 g
Total Fat 2 g
29% Calories from Fat
Cholesterol 6 mg
Fiber 0 g
Sodium 21 mg
Sugar 8 g

1   cup (2 sticks) AA-grade butter, melted
2   cups light corn syrup
1   cup sweetened condensed milk
2   cups sugar
2   tablespoons vanilla extract

Combine the butter, corn syrup, condensed milk and sugar in a heavy 3-quart saucepan. Cook over low heat to 348 degrees on a candy thermometer, caramel stage, stirring constantly. This will take about 40 to 45 minutes; the mixture must reach the exact temperature. Stir in the vanilla and remove from the heat. Pour into a buttered 9×13-inch glass dish. Cool until firm. Cut into 1-inch squares and wrap in waxed paper.

Popcorn Crunch

Serves 8

Per serving
Calories 242
Protein 2 g
Carbohydrates 31 g
Total Fat 13 g
47% Calories from Fat
Cholesterol 15 mg
Fiber 2 g
Sodium 154 mg
Sugar 13 g

1/4   cup (1/2 stick) butter or margarine
6   tablespoons light brown sugar
2   tablespoons light corn syrup
1/4   teaspoon vanilla extract
4   cups crisp rice cereal
4   cups popped popcorn
3/4   cup pecan halves or large pieces

Combine the butter, brown sugar, corn syrup and vanilla in a microwave-safe pitcher or container. Microwave on High for 3 minutes or until boiling, stirring after the first 1 1/2 minutes. Mix the cereal, popcorn and pecan halves in a large microwave-safe bowl or container. Pour the hot syrup over the popcorn mixture and mix well. Microwave on High for 4 1/2 minutes, stirring every 1 1/2 minutes. Spread on a baking sheet lined with waxed paper. Let stand until cool. Break into bite-size pieces.

Honey Candy

Serves 24

SIGNATURE RECIPE

Known as the Beehive State, Utah has a strong pioneer heritage of industry and economy. "Use it up, wear it out, make it do, or do without" guided early settlers, who made honey candy to be resourceful. Recipes passed from generation to generation are still a source of family fun for all ages. In Utah, where honey has always been a major staple and backyard beekeeping is gaining popularity, honey candy remains a deliciously delectable treat.

1   cup honey
3   cups sugar
1   cup cream

Pour the honey into a heavy saucepan. Stir in the sugar. Cook until the sugar dissolves, stirring constantly. Add the cream. Cook to 250 to 268 degrees on a candy thermometer, hard ball stage. Pour into a buttered 9×12-inch pan. Let stand until cool enough to handle. Butter your hands and pull like taffy until the mixture is porous and golden brown. Shape into ropes on waxed paper and score with a knife to the desired size. Let stand until cool and brittle. Break into pieces along the scored lines. Wrap each piece in waxed paper.

Per serving
Calories 281
Protein <1 g
Carbohydrates 12 g
Total Fat 27 g
83% Calories from Fat
Cholesterol 75 mg
Fiber <1 g
Sodium 168 mg
Sugar 12 g

Nutritional Profile Guidelines

The editors have attempted to present these family recipes in a format that allows approximate nutritional values to be computed. Persons with dietary or health problems or whose diets require close monitoring should not rely solely on the nutritional information provided. They should consult their physician or a registered dietitian for specific information.

Nutritional information for these recipes is computed from information derived from many sources, including materials supplied by the United States Department of Agriculture, computer databanks, and journals in which the information is assumed to be in the public domain. However, many specialty items, new products, and processed food may not be available from these sources or may vary from the average values used in these profiles. More information on new and/or specific products may be obtained by reading the nutrient labels. Unless otherwise specified, the nutritional profile of these recipes is based on all measurements being level.

- **Artificial sweeteners** vary in use and strength and should be used to taste, using the recipe ingredients as a guideline. Sweeteners using aspartame (NutraSweet and Equal) should not be used as a sweetener in recipes involving prolonged heating, which reduces the sweet taste. For further information on the use of these sweeteners, refer to the package.
- **Alcoholic ingredients** have been analyzed for the basic information. Cooking causes the evaporation of alcohol, which decreases alcoholic and caloric content.
- **Buttermilk, sour cream,** and **yogurt** are the types available commercially.
- **Canned beans** and **vegetables** have been analyzed with the canning liquid. Rinsing and draining canned products lowers the sodium content.
- **Chicken,** cooked for boning and chopping, has been roasted; this method yields the lowest caloric values.
- **Eggs** are all large, unless specified otherwise. If you are concerned about using raw eggs (egg yolks), use eggs (yolks from eggs) pasteurized in their shells, which are sold at some specialty food stores, or use an equivalent amount of pasteurized egg substitute.
- **Flour** is unsifted all-purpose flour.
- **Garnishes, serving suggestions,** and **other optional information** are not included in the profile.
- **Margarine** and **butter** are regular, not whipped or presoftened.
- **Milk** is whole milk, 3.5% butterfat. Low-fat milk is 1% butterfat. Evaporated milk is whole milk with 60% of the water removed.
- **Oil** is any type of vegetable cooking oil. **Shortening** is hydrogenated vegetable shortening.
- **Salt to taste** and **other ingredients to taste** as noted in the ingredients have not been included in the nutritional profile.
- If a **choice of ingredients** has been given, the profile reflects the first option. If a choice of amounts has been given, the profile reflects the greater amount.
- The **nutritional analysis** for each recipe represents one serving size.

Glossary of Cooking Terms

- **Bake**—To cook by dry heat in an oven, or under hot coals.

- **Bard**—To cover lean meats with bacon or pork fat before cooking.

- **Baste**—To moisten, especially meats, with melted butter, pan drippings, sauce, etc., during cooking time.

- **Beat**—To mix ingredients by vigorous stirring or with electric mixer.

- **Blanch**—To immerse, usually vegetables or fruit, briefly into boiling water to inactivate enzymes, loosen skin, or soak away excess salt.

- **Blend**—To combine two or more ingredients, at least one of which is liquid or soft, to quickly produce a mixture of uniform consistency.

- **Boil**—To heat liquid until bubbly; the boiling point for water is about 212 degrees, depending on altitude and atmospheric pressure.

- **Braise**—To cook, especially meats, covered, in a small amount of liquid.

- **Brew**—To prepare a beverage by allowing boiling water to extract flavor and/or color from certain substances.

- **Broil**—To cook by direct exposure to intense heat such as a flame or an electric heating unit.

- **Caramelize**—To melt sugar in a heavy pan over low heat until golden brown, stirring constantly.

- **Chill**—To cool in the refrigerator or in cracked ice.

- **Clarify**—To remove impurities from melted butter by allowing the sediment to settle, then pouring off clear yellow liquid. Other fats may be clarified by straining.

- **Cream**—To blend butter (usually softened), margarine (usually softened), shortening, or sometimes oil with a granulated or crushed ingredient until the mixture is soft and creamy.

- **Curdle**—To congeal milk with rennet or heat until solid lumps or curds are formed.

- **Cut in**—To disperse solid shortening into dry ingredients with a knife or pastry blender. The texture of the mixture should resemble coarse cracker meal.

- **Decant**—To pour a liquid such as wine or melted butter carefully from one container into another, leaving the sediment in the original container.

- **Deep-fry**—To cook in a deep pan or skillet containing hot cooking oil. Deep-fried foods are generally completely immersed in the hot oil.

- **Deglaze**—To heat stock, wine, or other liquid in the pan in which meat has been cooked, mixing with pan drippings and sediment to form a gravy or sauce base.

- **Degorge**—To remove strong flavors or impurities before cooking, e.g., soaking ham in cold water or sprinkling vegetables with salt, then letting stand for a period of time and pressing out excess fluid.

- **Degrease**—To remove accumulated fat from the surface of hot liquids.

- **Dice**—To cut into small cubes about one quarter inch in size.

- **Dissolve**—To create a solution by thoroughly mixing a solid or granular substance with a liquid.

- **Dredge**—To coat completely with flour, bread crumbs, etc.

- **Fillet**—To remove bones from meat or fish; or a boneless piece of fish, meat, or chicken.

- **Flambé**—To pour warmed brandy or other spirits over food in a pan, then ignite and continue cooking briefly.

- **Fold in**—To blend a delicate frothy mixture into a heavier one so that none of the lightness of volume is lost. Using a rubber spatula, turn under and bring up and over, rotating bowl one quarter turn after each motion.

- **Fry**—To cook in a pan or skillet containing hot cooking oil. The oil should not totally cover the food.

- **Garnish**—To decorate food before serving.

- **Glaze**—To cover or coat with sauce, syrup, egg white, or a jellied substance. After applying, it becomes firm—adding color and flavor.

- **Grate**—To rub food against a rough, perforated utensil to produce slivers, chunks, curls, etc.

- **Gratiné**—To top a sauced dish with crumbs, cheese, or butter, then brown under a broiler.

- **Grill**—To broil, usually over hot coals or charcoal.

- **Grind**—To cut, crush, or force through a chopper to produce small bits.

- **Infuse**—To steep herbs or other flavorings in a liquid until the liquid absorbs flavor.

- **Julienne**—To cut vegetables, fruit, etc., into long thin strips.

- **Knead**—To press, fold, and stretch dough until smooth and elastic.

- **Lard**—To insert strips of fat or bacon into lean meat to keep moist and juicy during cooking. Larding is an internal basting technique.

- **Leaven**—To cause batters and doughs to rise, usually by means of a chemical leavening agent. This process may occur before or during baking.

- **Marinate**—To soak, usually in a highly seasoned oil-acid solution, to flavor and/or tenderize food.

Glossary of Cooking Terms

■ **Melt**—To liquefy solid foods by the action of heat.

■ **Mince**—To cut or chop into very small pieces.

■ **Mix**—To combine ingredients to distribute uniformly.

■ **Mold**—To shape into a particular form.

■ **Panbroil**—To cook in a skillet or pan using a very small amount of fat to prevent sticking.

■ **Panfry**—To cook in a skillet or pan containing only a small amount of fat.

■ **Parboil**—To partially cook in boiling water. Most parboiled foods require additional cooking.

■ **Parch**—To dry or roast slightly through exposure to intense heat.

■ **Pit**—To remove the hard inedible seed from peaches, plums, etc.

■ **Plank**—To broil and serve on a board or wooden platter.

■ **Plump**—To soak fruits, usually dried, in liquid until puffy and softened.

■ **Poach**—To cook in a small amount of gently simmering liquid.

■ **Preserve**—To prevent food spoilage by pickling, salting, dehydrating, smoking, boiling in syrup, etc. Preserved foods have excellent keeping qualities.

■ **Purée**—To reduce the pulp of cooked fruit and vegetables to a smooth and thick liquid by straining or blending.

■ **Reduce**—To boil stock, gravy, or other liquid until volume is reduced, liquid is thickened, and flavor is intensified.

■ **Refresh**—To place blanched drained vegetables or other food in cold water to halt the cooking process.

■ **Render**—To cook meat or meat trimmings at low temperature until fat melts and can be drained and strained.

■ **Roast**—(1) To cook by dry heat either in an oven or over hot coals. (2) To dry or parch by intense heat.

■ **Sauté**—To cook in a skillet containing a small amount of hot cooking oil. Sautéed foods should never be immersed in the oil. Should be stirred frequently.

■ **Scald**—(1) To heat a liquid almost to the boiling point. (2) To soak—usually vegetables or fruit—in boiling water until the skins are loosened.

■ **Scallop**—To bake with a sauce in a casserole. The food may either be mixed or layered with the sauce.

■ **Score**—To make shallow cuts diagonally in parallel lines, especially meat.

- **Scramble**—To cook and stir simultaneously, especially eggs.

- **Shirr**—To crack eggs into individual buttered baking dishes, then bake or broil until whites are set. Chopped meats or vegetables, cheese, cream, or bread crumbs may also be added.

- **Shred**—To cut or shave food into slivers.

- **Shuck**—To remove the husk from corn or the shell from oysters, clams, etc.

- **Sieve**—To press a mixture through a coarsely meshed metal utensil to make it homogeneous.

- **Sift**—To pass, usually dry ingredients, through a fine wire mesh to produce a uniform consistency.

- **Simmer**—To cook in or with a liquid at or just below the boiling point.

- **Skewer**—(1) To thread—usually meat and vegetables—onto a sharpened rod (as in shish kabob). (2) To fasten the opening of stuffed fowl closed with small pins.

- **Skim**—To ladle or spoon off excess fat or scum from the surface of a liquid.

- **Smoke**—To preserve or cook through continuous exposure to wood smoke for a long time.

- **Steam**—To cook with water vapor in a closed container, usually in a steamer, on a rack, or in a double boiler.

- **Sterilize**—To cleanse and purify through exposure to intense heat.

- **Stew**—To simmer—usually meats and vegetables—for a long period of time. Also used to tenderize meats.

- **Stir-fry**—To cook small pieces of vegetables and/or meat in a small amount of oil in a wok or skillet over high heat, stirring constantly, until tender-crisp. Popular Asian technique.

- **Strain**—To pass through a strainer, sieve, or cheesecloth to break down or remove solids or impurities.

- **Stuff**—To fill or pack cavities, especially those of meats, vegetables, and poultry.

- **Toast**—To brown and crisp, usually by means of direct heat, or to bake until brown.

- **Truss**—To bind poultry legs and wings close to the body before cooking.

- **Whip**—To beat a mixture until air has been thoroughly incorporated and the mixture is light and fluffy, volume is greatly increased, and the mixture holds its shape.

- **Wilt**—To apply heat to cause dehydration and a droopy appearance.

Food Storage Guidelines

Product dates on meat products are not a guide for safe use of a product, so the following short but safe time limits will help keep refrigerated food (40 degrees F) from spoiling or becoming dangerous.

- Purchase the product before "sell-by" or expiration dates.
- Follow handling recommendations on the product.
- Keep meat or poultry in its package until just before using.
- If freezing meat or poultry in its original package longer than two months, overwrap the package with airtight heavy-duty foil, plastic wrap, or freezer paper, or place the package inside a plastic bag.
- Freezing at 0 degrees F keeps food safe indefinitely so the following recommended storage times are for quality only.

Cold Storage Chart—Be aware of how long foods have been in your refrigerator. When in doubt, throw it out!

Product	Refrigerator (40°F)	Freezer (0°F)
Eggs		
Fresh, in shell	3 to 5 weeks	Don't freeze
Raw yolks, whites	2 to 4 days	1 year
Hard-cooked	1 week	Don't freeze well
Liquid pasteurized eggs, egg substitutes		
Opened	3 days	Don't freeze well
Unopened	10 days	1 year
Mayonnaise		
Commercial, refrigerate after opening	2 months	Doesn't freeze
Deli and Vacuum-Packed Products		
Store-prepared (or homemade) egg, chicken, ham, tuna, macaroni salads	3 to 5 days	Don't freeze well
Hot Dogs and Luncheon Meats		
Hot dogs, opened package	1 week	1 to 2 months
Unopened package	2 weeks	1 to 2 months
Luncheon meats		
Opened Package	3 to 5 days	1 to 2 months
Unopened Package	2 weeks	1 to 2 months

Product	Refrigerator (40°F)	Freezer (0°F)
Bacon and Sausage		
Bacon	7 days	1 month
Sausage, raw from chicken, turkey, pork, beef	1 to 2 days	1 to 2 months
Smoked breakfast links, patties	7 days	1 to 2 months
Hard sausage—pepperoni, jerky sticks	2 to 3 weeks	1 to 2 months
Summer sausage—labeled "Keep Refrigerated"		
Opened	3 weeks	1 to 2 months
Unopened	3 months	1 to 2 months
Ham, Corned Beef		
Corned beef, in pouch with pickling juices	5 to 7 days	Drained, 1 month
Ham, canned—labeled "Keep Refrigerated"		
Opened	3 to 5 days	1 to 2 months
Unopened	6 to 9 months	Doesn't freeze
Ham, fully cooked vacuum-sealed at plant, undated		
Unopened	2 weeks	1 to 2 months
Ham, fully cooked vacuum-sealed at plant, dated		
Unopened	"use-by" date on package	1 to 2 months
Ham, fully cooked, whole	7 days	1 to 2 months
Ham, fully cooked, half	3 to 5 days	1 to 2 months
Ham, fully cooked, slices	3 to 4 days	1 to 2 months
Hamburger, Ground and Stew Meat		
Hamburger and stew meat	1 to 2 days	3 to 4 months
Ground turkey, veal, pork, lamb, and mixtures of them	1 to 2 days	3 to 4 months
Fresh Beef, Veal, Lamb, Pork		
Steaks	3 to 5 days	6 to 12 months
Chops	3 to 5 days	4 to 6 months
Roasts	3 to 5 days	4 to 12 months
Variety meats—tongue, liver, heart, kidneys, chitterlings	1 to 2 days	3 to 4 months
Pre-stuffed, uncooked pork chops, lamb chops, or chicken breast stuffed with dressing	1 day	Don't freeze well

Product	Refrigerator (40°F)	Freezer (0°F)
Soups and Stews		
Vegetable or meat added	3 to 4 days	2 to 3 months
Meat Leftovers		
Cooked meat and meat casseroles	3 to 4 days	2 to 3 months
Gravy and meat broth	1 to 2 days	2 to 3 months
Fresh Poultry		
Chicken or turkey, whole	1 to 2 days	1 year
Chicken or turkey, pieces	1 to 2 days	9 months
Cutlets	1 to 2 days	3 to 4 months
Cooked Poultry		
Fried chicken	3 to 4 days	4 months
Cooked poultry casseroles	3 to 4 days	4 months
Pieces, plain	3 to 4 days	4 months
Pieces covered with broth, gravy	1 to 2 days	6 months
Chicken nuggets, patties	1 to 2 days	1 to 3 months
Pizza		
Pizza	3 to 4 days	1 to 2 months
Stuffing		
Stuffing—cooked	3 to 4 days	1 months
Beverages, Fruit		
Juices in cartons, fruit drinks, punch		8 to 12 months
Unopened	3 weeks	
Opened	7 to 10 days	
Dairy		
Butter	1 to 3 months	6 to 9 months
Buttermilk	7 to 14 days	3 months
Cheese, Hard (such as Cheddar, Swiss)		
Unopened	6 months	6 months
Opened	3 to 4 weeks	
Cheese, Soft (such as Brie, Bel Paese)	1 week	6 months
Cottage Cheese, Ricotta	1 week	Doesn't freeze well
Cream Cheese	2 weeks	Doesn't freeze well
Cream, Whipped, ultrapasteurized	1 month	Doesn't freeze
Cream, Whipped, sweetened	1 day	1 to 2 months

Product	Refrigerator (40°F)	Freezer (0°F)
Cream, Aerosol can, real whipped cream	3 to 4 weeks	Doesn't freeze
Cream, Aerosol can, nondairy topping	3 months	Doesn't freeze
Cream, Half-and-Half	3 to 4 days	4 months
Eggnog, commercial	3 to 5 days	6 months
Margarine	4 to 5 months	12 months
Milk	7 days	3 months
Pudding	Package date; 2 days after opening	Doesn't freeze
Sour Cream	7 to 21 days	Doesn't freeze
Yogurt	7 to 14 days	1 to 2 months

Dough

Product	Refrigerator (40°F)	Freezer (0°F)
Tube cans of rolls, biscuits, pizza dough, etc.	Use-by date	Don't freeze
Ready-to-bake piecrust	Use-by date	2 months
Cookie dough *Unopened or Opened*	Use-by date	2 months

Fish

Product	Refrigerator (40°F)	Freezer (0°F)
Lean fish (cod, flounder, haddock, sole, etc.)	1 to 2 days	6 months
Fatty fish (bluefish, mackerel, salmon, etc.)	1 to 2 days	2 to 3 months
Cooked fish	3 to 4 days	4 to 6 months
Uncooked fish	14 days or date on vacuum package	2 months in vacuum package

Shellfish

Product	Refrigerator (40°F)	Freezer (0°F)
Shrimp, scallops, crayfish, squid, shucked clams, mussels, and oysters	1 to 2 days	3 to 6 months
Live clams, mussels, crab, lobster, and oysters	2 to 3 days	2 to 3 months
Cooked shellfish	3 to 4 days	3 months

Note: These short but safe time limits will help keep refrigerated foods from spoiling or becoming dangerous to eat. Because freezing keeps food safe indefinitely, recommended storage times are for quality only. Storage times are from date of purchase unless specified on chart. It is not important if a date expires after food is frozen.

Cooking Substitutions

Product	Substitution
Baking Powder	1 teaspoon = $^1/4$ teaspoon baking soda plus $^1/2$ teaspoon cream of tartar
Barbecue Sauce	1 cup = 1 cup ketchup plus 2 teaspoons Worcestershire sauce
Bread Crumbs, dry	1 cup = $^3/4$ cup cracker crumbs
Beef Broth	1 cup = 1 beef bouillon cube plus 1 cup water
Cajun Seasoning	1 teaspoon = $^1/2$ to 1 teaspoon hot pepper sauce, $^1/2$ teaspoon dried thyme, $^1/4$ teaspoon dried basil, and 1 minced garlic clove
Chicken Broth	1 cup = 1 chicken bouillon cube plus 1 cup water
Butter	1 cup = 1 cup margarine
In baking	1 cup = 1 cup solid vegetable shortening plus 2 dashes of salt
Buttermilk or Sour Cream	1 cup = 1 tablespoon lemon juice or vinegar plus regular milk to measure 1 cup
Chocolate, semisweet	1 square (1 ounce) = 1 square (1 ounce) unsweetened chocolate plus 1 tablespoon sugar, or 3 tablespoons semisweet chocolate chips
Chocolate, unsweetened	1 square = 3 tablespoons baking cocoa plus 1 tablespoon butter or vegetable oil
Cornstarch, as thickener	1 tablespoon = 2 tablespoons all-purpose flour
Corn Syrup, dark	1 cup = $^3/4$ cup light corn syrup plus $^1/4$ cup molasses
Corn Syrup, light	1 cup = 1 cup sugar plus $^1/4$ cup water
Cracker Crumbs	1 cup = 1 cup dry bread crumbs
Cream, Half-and-Half	1 cup = 1 tablespoon melted butter plus enough whole milk to measure 1 cup
Cream, light	1 cup = 1 cup half-and-half
Egg	1 whole = 2 egg yolks
Flour, cake	1 cup = 1 cup minus 2 tablespoons all-purpose flour

Product	Substitution
Flour, self-rising	1 cup = 1 1/2 teaspoons baking powder plus 1/2 teaspoon salt plus enough all-purpose flour to measure 1 cup
Garlic	1 clove = 1/8 teaspoon instant minced garlic or garlic powder
Gingerroot, fresh	1 teaspoon = 1/4 teaspoon ground ginger
Herbs, fresh	1 tablespoon = 1 teaspoon dried, crushed
Honey	1 cup = 1 1/4 cups sugar plus 1/4 cup water
Italian Herb Seasoning	1 teaspoon = 1/2 teaspoon dried oregano plus 1/4 teaspoon each dried basil and thyme
Lemon Juice	1 teaspoon = 1/4 teaspoon cider vinegar
Lemon Zest	1 teaspoon = 1/2 teaspoon lemon extract
Milk, skim	1 cup = 1/3 cup nonfat dry milk plus water to measure 1 cup
Whole	1 cup = 1/2 cup evaporated milk plus 1/2 cup water
In baking	1 cup = 1 cup water plus 1 tablespoon butter
Molasses	1 cup = 1 cup dark corn syrup
Mushrooms, sliced, cooked	1/2 pound = 6-ounce can, drained
Mustard, prepared	1 tablespoon = 1/2 teaspoon ground mustard plus 2 teaspoons vinegar
Onion, raw, chopped	1/3 cup = 2 tablespoons instant minced onion
Parmesan Cheese, grated	1/4 cup = 1/4 cup grated Romano cheese
Poultry Seasoning	1 teaspoon = 1/2 teaspoon rubbed sage plus 1/4 teaspoon dried thyme
Pumpkin Pie Spice	2 1/2 teaspoons = 1 1/2 teaspoons ground cinnamon plus 1/2 teaspoon each ground nutmeg and ginger plus dash of ground cloves
Sherry, dry	1 tablespoon = 1 tablespoon dry vermouth
Sour Cream for dips	2 cups = 1 cup plain yogurt plus 1 cup real mayonnaise

Product	Substitution
Sugar	1 cup = 1 cup packed brown sugar or 2 cups sifted confectioners' sugar
Tartar Sauce	3/4 cup = 1/2 cup real mayonnaise plus 1/4 cup pickle relish
Tomato Juice	1 cup = 1/2 cup tomato sauce plus 1/2 cup water
Tomato Sauce	15-ounce can = 6 ounces tomato paste plus 1 cup water
Veal Cutlets, 1/4 inch thick	1 pound = 1 pound boneless chicken breast, flattened
Whipped Cream for topping	2 cups = 1/2 cup nonfat dry milk plus 1/2 cup ice water, whipped, sweetened
Yeast, compressed	1 cake = 1 envelope active dry yeast

Measurement Equivalents

Dash or pinch	= less than 1/8 teaspoon
3 teaspoons	= 1 tablespoon; 1.2 fluid ounces
2 tablespoons	= 1/8 cup; 1 fluid ounce
4 tablespoons	= 1/4 cup; 2 fluid ounces
5 1/2 tablespoons	= 1/3 cup
8 tablespoons	= 1/2 cup
10 2/3 tablespoons	= 2/3 cup
12 tablespoons	= 3/4 cup
16 tablespoons	= 1 cup; 8 fluid ounces; 1/2 pint
7/8 cup	= 3/4 cup plus 2 tablespoons
2 cups	= 1 pint; 16 fluid ounces
4 cups	= 2 pints; 1 quart; 32 fluid ounces
4 quarts	= 1 gallon
8 quarts	= 1 peck
4 pecks	= 1 bushel
16 ounces	= 1 pound

Resources

Partnership for Food Safety Education-Fact Sheets, **www.fightbac.org**

USDA, Food Safety and Inspection Safety-Fact Sheets,
www.fsis.usda.gov

TX Beef Council, *Plating It Safe*

Certain items in the Home Safety checklists (page 24–29) were used with permission from the authors.

Home Safety—A Checklist for Parents; Mary Yearns, ISU Extension housing specialist, and Lesia Oesterreich, ISU Extension family life specialist. Iowa State University Cooperative Extension, **http://www.extension.iastate.edu/Publications/PM1621.pdf**

A Housing Safety Checklist for Older People; Sarah D. Kirby, Extension housing specialist, North Carolina Cooperative Extension Service, **http://www.ces.ncsu.edu/depts/fcs/pdfs/FCS-461.pdf**

www.health.gov/dietaryguidelines, **www.health.gov/paguidelines** and *My Bright Future: Physical Activity and Healthy Eating*, U.S. Dept. of Health and Human Services

American Dietetic Association. *Making the Most of Mealtime*. Last referenced January 31, 2008.

"A Healthy Harvest: Safe Handling of Fresh Fruits and Vegetables". Scott, A. R., and Van Laanen, P. C., TX AgriLife Extension, Revised November 2006.

Contributors

Theresa Cook Allan

Francis Alloway

Barbara Ames

Christene S. Anderson

Grace M. Angotti

Michelle Ashley

Kari Bachman

Karen Barale

Jeanne Baranek

Ella Mae Bard

Cheryl Aldridge Beck

Dave Beebe

Linda Beech

Brenda Bell

Regenia Bell

Jackie Benham

Harriett Bennett

Rhea Bentley

Melissa Bess

Brenda Bishop

Sara E. Bogle

Anita Boyd

Myra Braden

Judith Brelend

Andrea Bressler

Jennifer Bridge

Pat Brinkman

Ruth Brock

Marlene Buck

Joy Buffalo

Linda Burg

Margaret Burlew

Carla Youree Bush

Kathy R. Byrnes

Sandra Cain

Shirley Camp

Candace Carrié

Julie Cascio

Cheryl Case

Carol Chandler

Cindy Clampet

Lois Clark

Keith Cleek

Cynthia Clifton

Janet C. Cluck

Mary Sue Cole

Colorado Extension Agents for FCS

Denise Continenza

Susan Cosgrove

Debra B. Cotterill

Martha Cotterill

Alinda Cox

Nancy Crago

Jillian Davis

Nicky Davison

Debbie DeRossitte

Donna K. Donald

Kathy Dothage

Jan Dougan

Suzanne Driessen

Mary Duke

Christine Duncan

LuAnn Duncan

LaDonna Dunlop

Lorie Dye

Elizabeth P. Easter

Nancy Edwards

Amy Elizer

Kris Elliott

Jeanine England

Denise Everson

Katherine Farrow

Kathy Finley

Lisa Fishman

Cindy Fitch

Sue Flanagan

Mary Ellen Fleming

Florida Extension Association of
Family & Consumer Sciences

Heidi L. Flowers

Shenile Rothwell Ford

Inger Friend

Donna Fryman

Recia Garcia

Sally Garrett

Patricia Gerhardt

Mary Alice Gettings

Rosemary Gibbons

Mary Gosche

Jennifer Green

Heather Greenwood

Vickie J. Hadley

Johanna Hahn

Shewana Hairston

Susan Hansen

Mitzi Harness

Diana Hassan

Vicki Hayman

Mary Beth Henley

Barbara Hennard

Judy Hetterman

Johanna Hicks

Patricia Hildebrand

Sharon Hoelscher

Vanessa Hoines

Carissa Holley

Janet Hollingsworth

Shea Hornsby

Lora Lee Frazier Howard

Stephanie Howard

Theresa Howard

Cindy Hubbard

Genise Huey

Kara Hunt

Nancy D. Hunt

Linda Huyck

Lois Illick

Flo Jasper

Marcia Jess

Carrie Johnson

Janet H. Johnson

Lynda Johnson

Becky Hagen Jokela

Janet Jolley

Deborah Jones

Kathy Jump

Kimberly Kanechika

Naomi Kanehiro

Laura Jean Kawamura

Lorraine Keeney

Maude Kelly

Glenda Kinder

Jacqueline W. Kings

Elizabeth Kingsland

Mary Ann Kizer

Marciel A. Klenk

Christine Kniep

Chris Koehler

Judy Kovach

Rena Labat

Janet Lake

Dianne Lamb

Brenda Langerud

Rhea K. Lanting

Lisa Lao

Bobbi Larsen

Amanda Larson

Pamela Lee

Jeannie Leonard

Dana Lester

Mary Ann Lienhart-Cross

Pamela Lincoln

Contributors

Marsha Lockard
Vicki Lofty
Edith M. Lovett
Liat Mackey
Sharon L. Mader
Thelma J. Malone
Cathy Martinez
Bernice Mason
Debby Mathews
Theresa Mayhew
Louise W. McDonald
Liz McKay
Robbie McKinnon
Christine McPheter
Patricia Merk
Diane L. Metz
Daryl Minch
Diane Mincher
Sally Mineer
Angela Mitchell
Lisa Mitchell
Linda Mock
Marjorie Moore
Susan Morgan
Jess Morrison
Connie Moyers
Lou Mueller
Yvonne Mullen
Candace Murray
Jeanne Murray
Jo Musich
Treena Musselman
Lynn Nakamura-Tengan
Claire Nakatsuka
Rebecca Nash
Nebraska Beef Council
Nancy C. Nelson
Kara Newby

Jeannie Nichols
Kami Nishimura
Mary Novak
Nutrition Education for Wellness,
    University of Hawaii at Manoa
Dawn M. Olson
Kathy Olson
Ashley Packer
Mitzi Pate
Nori Pearce
Martha Perkins
Amy Peterson
Donna Peterson
Shelly Porter
Deloris Pourchot
Corinne Powell
Peggy H. Powell
Susan Quinn
Kathy Revello
Cynthia C. Richard
Caroline Richardson
Mary Kate Ridgeway
Ann M. Rinesmith
Paula Roberson
Crystal Robertson
Cora French Robinson
Jenny Rogers
Danette Russell
Eunice Sahr
Ruthann Sampson
Dolores Sandmann
Carol Schlitt
Nancy Schneider
Carol Schwarz
Linda Sebelia
Jan Seitz
Robin Seitz
Sheila Settles

Bobbie Dixon Shaffett

Brenda Sheik

Connie Sheppard

Susan S. Shockey

Kaye P. Shrout

Nancy Bradford Sisson

Denise Smith

Kathy Smith

Kaye Smith

Peggy Smith

Shawn C. Smith

Ida Marie Snorteland

Rita Spence

Kathleen Splane

Lori Sporer

Dale Steen

Patricia Steiner

Christian Still

Debbie Still

Janice Stoudnour

Paula Strawder

Kim Strohmeier

Debbie Stroud

Cheryle Jones Syracuse

Lisa K. Taylor

Susan Taylor

Crystal Terhune

Paula Threadgill

Janet L. Tietyen

Lisa Treiber

Deborah Unterseher

Valerie Vincent

Joan Vinette

Dawn M. Vosbein

Robbyn Wainscott

Lisa Wallace

Tracey Watts

Diana M. Weise

Laurie Welch

Cami Wells

Linda Wells

Diane Whitten

Brenda Williams

Gayle Williford

Laura W. Wilson

Mary Wilson

Wisconsin Milk Marketing Board

Carolyn Ann Wissenbach

Jane Wolery

Kathy Wolters

Vanessa Woods

Rhoda Yoshino

Maria Young

Martha Yount

Julia Zee

Deniese Zeringue

Index

Index

Index

Index

More Than a Cookbook

*For additional copies, please visit your local
Cooperative Extension Service or
our Web site (**www.neafcs.org**), or call the
National Association of Family and
Consumer Sciences at (972) 233-9107.*